Fresh Water

from

Old Wells

A 21st Century Woman's Visit to the Wells

Therefore with joy shall ye draw
water out of the well of salvation
Isaiah 12:3

Gwendolyn Persons
(Mrs. Fred K. Persons, Esq.)

Foreword by: Presiding Elder Harold C. Huggins
African Methodist Episcopal Church
Fourth Episcopal District

G Publishing LLC

Fresh Water from Old Wells
A 21st Century Woman's Visit to the Wells

All scripture quotations taken from the Holy Bible, King James Version. Songs of Praises taken from the African-Methodist Episcopal Hymnal. Pictures, quotes, letters, and written tributes used by permission.

Editors: Fran Carter
          Francene Ambrose Gunn

Cover Art: June Swad
Cover Design: SOS Graphics and Designs

Published by G Publishing, LLC
P. O. Box 24374
Detroit, MI 48224

ISBN: 0-9773267-3-X

Library of Congress Control Number: 2005933393

Printed in the United States of America

Author's Preface

Fresh Water from Old Wells sprang from my heart, mind and soul during the eleventh year of our marriage. It was at this threshold that financial reversals, sickness and old age hooked up and gave birth to trouble. The marriage vows, 'for better or for worse'; 'for richer or for poorer'; 'in sickness and in health', had come to pass and were being put to the supreme test. Life's challenges and reversals came knocking at our door.

For the sake of realism (my reality) and without tampering with the sanctity of the marriage vows, I needed to do a little transposing. I needed to ask the Spirit's permission to revise or to rewrite the marriage vows. I needed the Spirit's permission to play this tune in a different key. The Spirit said "Okay as long as you know what you are doing. "The vows now read; 'from richer to poorer'; 'from health to sickness'; 'from older to old'. For indeed, financial reversals, sickness and old age had taken up residence. Coping with these life changing circumstances presented a challenge for the writer. Medicating and pacifying on self-prescribed remedies became the order of the day.

Continuing to rely upon these self-prescribed remedies could only fan the flames of trouble. I needed an antidote for my trouble, I needed a prescription for coping. Fresh Water from Old Wells provided such an antidote. Medication through meditation, a twelve-step program for coping evolved.

Thomas O. Chisholm writes, "Great Is Thy Faithfulness, morning by morning new mercies I see." His mercies are fresh every morning. I invite all who suffer from an unquenchable thirst of the human spirit to join me each morning at the wells.

Beyond the gate you will find Fresh Waters of Comfort, Faith, Guidance, Hope, Joy, Kindness, Love, Patience, Peace, Strength, Truth and Understanding.

Jesus said to the woman at Jacob's Well, "If you drink this water you will thirst again, but whoever drinks the water I give will never thirst again." Drink this water and the vow 'to love and to cherish' will never change.

Keep drinking from old wells
wells that never run dry

From the Editor....

Subj. Way past time!
Date: January 6, 2005
From: Feliencarter
To: Gdpersons

Gwen, What a blessed gift you have!
Love _is_ eternal and time will not diffuse the command of your story. When I first met with you at the foot of your dollhouse I knew I was in for quite an emotional experience there that had its ultimate revelation as you sought for nourishment in the Fresh Water.

I've spent many hours with you and your Fred through your writing and have had to literally free myself from the personal into the abstract to order to continue.

Gwen, you do have a way of reaching into the deep places, in other words you reach out and touch! This was quite an experience! It's time to let the world know! It is way past time for publication. Is there not a hunger and thirst for Fresh WATER?

Thank you for the journey.

P.S.
He has a purpose and a plan so please continue to allow Him to lead you.

It really is way past time for the ultimate publication of your book.

Dedicated To:

Jesus Christ, author and finisher of my faith, thanks be unto to you for freely showering me with your grace and mercy ...Thanks be unto you for walking with me every step of the way; for being a light unto my feet and a lamp unto my pathway.

To: The Holy Spirit for inspiring and encouraging my heart and Guiding my thoughts

To: Oprah Winfrey
Thank you for all of the 'AHA Moments'
Thank you for sharing all the things you 'Know for Sure'
Thank you for all the 'Life Lessons' which have inspired me 'To Live My Best Life'
Thank you for the Courage to become honest and intimate enough with myself to embrace my own truth in order to write this book
The Oprah Magazine January 2002 Vol. 3 Number 1

To: My Soror Cathyrn Smith for being a conduit of the Holy Spirit. Thank you for these words sent June 17, 1999
Dear Soror Gwen,
Recall, I told you that we/you did not know of God's plans for you. It appears that you are to become a talented writer.
Thanks for my book on Forgiveness.
In Delta love,
Soror Cathy

To: Rosa Blake,
> Thank you for my gift, The Angel of Reflection Pin which reads "The Angel of Reflection will help you to search deep within for your own personal truth-to reach beyond your own imagination."

To: The Harmonaires of St. Stephen A.M.E. Church 'Fred's Choir'
> Thanks for inspiring my heart and spirit.
> WE LOVE YOU!!!

To: Dr. William Augustus Jones Jr., My Spiritual Mentor
> Bethany Baptist Church
> Brooklyn, New York
> Over the past several years, my husband and I have faithfully joined you in worship service on Sunday evening, via our local cable network in the city of Detroit. Dr. Jones, although you did not perform the marriage ceremony that united us in holy matrimony, your preached gospel has helped to weave and to strengthen the bond between us.
> We have purchased many of your tapes and have listened to them regularly. We have been blessed to worship with you whenever you visited our city. Your powerful, unadulterated preached gospel has been a mighty, mighty, blessing in our lives.
> I have properly acknowledged that all scripture has been taken from the King James Version of the Holy Bible.
> I wish to properly acknowledge that much of the content that lies within these pages has been resurrected from my heart and mind and taken directly from your preached word.
> My walk with Jesus Christ has been elevated, inspired and practiced, through the unbounded, unvarnished, unfettered, preached Word of God as only you are able to deliver. Therefore, I hope you won't mind that not only have I freely borrowed from that which saith the Lord, but also that which saith Dr. William Augustus Jones.

To: My Beloved Husband Fred K. Persons

WHEN GOD MADE YOU HE WAS AT HIS BEST!! I loved you, not only for what you made of yourself, but for what you have made of me. I loved you for the part of me that you brought out; I loved you for putting your hand into my heaped-up heart and passing over all the foolish, weak things that you couldn't help dimly seeing there, and for drawing out into the light all the beautiful belongings that no one else had looked quite far enough to find. I loved you because you helped me make the lumber of my life, not a tavern, but a temple; out of the works of my everyday, not a reproach, but a song.

ANON

"I love doing things to Gwen, for Gwen and with Gwen". "Love is a verb, love is something that you do." Fred you put these words into action everyday that we were together. Over the years no one could ever doubt our love. Your unconditional love brought so much joy, laughter and happiness into my life. I'll **be** forever grateful for each day you gave to me. Because of your belief, faith, trust and your wisdom, my life is a better place.

Fred, God blessed me with His greatest gift, 'Someone to love and someone to love me in return. I had your love, I had it all! I was abundantly blessed to have been loved by you.

Eternally yours,

Your Loving Wife

Mrs. Fred K. Persons, Esq.

P.S.

Fred, thanks for falling to your knees and praying *for* me and *with* me; then rising with these words on June 17, 1999:

"Write your Book."

Above All,

TO GOD BE ALL THE GLORY

A Tribute to Daddy

In spite of all the time I invested at the foot of my dollhouse, pretending and playing make believe, there was never anything that my little mind could do to turn my dreams into reality. No amount of make believing, pretending, or imagining could change the *who* and the *what* of my life. All the scripts that I wrote and rewrote in my mind for you, could not make you into the father that I needed and wanted you to be in my life. I could not dream, nor could I pray the truth away.

But thank God, the years have taught me wisdom. Looking back, I am made to realize that my reality and my truth were also the reality and truth of thousands of little black children growing up all around me. I was also made to realize that much of my disappointment, dissatisfaction, and discontentment with my world was fueled and poisoned by what came over the airwaves. I am young enough to have grown up with the *boob tube*. In all fairness to you Daddy, back then, not even with the help of my over active imagination, and under the most ideal of circumstances, could you have been expected to compete with the likes of Ward Cleaver or Ozzie Nelson. They simply were not our (black folks) reality. As a matter of fact, they were not their (white folks) reality either; not then and not now. If the truth be told, they were never anyone's reality!

Unfortunately, forty years down the road, with the saturation of all the reality shows coming across the boob tube, there still exists precious little reality for *black folks*. I cannot help but shudder when I think of just how many little black and white girls still look for, and sadly, too often find, their reality on television.

The years have also taught me that in spite of who or what you were or were not in my life, I was abundantly blessed and I had much to be thankful for in my life, even to you Daddy!!

Daddy, I don't ever recall thanking you for anything. Of course, that was part of the "treat daddy with disdain for walking out on you" syndrome. But wisdom has taught me that in spite of all the obvious bad, there was also much good. My DNA has been imprinted with both the good and the bad.

Reflectively, in all fairness I can recall your mother, my Grandma Harris, and my mother crediting you for your academic achievements. That was evidenced simply by virtue of where you attended school. In those days, not too many African-Americans attended, much less, graduated from Cass Technical High School. Daddy, your mind was indeed a terrible thing to waste. Here again, is just another one of those unfortunate realities so prevalent in our culture. But I thank God that gift was not completely wasted since that inheritance was passed on to your children.

I suppose one could say I was a late bloomer. I was considered an average student in elementary school. Unlike your two other daughters who have always had a passion for reading, perhaps I spent too many hours at the foot of my doll house playing make believe and not enough hours reading books. In any event it was not until I got to high school that I began to blossom. In spite of those extended years playing make believe at the foot of my doll house I was the first one in the family to go away and to graduate from college. Daddy, all three of your children as well as their children, your grandchildren, have all done quite well. Thank you Daddy!

My memory bank also holds deposits of your artistic genius. I can recall hearing and witnessing for myself just how artistically talented you were. Had that talent not been wasted, but nurtured and developed, perhaps my childhood dreams would have become realities. Nonetheless, I am thankful. I suppose I inherited those footprints as well. I'm sure my passion and creativity for decorating, my flair for fashion and perhaps now for writing all came from you. Thank you Daddy!

I can also remember looking at some early photographs of you as a much younger man. Daddy, you were some 'good looker.' Back then, you had it going on with the right skin color, and what black folks back-in-the-day called good hair. Growing up, especially on Colfax Street, I can recall always hearing these words, "She is the pretty one." "She is the sweet child." And let's not forget all throughout high school folks accused me of having 'good hair.' As the youngest, I was spoiled and indulged by everyone around me, even by my two older sisters, especially by your middle daughter who rescued and catered to her baby sister's whims. I was everyone's special child.

Although the years are beginning to rob me of my two most prized possessions, my hair and my good looks, they were, I suppose my crown and glory or my saving grace for years, until Amazing Grace found me. Thank you, Daddy, for passing on those imprints too!

Daddy, today I thank you for all the good you brought into my life and I also wish to thank you for all the bad as well. I suppose had it not been for all the bad I would not have spent those many extended years at the foot of my doll house trying to erase the obvious bad and trying to fulfill the missing void in my life. Had it not been for that void, that feeling of abandonment perhaps my life never would have taken the course that led me to the greatest joy in life.

Oprah, over the years I have never had an occasion to visit a psychiatrist's couch. But, of this I am sure. I am sure that all of the dime store shrinks, the naysayers, the skeptics, the critics, and let's not forget, the player haters, felt the day had surely dawned for me to make that appointment, the day I announced I was going to marry a man thirty-one years my senior. A man much older than my own father, and not even you, daddy could applaud my decision.

There was never a shortage of questions, accusations, doubts, skepticism and criticisms. Inquiring minds wanted to know. "Is she trying to fill a void from her childhood? Is that little girl, that baby inside of her looking for a father figure? Is she marrying for security?" If the truth be told, I suppose I did marry Fred for all of those reasons and so much more. But let the record reflect it was for the 'more' that I thank my Daddy for today.

Daddy, I am thankful for all that you were not able to be for me, and be to me at a time when I thought I needed it most in my life. My quest to fill that void, to find more in my life, led me to two of God's greatest gifts in life; someone to love me and someone to love in return. God blessed me with Fred K. Persons.

For that I say, "Thank you Daddy!"

Love,
Your Baby Daughter

Acknowledgements

Let me not continue without recognizing those who have stood by me and supported me with their prayers and their words of encouragement.

Rev. Delano Bowman
Rev. Juanita Bowman
Rev. Barbara Woodson
Rev. Clinton Hoggard
Carolyn Alexander
Soror Beverly Curry
Soror Beverly Sneed
Soror Deborah Sinclair
Deborah Brown
Carolyn Williams
Renay Pope
Lucille White
Charles Sanders
Orlando Brooks
Velva Gullatte
Pamela Cantrell
Antonio Harlan

I THANK YOU!

16   Gwendolyn D. Persons

Contents

OUR WEDDING DAY

JANUARY 12, 1988

FOREWORD

"Gwen," as I lovingly call her with tender regard, in this book tells of the blissful marriage between Gwen and Fred (Attorney Fred K. Persons). I met Fred many years ago at St. Stephen A.M.E. Church in Detroit, MI. It was some years later when I returned to St. Stephen as pastor that I met or rather became re-acquainted with Gwen, as they through marriage became one.

Fresh out of the seminary, March 1959, I was hired by the late Dr. Charles S. Spivey, Sr., one of the great pastors of St. Stephen A.M.E. Church, as his Youth Minister and Director of the church's community center. While serving in those capacities, I met Gwen and Fred who were members of the church. When I first became acquainted with them, neither of them actually knew the other. At the time Gwen was in her formative years and a member of the junior church. She was brought up at St. Stephen. Her grandmother, mother and sisters were members of that church.

In those days Fred was an up and coming member of the legal profession, one of Detroit's well-known lawyers and figures around the City County Building, known for his snazzy, sharp, and regal attire. Everybody knew Fred at St. Stephen, and Fred knew everybody at St. Stephen, except Gwen. He was the reader of church announcements, and a member of the St. Stephen's Steward Board.

In 1980, I returned to St. Stephen as senior pastor. Gwen was now all grown-up and was an active member in the church. I don't think Fred was acquainted with Gwen at the time.

Being members of the same church, one would think that at some time or another, their paths would have crossed.

But St. Stephen is a church with a large membership; its sanctuary seats about eighteen hundred people. It was a club centered church; one would perhaps, not be acquainted with other members outside of an organization or cell group, except casually or unofficially in passing. But through it all, Gwen and Fred met, not by accident, but by providence, somewhat separated by age, but inseparable by way of a predestination, pre-approved by power divine. This dapper Fred and this young, delightful queenly young lady met and the two became one. What God brought together, nothing could put asunder. Fred said to me, I don't know how many times, "She is the best thing that has ever happened to me." The feeling was mutual between the two of them.

For several years prior to Fred's death, he, Gwen, Martha, my wife, and I went out socially together. There's nothing like being out with Fred and Gwen. Their favorite place to dine out in those days was Joe Muer, a famous restaurant on E. Vernor Highway and Gratiot in the City of Detroit. But best of all, every year, for many years, Gwen and Fred ate Thanksgiving dinner at our home, prepared by my wife Martha.

I was the best man at their wedding and Martha stood up with Gwen. It was my privilege and honor to be the eulogist at his home going. Death could not separate them. Gwen and Fred will always be one in my mind as long as I live and even after my death if that be possible. The meaning of their oneness is what this foreword called 'The Two Became One" is about. The book, Fresh Water from Old Wells, is a testimony of what a good marriage is like when that marriage is put together in the board-room of heaven. Nothing on this side of life can put it asunder.

Jesus Christ reminds us that in the beginning God made us male and female, and said, "For this cause a man shall leave his father and mother and shall cleave to his wife; and the two shall become one flesh." Our lives find completion only as we love and are loved in return.

Whenever marriage is of God two always become one; they can become what they could never be separately. When marriage is of God, two become one ... Such as that of Abraham and Sarah, Isaac and Rebecca, Jacob and Rachel, Boaz and Ruth, Joseph and Mary, Aquila and Priscilla, and Fred K. Persons and Gwendolyn D. Persons.

Rev. Harold C. Huggins, Presiding Elder
Former Pastor of St. Stephen A.M.E. Church
Detroit, Michigan
October, 1980-June 1999

To Gwen and Fred.....

MAY YOUR MARRIAGE BRING YOU...
- ENOUGH HAPPINESS TO KEEP YOU SWEET
- ENOUGH TRIALS TO KEEP YOU STRONG
- ENOUGH SORROW TO KEEP YOU HUMAN
- ENOUGH HOPE TO KEEP YOU HAPPY
- ENOUGH FAILURE TO KEEP YOU HUMBLE
- ENOUGH SUCCESS TO KEEP YOU EAGER
- ENOUGH FRIENDS TO GIVE YOU COMFORT
- ENOUGH WEALTH TO MEET YOUR NEEDS
- ENOUGH ENTHUSIASM TO LOOK FORWARD
- ENOUGH FAITH TO BANISH DEPRESSION
- ENOUGH DETERMINATION TO MAKE EACH DAY A
  BETTER DAY THAN YESTERDAY!

WE TOAST YOU!!!

(written by Soror Evelyn Browne)
4/29/88

Introduction

Phase One: The Bare Truth

And ye shall know the truth,
and the truth shall make you free

John 8:32

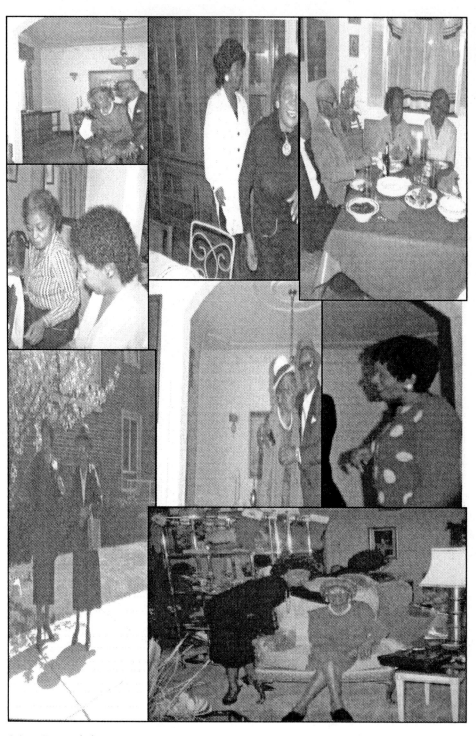

24   Gwendolyn D. Persons

The Bare Truth

I dare say that not a one among us can go to the museum of memories and depart without a catalog of unfinished business. Khalil Gibran asked in one of his musings, "Are you one who was born in the cradle of sorrow and reared in the lap of misfortune and in the house of oppression?" Are you eating the dry crust moistened with tears?" "Are you drinking the turbid water in which are mingled blood and tears?" To this trilogy of queries, if the truth be told, most of us would have to answer 'yes'.

I grew up in an extended family household, headed by a loving, God-fearing, maternal Grandmother, Loretta Jones. I was the youngest of three girls, Judy, Diane (Carolyn) and Debbie (Gwen). My parents tried to make a go of it, on and off, mostly off, so with the support of her mother and father, and little or no help from Daddy, Mama raised her three girls as best as she knew how. She did the best she could until she knew how to do better (thanks, Oprah for teaching me this life lesson).

My museum of memories has recorded a childhood replete with both good and bad, both happy and sad memories. Growing up we were never close to my father's side of the family. We would visit Grandma Harris's house once or twice a year. We would spend the night only on occasion. It seemed as though Daddy and his two brothers, Uncle Raymond and Uncle Milton, the Harris men, along with his sisters, Aunt Marion, the twins, Lessie and Jessie, all lived with Grandma and Grandpa Harris. Daddy was the oldest of the Harris clan. We had a plethora of first cousins, but we never got to know them except by name and to whom they belonged. I never heard of family reunions until the seventies. To this day, I've never participated in or attended a family reunion, my own or anyone else's.

The Harris household was also headed by a God-fearing matriarch, Mabel Harris. Although Grandpa Harris was in the home, he was not the head of this household. Grandma Harris raised her sons with a fist of iron. On the other hand, or should I say with the other hand, my aunts were raised with their mother's hand of tender loving care and kindness. She raised them all with the Word on her tongue. She was a strong church going, God-fearing, Baptist woman.

Unfortunately, Grandpa Harris was not a team player in the raising of his clan. The only thing he was good at was raising all sorts of hell. He was one of those weekend *hell raisers*.

I guess it would be an accurate statement to say that my aunts inherited their mother's legacy; they were raised to become God-fearing, Bible, tea tottery women. They loved the Lord. They were their mother's daughters. Whereas, my father and his two bro-thers evidenced little acquaintance with the Lord or anything else resembling holiness in their lives. In fact one might say that they despised and rejected my grandmother's teachings and preaching of the religion of Jesus Christ. Their rebellion and rejection of their mother's influence manifested in their adult lives. Without question, the boys inherited their father's legacy. They, too, were master craftsmen at raising all sorts of hell.

Those infrequent visits to LaSalle Street revive memories of much strife and contention between my grandmother and the men in her household. There was always their drinking, their cursing, their fighting, their stumbling, their staggering, and Grandma Harris's yelling. When they could drink, curse, fight, stumble and stagger no more, the yelling for some other reasons seemed to continue. I hated being around those barroom brawls. I hated those times when my grandfather would set me on his knee and call me that 'special child.' I don't know what the weekdays were like on LaSalle for the Harris clan, but if I had to give title to those weekends, I would entitle them "Good vs. Evil: the Lost Weekend."

Over the years my walk with grace has taught me to hate the sin and to love the sinner. As a child, I hated those Harris men. I hated the way they lived and the way they treated their mother. I hated being around my father when he was drinking. I hated seeing my father drunk. But, unlike my sisters, in spite of who and what our father was or was not to us, in my heart I know I never hated my father.

Reflectively, I am sure the Lord came to see about me and laid His hands on me at the foot of my dollhouse. I suppose He was working in me and on me getting me ready on the inside, so that He could use me at His appointed time. My Daddy and his father grew old and sick together. All those years of self abuse, misuse and neglect had come home to roost. My grandfather and my father were sick and they were dying.

In spite of all those unhappy and misunderstood childhood memories, I was there for my father and my grandfather when they needed someone most in their lives. There is something about God's Grace. It is only His Amazing Grace that enables you to love freely to give freely and to freely forgive. He gives it to you long before you even know that you have it and long before you even know you will need it! So it was with me. My love for my grandfather and my father showed up when they both needed it the most. I went to see about them.

I can recall one summer afternoon after his stroke I picked my Daddy up from the nursing home and took him out for a ride. Of all the places I could have taken him, I took him on Colfax, over to my mother's house. Shortly after our arrival, I overheard my mother saying to Grandma, "There is something special about that child," Hmmm. Now where had I heard those words before? My Daddy was finally sober. He was sick and dying, but at last he was sober. I loved him then and I love him now!

In many respects, the family dynamics were not much different on Colfax Street. Grandma Jones was also the head of the household. Consequently, we were raised in a home with strong Christian principles and values. Much like LaSalle Street, Grandpa Jones did not embrace or practice religion in his life either. The only time in my seventeen years growing up in his presence that I can recall him at a church service was on the day of his funeral. Grandpa Jones was also afflicted and possessed by that damnable demon. However, in the case of Grandpa Jones those weekend barroom brawls too often carried over into the middle of the next week.

With Grandpa Jones, however, there was no escaping his drunk and disorderly conduct. We were stuck with it; we lived with him. I suppose Grandpa Jones duly earned the title of the 'neighborhood lush.'

During the times when Mama and Daddy would try to make a go of it, the fact that Daddy and Grandpa Jones would be under the same roof spelled a double dose of trouble. Loretta Jones could not and would not allow such a double portion of the devil's vices to dwell in her household. Something or somebody had to go, and who do you think got handed his walking papers? You guessed it! Certainly not my grandmother's husband.

For years I have struggled with the question, "Why and how did both of my grandmothers unite in holy matrimony to men whose lives were so diametrically opposed to everything they held sacred?" This is without question another one of those unfortunate statistics that too often rears its ugly head in African-American culture. The bare truth is that historically many African-American women have had to endure toxic relationships in order to survive and raise their children. Both of my grandmothers were strong black women grounded in their faith. Did they remain in those relationships in order to survive? Or did their faith instruct them to stand by their men 'til death will they part? I sometimes wonder if our religion is at times a two-edged sword. I suppose that is a subject for a whole other book! In any event, that's exactly what Grandma Jones did. After Grandpa Jones got cancer, Grandma kept him home and cared for her husband without any assistance until she was no longer able to do so. When conditions became unmanageable for her, Grandma put her husband in a nursing home. There he remained until his death.

Grandma and Grandpa Jones had two children, Louise and Jackie. Louise and her baby sister, Jackie, were several years apart, consequently they were not very close as sisters. In fact it was sometimes suggested that the separation in years was such that Louise could have actually been Jackie's mother. The fact is that I only heard that suggested from just one person and that was from Mama (Jackie) herself. As a child, and throughout her teen years, Mama was never close to her mother, either. I have more remembrances than I choose to recall of Mama saying she never felt her mother's love. As a consequence, she grew up closer to her father and estranged from her mother. I suppose Mama could have been a poster child for the expression, "Daddy's little girl." Not unlike the man she would eventually marry, Jackie also bore her father's inheritance.

I have always taken exception to the expression, 'The apple doesn't fall far from the tree." This would suggest that one is the product of a single set of genes. We are not. We are the product of two sets of genes. The fruit that falls from that tree can yield either sweet or bitter fruit. Having said all of that I suppose God planted the seeds, but perhaps it was her close relationship with her father that aided in fertilizing the bitter seed and eventually giving root. Jackie could not escape her genealogy. The inheritance of her father's legacy would be upon her. With the advancement of years, that bitter seed eventually ripened and evidenced itself in her adult life.

Although much smaller in size, in terms of closeness our relationship with my mother's side of the family was not much different than Daddy's side of the family. My mother's sister, Aunt Louise, was married to Uncle Watson. Uncle Watson was one of those rare breeds at least in my limited world. He was a hardworking, church going, family man, a devoted husband to Aunt Louise and a good father to their only daughter, Cheryl

Louise. Uncle Watson had all the makings for a black version of an Ozzie Nelson or a Ward Cleaver.

We saw them more frequently than Daddy's side of the family. Every year we would have Thanksgiving and Christmas dinner together. On unspecified Sunday afternoons, they would drop by the house after leaving church. Back in the day when gas was cheap, folks would pile up in the car and go for rides. Of course, we did not have a car, so Uncle Watson would, on rare occasions, surprise us and come by to take us all out for a Sunday afternoon excursion. Those infrequent contacts with the Watsons seemed superficial, so stuffy, so fake, so disingenuous that, as a result, we never bonded with them, either. To make a bad situation worse, my Aunt Louise had an uncanny talent for making my mother's girls feel like step-children, a station or two beneath her beloved, privileged, Cheryl Louise.

Once a year, Aunt Louise would bring a bag of hand-me-down clothes over to the house; clothes that Cheryl had either out-grown or just no longer wanted. For the life of me I still don't know why she felt so compelled to do that. Perhaps it made her feel more charitable and benevolent toward her less fortunate baby sister's girls. One thing about Mama, she did not need any help dressing her three girls. Mother was so very proud of her girls. Jackie's daughters were always the best dressed girls in the neighborhood and in school. My fondest childhood memories were of going back to school each fall. I absolutely loved and lived for back-to-school clothes shopping. The fall still remains my favorite time of the year. Mama did all of our shopping in downtown Detroit. My museum of memories is replete with those carefree, fun filled days spent downtown. As I grew older, I would catch the Tireman bus alone and spend my Saturday afternoons downtown in J. L. Hudson's. Many times I would depart with only a box of Fannie Farmer candy or a bag of Otto's popcorn, cheese was my favorite. This was the only evidence of my having been downtown all afternoon. To this day, my heart and soul, as well as my body, dwell in downtown Detroit.

At Christmas, all the kids waited anxiously to see what the Harris girls were getting for Christmas. Jackie never disappointed them, nor us. We always seemed to have the biggest Christmas on the block.

Both our mother's and father's genealogy contributed to our academic successes. However, mother denied, too often, her contribution to her girls' academic success. Daddy's intelligence was the one thing for which Mama gave Daddy his *propers*. Daddy's mind *was* a terrible thing to waste. But with little or no contribution from Daddy, Jackie saw to it that her girls had the same advantages and exposure as other kids in the neighborhood. In many instances, we may have had more. Mama saw to it that her three girls were exposed to all of the learning opportunities that were offered outside of Sampson Elementary school. She would bundle her three girls up, and hand-in-hand, the four of us traveled the city using public transportation. Mama took her girls everywhere on the bus, amusement parks, the Detroit Zoo, the Main Library, the Historical Museum, the Art Institute, and all the theaters downtown.

Grandma Jones saw to it that we got our religious training and all the other social morals that define human decency and good 'rearin.' Loretta Jones didn't play! Grandma Jones's voice never resonated as loudly as my Grandmother Harris's, but make no mistake, she was heard loud and clear! One of the constant messages I recall echoed by my grandmother was that Jackie did not know what to do with money. She spent money foolishly on herself and her daughters. She lived from paycheck to paycheck. According to my Grandmother, Mama was always head over heels in debt. Grandma pontificated this over and over and over. Unfortunately, to our own detriment, it is usually those repeated messages to which we turn a deaf ear. For as long as I can remember money was always a bone of contention between my Grandmother and my mother.

I suppose Aunt Louise was my Grandmother's drum majorette. There was never a shortage of her condescending opinions toward my mother's lifestyle and the way she was raising her three girls. I would later learn that Mama had lived with her older sister's critical, holier-than-thou, self righteous analysis of her life for as long as she could remember; long before she had her three girls.

I'm not quite sure how old I was when 'it' first arrived at our doorstep. In the earlier years the visits from that unwanted intruder were less regular than it would become in later years. Nonetheless, I resented and hated each and every time 'it' showed up. The incessant movement of time found that intruder taking up permanent residence. My mother's life was turning into a nightmare for her and for me. Try as she may Grandma could not pray, preach or pontificate that unwelcome intruder out of her daughter's life. That damnable demon was back and it out stayed its welcome. It was never invited in the first place.

Unlike my father, not only did I hate what those intruders did to Mama, I think they caused me to hate Mama. I hated her for caring and spending more time with that unwelcome intruder than with me, her baby. I felt I needed my mother more than my sisters; after all they were older, they had each other. I needed my Mommy. It was during those times that I would retreat more and more into my world of make believe. All of my dreams came true and my troubles vanished, if only temporarily, at the foot of my doll house.

Mama always worked outside of the home to support us; yet another competitor in my life. In addition, Mama was the victim of one failed relationship after another. With all of that to compete with, I guess it was no wonder I developed such a close and loving relationship with my dollhouse and my Grandmother. Long before I started kindergarten, my days were spent 'up under' my Grandmother. Whatever wicked and evil things were going on around me I always felt safe and secure as long as Grandma was close by. I trusted my Grandmother to take care of me to calm the storms and bring sense into my world. I was the apple of her eye. Loretta Jones was our 'Rock of Gibraltar.' She was there for us all! Grandma taught me early to "Hold to God's unchanging hand."

One of my most precious childhood memories is of my black baby doll. I had one of the first, if not the only black baby doll on the planet. When her skin started to peel, my grandmother found a doll hospital in the yellow pages. We boarded the Tireman bus and took my black baby doll to the doll hospital located on West Grand Blvd. Once her black skin had been restored, we picked my doll up and brought her home. My grandmother was a jack of all trades. Grandma knew how to do it all, and she did it all quite well. Shortly after picking up my doll, Grandma began making me or rather, my doll a whole new wardrobe. That little black baby doll had more clothes than I did.

I learned so much being around my Grandma. Grandma taught me how to cook, bake, clean and pray. I loved hanging out with my grandmother; I was her favorite companion. She took me everywhere she had to go. We took special shopping trips downtown to Crowley's (her favorite store), to the A&P store (which was out of our immediate neighborhood) and to the Green Stamp store on the Boulevard. The Green Stamp store was where folks would go to redeem the green stamps for merchandise.

My grandma and I attended special teas and programs at her church, St. Stephen A.M.E. During our early years, my mother took her girls to Second Grace United Methodist Church located near the house on Tireman Street. It was later on that we joined St. Stephen A.M.E. Church. I have fond memories of going to Good Friday services with my grandmother. We would even board the bus to visit her best friend, Nancy Feggans.

The years advanced. I graduated from high school, went away to college and in 1973, got married the first time. The following year mother took a giant leap in her life. Still visited by those damnable intruders, for the first time in her life Mama took a chance on herself and a chance on love. In 1974, Mama moved to Los Angeles, California. One year later my middle sister, Carolyn, moved into her own apartment leaving Grandma all

alone for the first time in her life. Although still quite independent, adjusting to being alone was not easy for Grandma.

My first marriage proved to be a game of smoke and mirrors
from the onset. This charade of a marriage allowed me and
afforded me the opportunity to spend much time away from
home. I found myself spending lots of time with my Grandmother. It was easy for me to step into my mother's shoes and do
the things for Grandma that she had become accustomed to
mother doing for her. It was during that same period that I began
to experience some of the most difficult trials in my adult life.
Troubles and tribulations had descended upon my life, once
again I felt abandoned and all alone. In my mother's absence, I
grew closer to my grandmother.

The advancement of time perhaps five to six years later
found me divorced and Grandma growing older and her health
beginning to decline. It was becoming clear to all of us that she
was no longer able to live in her house alone. At the ripe age of
eighty four Grandma was becoming more and more dependent
upon others to take care of her. Mother had taken a chance on
love, life and herself. She lost at all three. Six years later, Mama
packed up her bags and moved back to Detroit to care for her
aging mother.

Grandma and her baby daughter were reunited. They were
together again, just the two of them. Unfortunately, it was difficult
for either one of them to verbally express their love. How sad it is
that this gift that God gives to us so freely is not so freely
expressed in many mother-daughter relationships. This sad
commentary is not one just confined to the African-American
culture. It is one that transcends all socio-economic barriers. I
shudder to think how many daughters die without ever hearing
those words, "I love you" spoken from their mother's lips. Put
another way, how many mother's die, never hearing those same
words spoken from their daughter's lips. What a sad tragedy!

Regrettably, the same baggage Mama took with her returned
with her and for the next thirteen years the responsibilities of

caring for her aging mother grew to almost insurmountable proportions. Mother did the best she could at the time. The road was not an easy one. Coping with these daily challenges proved to be one of the most difficult periods in her entire life. The demons were relentlessly ravaging her soul. Her soul was forever restless, her spirit defeated and broken. Darkness had veiled its lovely face all about her. Mama was at the lowest point in her life; she was standing at the crossroads of her very existence and at a time when her mother needed her most.

I was witness to one of those dark days. By then I was married to one of God's best, Fred Persons. That day will always be recorded as one of the darkest days in my life also. It happened one Sunday afternoon in 1992. Fred and I had stopped by after leaving church service. It was a summer afternoon but still very early in the day. It did not take long after our arrival before I discovered mother was having a pretty rough time with Grandma on that fateful afternoon. We found my mother in the battle of her life. Like a sweeping prairie fire, weariness was plaguing her very soul and the law of kindness was not upon her tongue that day. We found her verbally abusing her mother. The words my mother spoke to her mother that day will remain permanently etched in my memory. The moment I heard my mother say to her mother "I wish you would die" broke my heart in two. How could she speak such evil to her mother, to my beloved grand-mother? If I thought I hated her as a little girl for abandoning me, the jury was finally in; those words convicted her instantly. I hated my mother at that very moment in time and I wasted no time letting her know how I felt. The law of kindness dismissed itself from my tongue on that fateful Sunday afternoon as well. A flurry of evil words was hurled between us escalating to a level that Fred could not allow to grow in his presence. The master of wisdom, truth and love intervened. In no uncertain terms, my husband ordered me to stop.

His chastisement towards me went something like this, "I don't care what you think your mother has done, Gwen. As long as you are my wife and in my presence, you will never speak to your mother like that! Jackie is not well, and you should know that. In spite of what she is going through in her life, Jackie loves her mother." After my husband had finished admonishing me, my mother issued the following forecast upon my life. "You just wait, your day will come." I continued to protest his defense of my mother, and his conviction of me. How dare he take this position after hearing what she just said to my Grandmother. Of all people, Fred has lived by the Word all of his life, Honour thy father and thy mother: that thy days may be long upon the land which the Lord thy God giveth thee. (Exodus 20:12, KJV).

Enough said, that was all the defense Attorney Persons needed to defend his position that afternoon. I thank God Grandma did not hear or understand any of what had taken place in her living room on that fateful Sunday afternoon. Before leaving, Fred prayed and we left the two of them together, but not alone, we left them in the hands of the Lord.

The most troubling question in the classroom of affliction is not 'why', nor is it 'how much', rather it is 'how long? It's not the depth, but rather the duration of distress and sadness that produces despair (taken from *Rahab, the Harlot*, by Dr. Jones).

I thank God for opening up my heart and soul in time and pouring in His blessings of wisdom and truth. Fred was altogether correct. Jackie did love her mother. Jackie did the best she could for her mother and for her three daughters. Of one thing I am sure, at that time Jackie just could not do better. Oh, I'm sure, Jackie always knew better, after all she was Loretta Jones' daughter. Loretta Jones lived by the Word. Much like Jochebed, Moses' mother, Loretta knew that if you train up a child in the way she should go, even if she departs from it, she will eventually find her way back home. As with Moses, the visible fruits came later for Jackie.

"Jochebed knew that the roots had to be right in order for the fruits to be right. So she nursed him in infancy and guided him in his youth. She remained there all the time to impose whenever necessary a reality

check. Do's and don'ts, and yea's and nay's were part and parcel of the daily diet. Commitment to the God of the ages was primary in the curriculum. She knew what every mother should know, namely that faith has historic roots. "Train up a child in the way he shall go and when he is old he will not depart from it." Proper roots make for good fruits and the fruits spring forth from the roots. Nurturing roots is primarily a faith venture. Fruits is the thank-you tribute to roots. The visible fruits came later for Moses. Sometimes they come a long time after the roots have been planted. But the dictum remains true, by their fruits ye shall know them. the test of the roots is in the fruits.......it's roots that produce fruits and it takes good roots to produce good fruits. If you plant properly and nurture properly God will bring it all to proper fruition and you will see evidences of affirmations of identity, of assertion of independence and of acknowledgement of idealism. It is a truism, 'a tree is known by the fruit it bares..'" (On Roots and Fruits, Dr. William A. Jones)

The sad truth was that for Grandma, for her three girls and especially for herself, Jackie simply could not do better until her mother's death. Grandma died on April 18, 1993. One week later, Mama surrendered her life to God. She joined a twelve-step program and for the next eight years Jackie's life was a living testimony that the apple that falls from the tree is a product of two sets of genes. Jackie turned into her mother. Jackie was finally able to live her best life.

Jackie went home to be with her mother and father on October 2, 2001. To Grandma and Mama, I owe you both so much. I love and miss you much!

Phase Two: My Defining Moments

To the praise of the glory of his grace,
wherein he hath made us accepted in the beloved.

Ephesians 1:6

40   Gwendolyn D. Persons

My Defining Moments

Like most folks who own and accept their personal 'bare' truth, I realize that I grew up in a dysfunctional household (thanks Oprah for another life lesson). Like mother, like daughter, I also grew up with a certain feeling of separation and a feeling of disconnect. But much unlike my mother it certainly was not due to a lack of being or feeling loved. I have always felt a strong sense of love and caring all around me, not only from family, but from just about everyone in my life. For as long as I can remember, I was treated just a bit more special than my two sisters. Early on I was labeled that 'special child'. Everyone loved that 'baby girl'.

So why then if love truly does conquer all did I have such a strong sense of disconnect so early in my life? Why did those feelings of self-worth and self-validation refuse to make an appearance early on? In spite of all the love that was showered upon my life it just did not seem to be enough. I did not feel whole. I was not satisfied. There was a void in my life. Surely I was born for more than this. I wanted more.

Those hours spent playing make believe at the foot of my doll house probably extended far beyond the age that such imaginary play was expected. Perhaps it did, but as I stop and take a backward look at my life, I thank God for those expanded years spent up under my grandmother, and at the foot of my doll house. Those imaginary moments gave me a great deal of satisfaction and contentment, and they set my focus early toward turning those dreams into reality. Those dreams laid the foundation as I embarked upon the journey that would eventually fulfill that sense of self-worth and wholeness that was missing in my life, ultimately uncovering what would be my life defining moments.

I strongly believe God did come to see about me at the foot of my doll house. I believe God laid His hands on me at the foot of my doll house. He came to see about *His child* way back then.

The prelude to this connection came when I entered Chadsey High School and the friendships I made with five other freshman girls, Sybil, Sheila, Terri, Beverly and Cynthia. I was the only one of the six who was not only from a single parent home, but an extended family as well. They were all from homes where there was both a mother and a father. They did not live in the Chadsey High School boundaries; they each had to travel to school by bus. They lived in what was then considered to be middle class neighborhoods. We formed a club in the ninth grade and called ourselves the Chantelles. The club remained active for the entire four years of high school. We met for club meetings regularly. Whenever it was my turn to host the club meeting, I was always a bit ashamed and embarrassed to meet at my house. We did not have fine accommodations, unlike their homes with their finished basements or recreation rooms, if you will. It was impossible to ever find a private spot to meet at my house. However, they never seemed to mind coming to my house.

During our high school years, there were two distinct groups of students, the 'grease' and the 'frats'. The frats consisted of students who had been tracked into a college preparatory curriculum. The 'grease' on the other hand, were not expected to go on to a four year college upon graduation. In the west side high schools and the big CT (Cass Tech), there existed more structured and formal clubs. Clubs sponsored or at least in practice, fashioned themselves after the college sororities and fraternities. For the females there were the Delsprites and the Co-eds. For the fellows there were the Pre-Omegas and the Epsilons. During our high school years these groups at least the fellows often sponsored dances at some of the finest hotels in downtown Detroit. In those days, it was the Statler Hilton, the Pick Fort Shelby or the Sheridan Cadillac Hotels. We had our introduction to these groups and their functions in our sophomore year at Chadsey. We were not dating at the time of our introduction to these functions; therefore, we relied upon our mother's to transport us to and from these Friday night dances. More accurately stated, we relied upon their mothers to transport us.

The Chantelles never seemed to mind. They never once in the four years we were together at Chadsey High School made me feel any different. I was treated just the same at all times. I suppose this was my first recognition and introduction to my own self worth and self validation. I was accepted by them and loved by them for who I was and not for what I had. The friendships of these five girls along with the influences from the strong role models, mentors and our teachers, Sam Walker, Acie Meekins and Soror Pearl Johnson (just to name a few) at Chadsey High school laid the pathway for the events that would lead to my first life defining moment.

The first life defining event occurred on the campus of Western Michigan University. No, it was not the fact that I was the first in my family to attend and graduate from college. And no it has not been this twenty eight year career as a Public School Speech and Language Pathologist that I currently enjoy. One would think that a twenty-eight year career would surely define who one is. As strange as it may sound, I don't think that I ever connected with my profession. Make no mistake about it, I've enjoyed my career and I've been blessed to have had it for all of these years. But believe me, there lies a vast difference between enjoying what you do and loving or having a passion for what you do. The passion never flourished in me.

Having said that, I suppose, I have not yet lived my best life. If the opportunity ever arose for me to do what I absolutely feel passionate about, my chosen career would be in the area of interior design. I love to decorate my home. I can sit for hours just looking through catalogs, Gumps, Winterthur, Crate/Barrel and my absolute favorite, Horchow. I would love to own a store such as that in Downtown Detroit one of these days. If realizing or accomplishing one's ultimate career goal defines living your best life, then I have not lived my best life.

Now let's get back to my first life defining moment.

The first significant life defining event that took place on the campus of Western Michigan University was recorded on September 20, 1969 when I was inducted into Delta Sigma Theta Sorority, Inc. Delta Sigma Theta Sorority, Inc. was created to change and benefit individuals rather than society. As a sorority it was formed to bring women together as sisters, but at the same time to address the divisive, often class-related issues confronting black women in our society.

Delta Sigma Theta fulfilled its intended purpose in my life. My eight month pledge period and my years as an under-graduate soror certainly did change and benefit me as an indivi-dual. I was challenged to a degree beyond anything I thought possible or achievable for me. These experiences resulted in a more confident, courageous, positive and self assured me. My self worth and self-validation skyrocketed with my membership in Delta Sigma Theta Sorority, Inc. The bonds that I formed within the sorority have been closer than blood, bonds that will last a lifetime.

In more recent years, my opportunities to serve and to lead in the Detroit Alumnae Chapter, have without a doubt, encapsulated some of the proudest and most rewarding experiences and achievements in my life. The position that has been most reward-ing for me was serving as the chapter chaplain. It was in this position that I did some of my earliest writings. In 1998, I was inspired to write a litany in honor of our founders. The following year I wrote a little book on forgiveness for my sorors entitled, *Prayers of Forgiveness for My Sisters*. In 2000, the Holy Spirit, instructed me to write *God's Got A Word for Delta Women*. Who knows, maybe I may have to revisit this one. Could it be that writing might one day evidence itself as living "My Best Life?"

Unashamedly, and without apology, I am proud to say my search for a connectedness and a sense of belonging was first fulfilled when I answered the call to Delta. I could not have found a more meaningful and purposeful connection than membership in one of the largest black women's organizations in the United States. For me, answering the call to Delta was a spiritual calling. For when the call to Delta is answered in earnest, serving Delta through faithful and committed service will continue to lift you to higher ground and the rewards will last throughout a lifetime.

In the sixties, Delta's had a saying "Many are called, but few are chosen" (Matthew 22:14). I thank God I was chosen. My experiences will be indelibly carved into the archives of my heart and soul. I'd take nothing for my journey with DEAR OL' DELTA!!

Ask me who I am. I will reply, loudly and proudly,
I am a 'Delta.'

Something else happened to me on the campus of Western Michigan University. I fell in love during my freshman year. I don't recall when I first saw or met him. I don't even know when it happened or even why or how it happened. But it happened, I was in love for the first time in my life. You know, that "can't-live- without-him" kind of love. That "will do almost anything for him" kind of love. That "just don't know any better" kind of love. That toxic, self-destructive, one-sided, lopsided, insane kind of love.

When I met him he was already a senior. I don't recall that we ever had a single date while he was still on campus. I left for the summer at the end of the Winter term (April). He remained on campus for the spring and summer term, graduating at the end of the summer term, August 1969. I can remember it just as though it was yesterday. His favorite aunt Fennie, picked me up on Colfax in her Cadillac the morning of his graduation and the two of us drove to Kalamazoo for his graduation. That was my first introduction to the Cadillac experience. I am not sure whether I met the rest of his family prior to that day, but when we arrived in Kalamazoo they were all there at his apartment, his parents, his brother, his sister and his sister's best friend. All afternoon I wondered to myself, is this what family feels like? Well if it is it sure feels good to me. I don't recall spending five minutes alone with him that entire afternoon. When we got ready to drive back to Detroit, he stayed behind to finish packing up his things. Only two more weeks remained before the beginning of the fall term and I would be returning to campus. I so looked forward to his coming home these last two weeks and spending the remaining of my summer vacation with him. It never happened. The days passed and I had returned to campus to begin the fall semester (1969). I never got as much as a phone call from him. That fall, he began teaching at an elementary school in Detroit, moved out of his parents home, and got his own apartment on LaSalle Street.

Upon returning home in the spring of 1970, I can recall his picking me up and taking me to his school one evening for an end of the year program. That evening was a major event in my life. I knew I had arrived. I was out with a real, certified, grown-up school teacher. At that moment, my life was looking pretty good to me.

When the evening ended, he dropped me off at home and kissed me gently on my lips. I did not see him anymore that entire summer. I never did see his apartment. Surprisingly, when I returned to campus to begin my junior year, he started to return my letters. I was beginning to hear from him on a regular basis. I lived to receive his letters, cards and phone calls. He had thrown out a life line to me.

Sometime during the course of that year, 1971, his family purchased a two-family flat for him and his brother on Lakewood Street on the far east side of Detroit. It was the furthest east I had ever been in my life, less than half a mile from the Grosse Pointes. It was a lovely neighborhood, still partially integrated. In those days, I guess you could describe it as a middle class neighborhood, a far cry from Colfax. He resided in the lower flat, while his brother's family occupied the upper flat.

For the next two years, I am not sure just how we defined the relationship. We were in constant communication while I was still on campus and we went on dates on the occasions I was home. It was during this time that those visits home found my mother's life taking a downward spiral. I hated to go home. However one chose to define the relationship, it was safe to say, it felt all good to me. I was in love and I was just happy. I was happy that he allowed me to participate on his program. But even through my love-struck vision, it was clear that this was a one-sided, lopsided arrangement.

When I returned to campus for my senior year, my trips home to Detroit became more frequent. However, my time was not spent on Colfax. My weekend trips to Detroit found me on Lakewood Street. On those ever increasing, secret visits to Detroit, he never once drove me back to Kalamazoo. The furthest he drove me was downtown Detroit and dropped me off at the Greyhound Bus station. But I did not mind, I was in love with him and I was grateful he was still allowing me to participate on his program. Being someone's doormat started to feel pretty damn good.

Those secret weekend visits brought me closer to his family. I looked forward to spending time in that house and playing grown-up make-believe. I was living out my childhood fantasies. I had the house and the family I dreamed about all the years ago at the foot of my dollhouse. Only this was not a game and I was no longer a child. There remained missing one obvious ingredient from this grown-up game of make-believe. The entire time I was sneaking to Detroit on the weekends to be with him, he never once tried to advance our relationship to the next level. Mind you now, neither one of us were born again Christians and we were in an era which was defined by the rising civil rights movements and sexual and drug upheavals on college campuses throughout this country. However, make no mistake I was certainly no flower child by anybody's stretch of imagination, but I was not God's little Angel either. So why didn't the red flag go up before I decided to make the biggest mistake of my life? Oprah was not around then so I didn't know what an "Aha Moment was."

As strange as it may sound I don't ever recall getting a proposal from him. We never sat down together to plan our wedding or to discuss future plans. It just happened. It was a given, upon my graduation from Western Michigan University we would be married.

But what was there to discuss. He was giving me the opportunity to continue to participate on his program, for the rest of my life. I knew all that I needed to know. I was in love and this I knew for sure, I did not want to return to life on Colfax as I had left it four years ago. My doll house dreams were coming true for me. He had offered me my Great Escape. I was not about to let this opportunity of my lifetime pass me by! What else did I need to know?

In April, 1973, I walked up one aisle and in September, down another aisle. I had the biggest wedding any poor black girl from Detroit had ever seen! My doll house dreams had finally come true. Or had they? What else did I need to know?

The honeymoon didn't last very long, in fact it never got off the ground. IT never happened. I kept waiting. Weeks passed. IT never happened. I kept on waiting for IT to happen. IT never happened. When I found the courage to ask him about IT, he became verbally abusive. His exact words to me were, "Is that all I'm here for is to give you some motherfuckin dick?" Those words were the beginning of my demise. I had the answer to that question, "What else did I need to know?" My husband was gay. I never brought IT up again. I went from a doormat to wall to wall carpet.

The first time I flew to Los Angeles to visit my mother, my best friend, Sheila, drove me to the airport. When I arrived back to Metro Airport there was no one there to meet me. Fortunately there was a ram in the bush. Stacey Brackens just happened to be there that evening and offered to drive me home. When Stacey brought my luggage into the house my husband never once acknowledged my return or thanked Stacy for bringing me home. I can not recall that we ever once sat down together to eat a meal. The only time we were in the Lord's house together was on our wedding day or someone else's wedding day. He never once brought me a Christmas or birthday present.

I laid down and allowed him to walk all over my heart and soul. I put on the greatest masquerade ever! In front of an audience we both put on the performance of a lifetime. I should have won an Oscar for my performance, and been crowned the Queen of Denial. Beneath a mountain of hurt and pain I wore my crown proudly. No one need ever know that behind closed doors he treated me with utter disdain.

As long as he allowed me to participate on his program I was more than willing to live his lie and to keep up his great masquerade. After all, my doll house fantasies had finally come true. And what a doll house I turned it into! I absolutely loved buying new things and decorating my real life doll house. I turned one of the bedrooms into a den. I was so proud of that room it was perfectly coordinated. I don't think we ever spend five minutes in that room together. If I got there first, he would walk by as though I was invisible. If he got there first, he would always close the door behind him. Just another one of his ways of shutting me out.

Although it was never truly my house, I had a place to put all of my pretty things. I had the house, the father and the family I had longed for all those years and I was not willing to lose either! I wanted to hold on to all three. And hold on, I did. I took it all.

My life was torn by domestic disaster, moral madness, and ethical improprieties. I lived with every conceivable sin known to man and woman from sloppy sin to sophisticated sin. I lived with my own lies, deceit and infidelities. I lived with his lies, deceit, his verbal abuse, his emotional and physical rejection, his use of illegal drugs; he gave it all to me, everything but his love. I was a walking time bomb, headed for self-destruction. If I was not careful I would lose every vestige of self-respect, self-worth, self-validation that I thought I had found. Yes, even my soul! My spirit was dying a slow death.

Once again I felt abandoned, lost and all alone. It was during those very difficult times I would get in my car and drive through the Pointes. I discovered that a whole new world existed and what a world it was! Driving through this exclusive east side suburb, Grosse Pointe took my breath away. My childhood dreams escalated to monumental proportion. All of my troubles seemed to be cast into a sea of oblivion, better yet, into the Detroit River. I found great solace driving along Lake Shore Drive. Regrettably, the hurt and pain reared its ugly head once I returned to my grown-up doll house on Lakewood Street.

That same question that plagued my mother's spirit now loomed over my life. The most troubling question in the classroom of affliction is not 'why', nor is it 'how much'; rather it is 'how long'? It is not the depth, but rather the duration of distress and sadness that produces despair.

Thanks be to God, He did not let the big lie live forever! One day my tortured soul opened up and cried out to the God of my childhood. The Lord heard my cries and came to see about His child. Thus, the second life defining event. On September 3, 1976, I went back to the church of my rearing and joined or rather rejoined St. Stephen A.M.E. Church. The following week, September 10, 1976, I was baptized and accepted Jesus Christ as Lord and Savior of my life. Indeed, I am proud of the rich legacy of the A.M.E. Church as the oldest African-American organization in this country. But the connection that has been far greater than any church membership, has been my personal relationship and connection with God, the Father, God, the Son, and God, the Holy Spirit. It was this "vertical connection" that saved a wretch like me. Looking back, I have felt the hand of God on me all of my life. I know He came to see about me years ago at the foot of my doll house.

I don't have a clear and precise time as to when it happened, but it did happen. One day grace showed up and I was able to forgive my first husband. Wisdom has taught me that in spite of who and what he was or was not, my first husband was a victim of his own unfortunate imprints. I owe him a tremendous debt. Not only does he have my forgiveness, but he also has my gratitude. Thanks to all the unhappiness, grief, pain and rejection that he gave to me I found my greatest life defining moment.

Ask me who I am I will reply loudly and proudly,
I am a "Child of the King!"

Little did I expect that eight years later after returning to the church of my rearing, it would lead me to my third life defining moment. It was there that I became acquainted with Attorney Fred K. Persons. I say became acquainted with because I had known Attorney Fred Persons practically all of my life. I had joined this church at an early age and he, (and only he) read the morning announcements and welcomed the visitors to each and every worship service. Fred Persons had been a member of the Steward Board of St. Stephen A.M.E. Church since 1945. He had been a pillar in the church for as long as I can remember. Fred Persons was Mr. St. Stephen.

Not only had Fred had a rich history in his church, he had been a practicing attorney in the city of Detroit since 1955. He had been actively involved in both and had in many instances been a trailblazer for those who came behind him. Fred Persons, an accomplished, respected attorney was clearly a man of distinction and class, a real people person in every sense of the word. Fred loved to be around people and people loved to be around Fred Persons. He was always upbeat with a kind word for every one he met. He was a sharp dresser too! He most definitely set the bar, if not raised it, in that area. Over the years Fred had been tagged the sharpest lawyer in downtown Detroit.

Fred K. Persons, a successful attorney, was living in the palatial white house at 1600 Lincolnshire and was married to a beautiful, elegant, high society sophisticate. According to the world's standards and perceptions, Fred had all the trappings of the good life. Fred Persons had it all! Or did he?

The answer to that query was evidenced in 1983. It was in that year that Fred Persons discovered that he had been living a lie. Fred had been living someone else's lie. Their lie was not his truth. Fred Persons did not have it all. Fred was not happy. Fred was a man of God. He had strong faith in the Lord. He had been trying to make heaven his home all of his life. He could not and would not let the enemy destroy him now. In May of 1984, Fred asked his wife for a divorce.

Fred Persons was now an eligible bachelor, and most certainly marketable. So then, when cupid's arrow began to shoot his interests and unmistakable advances in my direction, why did I not readily respond? I queried, "What in the world do I have in common, with this pompous, self-possessed, holier-than-thou, elitist, ol' man?" Yes folks, those were my exact thoughts toward Fred. Not only were those my thoughts, those were also some of the first words I uttered to him. What a big flirt he was and everybody knew it. However, my lack of interest and no responsiveness to his flirtations did not discourage or dissuade his advances. Always a gentleman, the dinner invitations and the polite verbal overtures kept right on coming. He was relentless. His interest became obvious to others as well!

His persistence finally paid off. After six months of this cat and mouse game, my closest friend Sheila encouraged me to go out with him and I finally accepted one of his dinner invitations. I've always heard that whatever God has for you He has ten thousand ways of getting it to you. It did not take very long. Being around Attorney Persons was infectious. He was always the consummate gentleman, that award winning smile, that great sense of humor, charm, his style and grace accompanied him everywhere he went. My perceptions of him were quickly being redefined and refined. He was not that stuffy "elitist ol' man" I had perceived him to be during my formative years growing up at St. Stephen A.M.E. Church. Fred knew how to treat a lady. He knew how to put a smile on your face and laughter in your heart. But above all, Fred was a man with strong faith in God.

I don't know which is more accurate, but as the months passed, either the hunter got captured by the game or the game got caught. However you choose to put it, God had put it all together for us long ago. We grew madly in love. With four years of a courtship and many trials and tests behind us, we discovered that in spite of our age differences, we were both willing to make an investment and a lifetime commitment to our love. On Sunday afternoon, November 15, 1987, walking down the front steps of my Grandmother's porch on Colfax, Fred Persons asked me for my hand in marriage. As the saying goes, "The rest is history." On January 12, 1988, I became Mrs. Fred K. Persons, Esq., thus my third life defining moment.

Ours was a fairy tale marriage from the beginning. It had all the makings for a tinsel town romance, ripped straight from the pages of a Hollywood script, the perfect May/December love story.

Someone has said that you unconsciously choose a partner who has the potential to help you heal the unresolved pain from your childhood. When I married Fred, I found everything that I had been searching for at the foot of my doll house. At last I was whole. We were truly blessed. God shined down on us. God had been good to us! There were so many memorable events in our eleven year marriage, it would be utterly impossible for me to describe them all. However, allow me to lift up two of the most memorable.

The first was the 75th surprise birthday celebration I gave Fred on Sunday, June 19, 1994. I invited a host of friends and family members to join us at the 10:45 a.m. worship service. Afterwards, we gathered in the fellowship hall to continue the celebration.

I presented Fred with the following words:

We gather today to celebrate and give honor to this most auspicious occasion in the life of my husband, Fred K. Persons. I wish at this time to collectively thank each of you for your presence here today. I have four gifts to present to Fred today.

The first has been presented and evidenced to him through your acceptance of this invitation. Thank you from the bottom of my heart. The second gift is my heart. However, I could not figure out how I could pluck out my heart and present it to Fred, yet, at the same time be here with him today. Consequently, I hope that the words I have prepared will in some small measure speak to what lies within my heart.

As many of you are aware, Fred professes to be an expert in many matters. One of these areas of expertise lies in the area of mathematics. It was during one of our late night discussions that Fred *reminded me that mathematics has always been and continues to be the only exact science. Yes 2+2 will always equal 4, and 4+4 will always equal 8. 64-33 will always equal 31. Ten years ago when we embarked upon this relationship that latter equation represented the difference between our ages. That gap may just as well have been a millennium in terms of the differences we brought into this relationship.*

However, as time passed we discovered, we shared many of the same interests. Our commonalities grew more apparent and the differences grew less apparent. And though the years have not narrowed the gap our lives grew closer and closer and our hearts grew fonder and fonder. Four years later we decided to fully embrace the love we had created, nurtured, injured, mended and yes even defended,

Believing as the scripture teaches us in Mark 10:27,'with men it is impossible, but not with God, for with God all things are possible." Thus, recognizing the possible obstacles that stood ahead of us we released all reservations and became man and wife.

I would be remiss this afternoon, if I did not remember my dearly departed, but forever beloved grandmother. Grandma loved Fred, and Fred loved my grandmother. Those of you who knew her, knew how much she loved her baby granddaughter. Grandma fully sanctioned and blessed our union. She always taught me to "Hold to God's Unchanging Hand"

Fred, we have put our faith and trust in the Lord, and He has truly blessed us with a rich and loving marriage.

Fred, I thank God each day for you.

As I attempt to bring these remarks to a close, I wish to leave you with one clear message. However, in order for me to conclude, I must first remind you of an incident that occurred two weeks ago. We were invited to an Open House at Hot Sam's Clothier. There you were asked to deliver some words of encouragement and support to the new owners. Fred, you prefixed your remarks with these words "My wife is in the audience and I hope she doesn't mind me saying this, but in two weeks if the good Lord blesses me to be here, I will be 75 years old. " You continued on with your remarks.

Dear husband, to that remark, I wish to simply reply to you that the only thing I minded was the thought that you thought I minded.

As I stand beside you this day, I wish to remove any and all doubt in that regard. Let it be recorded on this 19th day of June 1994, I Mrs. Fred K. Persons unashamedly announce very loudly and proudly "HAPPY 75th BIRTHDAY, Fred. I am proud to be your wife; I could not have been blessed with a more wonderful husband.

I love you dearly,

As the songwriter put it "Many things about tomorrow I may not seem to understand, but I know who holds tomorrow and I know who holds my hand'

May we lift our glasses as we salute and honor Fred K.

Persons on this most Auspicious Day, and wish him a

Blessed and Happy 75th Birthday, and many more returns.

Fred, I love you, We love you, Most of all

GOD LOVES YOU!!!

The third gift was dinner out with three close couples.

The fourth gift was presented to him upon our return home. (*I hear you Oprah; tell what I know but not all I know*)

The second most memorable occasion was in November, 1999. St. Stephen A.M.E. Church would be celebrating its 80th anniversary. Fred was to be recognized and honored for his fifty years of faithful service to the Steward Board. The presentation of this recognition would take place at the closing banquet on Friday evening, November 12, 1999.

Fred has never stood on ceremony nor did he take to flowery and showy displays, especially when he would be the one put on display. In fact if left up to his own devises, Fred would have much preferred to have stayed at home and leave the celebrating to others. Those days, that is where he preferred to be anyway. He certainly would have objected to my plans to turn this into such a special night for him. But I was proud of this recognition and like a proud mother I wanted others to share in the occasion. Not only that, five months earlier Fred had also celebrated his 80th birthday. Unfortunately, at the time, I was unable to give him an 80th birthday celebration. So without his knowledge or permission I invited family and friends to join us in this celebration.

With the recent announcement of prostate cancer staring us in the face, I thought it would be a great idea to invite his sisters to come for the occasion as well. It had been nearly five years since his mother's home going. That was the last time Fred had seen his sisters, Louise, Joyce and Frances. Joyce had not been to Detroit in over forty years, and I don't think his sister, Louise, had ever been to Detroit. Furthermore, she did not fly, period! If anyone would come I suspect it would have been Frances. What are the chances they will come?

Joyce and Louise arrived on the Friday afternoon of the banquet. Needless to say Fred was blown away by their arrival. For the first time in his eighty years, Fred Persons was just about at a loss for words. The banquet paled in comparison to the celebration the three of them shared that weekend. I had never seen my husband so happy and so surprised by anything. This has been duly recorded in my archives as one of the most cherished memorable gifts I have given to my husband.

Little did I know that would be the last time Fred saw his sisters and it would be the last time on this side of heaven that his sisters would spend with their most highly regarded, greatly admired, deeply loved and respected 'big brother', Fred.

Ask me who I am. I will reply loudly and proudly,
I am Mrs. Fred K. Persons, Esq.

Gwendolyn D. Persons

Part One

Trouble

Then they cry unto the Lord in their trouble
and he saveth them out of their distresses.

Psalm 107:19

60   Gwendolyn D. Persons

Trouble

My day began each afternoon at 3:00 o'clock. It was at this hour I would leave work and anxiously head home to be with my husband. As a general rule I was the first one to arrive home. Although there were many days when Fred's work day ended before mine, he would always wait until he thought I had arrived home before coming himself. Fred simply did not like coming home to an empty apartment. I think this in large part was a carry over from his childhood. Fred had often told me that never once while he was growing up, did he arrive home and his mother was not in the home.

While waiting for Fred to come home each afternoon my routine generally consisted of sitting down to read the mail, do the crossword puzzle in the paper and watch Oprah. This hour was mine. It was my downtime or my d-stress time.

Occasionally if I really needed it, I would leave Fred a note and head down to the gym or the Jacuzzi for a thirty to forty minute workout.

Whenever Fred Persons walked through the door, no matter what kind of day I had Fred would make everything right in my world. Fred never entered this apartment in a bad mood. He never brought the problems of his day home. He was always upbeat, jovial, full of joy. Fred entered the apartment calling my name, "Perci," "Persabol," "Baby Persons." Over the years I had coined several cute nicknames for Fred. It wasn't long before Fred had begun calling me those same nicknames. Often when I heard him coming into the apartment I would rush to hide. I loved greeting him with that element of surprise. Fred, too, was full of surprises for me. When we were first married Fred would surprise me with bouquets of beautiful tropical flowers every week. In 1990, I quit smoking and joined Weight Watchers at the same time. When Fred discovered that chewing sugarless gum seemed to help curb my appetite and subdue my craving for cigarettes, he must have bought all the sugarless gum in downtown Detroit. I entered the apartment one afternoon and a trail of gum met me at the door. Fred had literally made a gum trail throughout the apartment. The trail ended in our bedroom and there I found the bed covered with boxes and boxes of carefree sugarless gum.

I loved living in downtown Detroit. Soon after moving downtown I discovered some wonderful hidden shopping treasures. Introducing my friends to these hidden treasures became my mission, my obligation if you will, in bolstering the crippling downtown revenue. During the summers I organized shopping tours uncovering these well hidden treasures. Fred was also introduced to these hidden treasures and became well acquainted with the owners. He would frequent the shops and inquire, "Has my wife been in here lately?" "Does she have anything put aside?" If I did happen to have something put away it was not unusual for Fred to surprise me and bring the item home. Then, in his lawyer, matter-of-fact demeanor, he would admonish me with these words, "Now Gwen, you can't keep these downtown merchants in business all by yourself."

A favorite surprise of mine was always dinner out in the middle of the week. This was always an unexpected surprise. Of course, every Friday night without exception for the past fifteen years (the tradition started before we were married) we dined at Joe Muer. This was the highlight of our week. We looked forward to meeting our friends the Muics' at the bar for cocktails and fellowship before dinner. Over the years we developed some very close friendships and met many wonderful people at Joe Muer.

It saddened our hearts deeply when they closed the doors in 1997. Our Friday night ritual had come to an end. How we loved and looked forward to bringing our work week to a close at the corner of Vernor and Gratiot.

But no matter if we were dining in or dining out, the dinner hour was a special time of the day for us. It was, after all, our first chance to reconnect, to catch up, share our day, share some laughter and to give thanks. It was Fred's role to say grace before each meal. On occasion however, he would ask me to say the grace. During the dinner hour without fail, Fred would always take the opportunity to inquire, "Have you talked to Jackie today?" I enjoyed preparing Fred's meals; he always showed his appreciation for my efforts. After dinner I would leave Fred to clean the kitchen while I put on my walking shoes and headed out the door to do my evening stair climbing routine. Fred felt that if I could work all day, come home and prepare dinner, the least he could do was to clean the kitchen and clean it he did. Cleaning the kitchen was indeed a job for Fred. He approached it with the same dedication and philosophy that he applied to everything he did. "If you're going to do it, do it right." Fred always said he cleaned like Mr. Wheat called clean and he didn't turn that kitchen loose until it passed the white glove test. Mr. Wheat by the way, was a Caucasian man who owned a jewelry store in Columbus, GA. As a teenager, growing up in Columbus, Fred learned to clean while working in that jewelry store.

I suppose our evenings throughout the week were pretty routine. After dinner we would each retreat to our separate quarters to do our own thing. For me that entailed talking on the phone, calling Mama, (admittedly, not every night as he would have liked me to do), school work, planning a sorority activity, checking my e-mail (that came later) catching up on household chores, reading or writing. Later on, after my writing took off, Fred would often walk into the room where I would be sitting at the computer and inquire, "Baby, are you working on your book?"

Evening T.V. held very little entertainment value for me with one exception. I absolutely looked forward to tuning in to the

Detroit City Council. I love to see my tax dollars at work. I have a secret desire in my heart to one day run for the City Council. Whenever I made even the slightest mention of this to Fred, he would respond, "If you do, you'll have to get a lawyer." Fred held a much different opinion about the Common Council. In Fred's estimation the Council served very little purpose. But in spite of his less than favorable opinion toward the Common Council, Fred would without warning, clearly out of the blue, with genuine sincerity and concern for me, ask "Baby, would you really like to be on the Council?" He was just that kind of a guy. Fred was a jewel!

Fred's evenings were much more routine than mine. They were basically the same each evening. He settled in his favorite 'big chair' and watched *Moneyline, Crossfire,* and *Jeopardy,* then the remainder of the evening was spent watching a sporting event. Fred loved sports, and had very little tolerance for most anything else that came over the airways including the evening news. I was not by any stretch of the imagination a sports enthusiast, consequently we seldom spend time during the week watching TV together. However, just as sure as the sun rises in the east and sets in the west and we were at Joe Muer every Friday night, when Sunday evening rolled around everything in the Persons' household came to a standstill. Folk, who knew, knew not to call during the 7:30-8:30 hour. That was the hour we came together and turned our hearts and turned our TV channel to the 'Bethany Hour' from Bethany Baptist Church in Brooklyn, New York, Dr. William Augustus Jones, pastor.

Dr. Jones had become my spiritual father. His teachings and preachings had become a source of inspiration not only in our marriage, but in our daily lives. We had been abundantly blessed through his television ministry. We never missed an opportunity to see him whenever he came this way.

Unless Fred was out of town, (in the eleven years of our marriage, with the exception of a special, evening call meeting of the Steward Board or a special church conference), Fred Persons was home with me every evening. There was very little that we didn't do together. We had even been accused of being joined at the hip. See one, see the other. This was no surprise to us; after all when were joined 'in holy matrimony 'the two became one'.

Retiring together had become a routine, a habit. It gave yet another chance for us to reconnect not only with each other, but with the Master. We prayed together every night before crawling into bed. Once in bed, we talked. Fred loved to talk. We talked about everything under the sun. Fred loved to tell me about the early years of his law practice. How many times had he told me how as chairman of the penal code he put the bondsmen out of business. Judges were forced or ordered to let first time offenders out on their own recognizance. Fred was proud of his legal accomplishments. Another one of his treasured accomplishments was boycotting Briggs (Tiger) stadium during the forties, when the owners would not allow Negroes to play in the national leagues.

Among Fred's other accomplishments was that of defending the young man who was charged with inciting the 1967 riots in Detroit. He absolutely loved to share these stories with me and I loved hearing them. I don't think I could have loved him more, but listening to his many, many accomplishments, long before I was a part of his life, made me very proud to be Mrs. Fred K. Persons.

Every night Fred had something to say about the goodness of the Lord in his life and his faith in the Lord. Fred's favorite faith story happened in Columbus, Georgia, at seven years of age. Fred was the son of an A.M.E. preacher. On a hot, stormy summer night in Columbus, Georgia, Fred was instructed by his father to assist him in sawing some wood. The thunder was roaring, the lightening was flashing and by Fred's account the storm was relentlessly raging in Columbus on that fateful night.

Having been double promoted twice, once in the kindergarten and again in the first grade, Fred was a bright child. He knew at the age of seven that metal attracted lightening. Fred was scared to death. He said to his Papa, "Papa I'm afraid of the lightening striking the saw. Let's stop and go inside." Fred's Papa never stopped sawing. He very simply and calmly said to his son, "God is just lighting up the sky so I can see how to cut this wood. Keep holding on." The next Sunday, at the age of seven, Fred gave his life to Christ and had been putting his trust in the Lord and holding on to his faith and to God's unchanging hand ever since.

I'm not exactly sure when I made up this game, but often before falling off to sleep we played *Pick a Hymn*. It went something like this. One of us would pick a favorite hymn and then we would take turns singing a verse. Of course neither one of us could carry a tune, but you could never convince Fred of that. Some of our favorite hymns were "God Moves in a Mysterious Way," "Blessed Assurance," Fred's favorite, "Great Is Thy Faithfulness" and 'We'll Understand it Better By and By." This was just another way we enjoyed praise and worship together. We loved the Lord; God had been good to us.

Before concluding these nightly or midnight discourses, I often asked Fred, "Fred, what if you get to heaven before I do, how will I find you?" His reply was always the same, "Baby, you won't have to look for me, I'll be that bright and shining star waiting for you when you get there." Those words were so reflective of how things were for us down here at pavement level. Whenever I took a trip out of town without Fred, upon my arrival home Fred was always right there to meet me. When I approached the end of that runway, he would be there, standing, waiting with that big smile on his face. I never had to look for him or wait for him. He was always there. He promised me it would be the same way in heaven.

In recent years, before falling off to sleep, Fred's words to me had been, "God has been good to me and you are the best thing that ever happened to me." Tears of joy filled my eyes and thanksgiving my heart. Hearing these words uttered by my husband was the most valuable and precious gift that I could ever hope to receive from my husband. I have been blessed to have received this gift over and over and over again. I was blessed in a mighty way to have been married to Fred K. Persons for eleven years. They were without a doubt the best years of my life.

"It doesn't matter how right any of us think that we are. God is not arbitrary to what He meets out. He allows His rain to fall on the just and the unjust alike. Jesus told us that in the world we will have tribulations. We don't always know when trouble will arrive, nor from what quarters it's coming. Just be sure that it is en route to your doorstep.

Sometimes trouble creeps up on you and at other times, it meets you head on like a monstrous headwind. Trouble can descend on you like a bolt-of lightening out of the blue. Trouble comes in so many ways and in many forms. Believe me, one of them will surely knock on your door. It is for certain no one is exempt. (Dr. William Augustus Jones)

Out of the blue and unanticipated, trouble descended on our lives. I hadn't expected or prepared for such a sudden reversal in our finances. Fred had always treated his body like a temple never misusing or abusing it. Consequently at the age of eighty, I never expected Fred would be diagnosed with cancer.

But above all the unanticipations and perhaps the most paralyzing and the absolute toughest to accept, was the aging process. I had never thought of or envisioned Fred as an 'old man'. Scripture teaches us to honor thy father and thy mother, that our days shall be long upon the earth that the Lord has given us. God has only promised three score and ten. Fred was now in his tenth bonus year. God had truly been faithful to His word and to Fred. (I pray that the Lord's blessings shall also be upon my life).

One of my all time favorite songs from the sixties was by the Four Tops, 'The Whole World is a Stage'. Well, if I was playing a part, no one had prepared me for this scene in our lives. I was not rehearsed for this role. I was Fred Persons' darling wife, his queen, 'his baby.' I had counted on this fairy-tale marriage to last forever. I don't think Fred the eternal optimist, forever young at heart was prepared for it either. If his heart could control his mind and body, believe me Fred would have never grown old.

Now I know what some of you may be thinking. You're thinking, Fred was an old man when I married him. No, when I refer to him as old I'm not referring to chronological age, but rather to his actions, behaviors, and his mental functioning. The incessant movement of time had brought Fred to the fulness of years, and with it an unexpected crop of misunderstood and oftentimes unforgiving behaviors.

Fred K. Persons was always a man with unique and uncompromising attributes. He was a strong and proud man, a role model for everyone who came into contact with him in both his professional and personal life.

Intellectually, Fred was a natural born leader, a genius at his craft, a master in the courtroom. He loved the practice of law. Up and coming attorneys would frequent the courtroom just to see him in action. Fred knew the law and he loved the practice. There was never any doubt or misunderstanding on where he stood on any issue. Whenever Fred took a stand he did not waiver; he stood by it. Perhaps it was not always the popular stand, but always the right one. Fred was a fighter, a warrior and a pioneer in the practice of law in the City of Detroit. He was known for his strong convictions and opinions.

Fred told me about the time he argued a case in front of a white judge. The judge told Fred that he did not like the way he was applying the law in that particular case and if he continued in that vein, he would have Fred locked up and held in contempt of court. Fred told the judge that he did not care whether he liked it or not, he did not write the law. He further told the judge that he did not like it when he was a boy growing up in Georgia and he had to take his mother to the 'colored only water faucet' and that black people had no rights that the white man had to honor. Fred said to the judge "I didn't like that law judge and I held it in contempt. But I had to live with it." Fred was indeed a man of uncompromising character.

Pardon me for saying again, but Fred Persons was a sharp dresser. He had a reputation of being the sharpest lawyer in downtown Detroit. A proud soul! Over the years Fred Persons became known as the lawyer with the white shirt and the white tie and was a fixture in the City County Building. Fred was an ambassador for the City of Detroit, always there spreading good-will to all who came in contact with him.

Physically Fred kept himself in tip top shape. He loved to walk all over downtown Detroit. For years, throughout the course of a day Fred walked from one courtroom to another and back to his office. Fred loved the game of golf. At the age of seventy-nine Fred could still play 18 holes without a cart. For a man in his golden years Fred was in excellent physical shape. Fred lived like a king and treated his adoring wife like his precious queen. He loved life and knew how to enjoy it. I use the past tense because time robbed Fred of many of his unique, defining and uncompromising attributes. Time caught up with Fred and time brought him in.

But of all Fred's unique, defining, uncompromising attributes, it was his unwavering and abiding faith in God that had grown stronger as the years went by. Fred Persons was a witness for the Lord. Fred loved to tell others about the goodness of the Lord; he loved to spread the good news of the gospel. His testimonies of the goodness of the Lord inspired many to seek their own personal walk with God. Fred talked about God's goodness from the church house to the courthouse. Even now, as an old man, he had fresh faith.

My Knight-in-shining Armor, my rock, 'the wind beneath my wings', my best friend, the one who could right every wrong, could move every mountain in my life, the one I had learned to lean and depend on, was slowly drifting away from me. I looked for him and expected him to be there for me. But one evening I looked for him and he was not there. He had stopped showing up at the dinner table. My earthly king had vanished right before my very eyes.

Those much anticipated evening encounters at the dinner table had become almost dreaded encounters. Fred's mind was beginning to play an illusive game of hide and seek. That great mind that used to meet me every evening stopped making an appearance at our dinner table. Our discussions and dinner conversations had become scripted, predictive and superficial. Our conversations suffered. Fred was no longer an active participant and contributor to these discussions. We no longer connected. That bond, that oneness, seemed to have divided in two. I had lost my best friend. The man I had married eleven years ago was no longer there for me. It was as if I was mourning his death while he yet lived. I almost felt as though he had abandoned me, stopped caring about me. I felt as if he had left me there all alone. I felt betrayed.

Fred used to be my worst critic. My appearance was always important to Fred. But it seemed that Fred no longer even noticed me. My weight was at an all time high and Fred did not even seem to mind.

It was all so easy for me to lose the weight when we were first married. I carried not a care in the world. Fred carried the load for us both. The table had turned and I was finding more and more on my plate, both literally and figuratively I was overeating and the weight was beginning to mount. If that was not enough, at a time when there was already a financial 'famine in the land' I began to overspend. These two uninvited intruders took up residence in my life.

This was an "Aha moment," if ever there was one and the illumination was crystal clear! Weight is never the real issue, and it was perfectly clear to me what my issues were. I had made the connection, but I was helpless to do anything about it. What was worst, I didn't even seem to care.

Dealing and coping with these circumstances was becoming more and more difficult. One evening some more uninvited guests knocked at our door. An Australian fellow named Merlot and two of his Italian sidekicks, Martini and Rossi. I invited them to join us at the dinner table one evening and their visits became more frequent. Their company at the dinner hour made those dreaded dinner encounters easier to bear. We seemed to be developing quite a close relationship. Before too long they started arriving before dinner and too often remaining well after dinner was over.

Insulating and medicating my pain with these uninvited guests became the order of the day. I should have seen them each to the door months ago. I was growing weary, angry and afraid. Our critics and skeptics forecasted it years ago. They said that one day the money would run out and Fred would get old. Had the player haters been right? The aging process was indeed taking its toll on our relationship. The devil was rearing its ugly head in my life once again. Without our consent the genealogy of addiction hooked up with the genealogy of longevity, and the resulting offspring of this marriage was 'trouble'. I was at a crossroad in my marriage and it marked crisis. Old age and sickness had broken my dreams and shattered my spirit. Life had lost its sweetness. All of my adult life, I had been vigilant and kept a prayerful watch over my rich inheritance of addictive personality. Over the years, time and time again, I had been witness to its effects in my immediate family. I declared early on I would never allow the genealogy of addiction to overtake, control and ruin my life the way it had so many before me.

Those terrible demons had paid me a visit twenty four years ago. I cried out then to the God of my childhood. He heard my cries and rescued me. I knew that as long as I allowed the devil to be in the driver's seat I was an accident waiting to happen and happen it did. It was a head-on collision. One that could have very well been a fatal accident. And where did it happen? It happened at that proverbial dinner table one evening.

It had not been a particularly good day at work. The end of the year was at hand. It had been one of those days that I had precious little tolerance for little people masquerading as students and big people masquerading as parents and educators. There were days you are made to wonder if it's worth the effort, days when there seemed to be absolutely nothing rewarding, satisfying, or redeeming in the job of a Detroit Public School educator.

Fortunately, these days have been few. Lately however, everything seemed to be closing in all around me. I longed for those days when I anxiously looked forward to 3:00 p.m., rushing home to end or rather, begin my day with Fred. Once Fred could right the wrongs; once Fred could make me forget about the 'troubles of de world'.

On this fateful day I left work and headed for home. Fred's trips to court had gotten fewer and fewer. He would pick up an assignment every now and then just to keep his feet wet. However, for the most part, Fred's days of practicing law were behind him. His days were generally spent running an errand or two for me, walking over to the Ren Cen and just hanging out there or walking down to Hot Sam's to visit the boys. It saddened me and hurt my heart to see this once active, vital man with so much idle time on his hands. By 2:00 p.m. most every afternoon Fred was back home and had positioned himself in his favorite spot in the lobby of the Millender Center anxiously waiting for me to return home to be with him.

Fred loved to people watch. Fred loved people. He sat in the lobby and greeted the residents as they came through the door. Everyone looked forward to and expected to see Mr. Persons sitting there with a smile on his face a friendly word for all.

However this fateful day I did not find Fred sitting in his favorite spot so I headed up to the apartment. When I entered the apartment the heat just about knocked me out. I checked the windows, they were closed. I checked the A.C., it was off. Fred was not in the apartment either. I immediately turned on the air and I headed back down to the lobby. Fred had still not returned to his expected position. I retrieved the mail and took a seat in the lobby to wait for his return.

There was an envelope addressed to Fred and Gwendolyn Persons from the Internal Revenue Service. I could hardly believe what my eyes had fallen upon, an overdue tax notice from the

Internal Revenue Service. Clearly this was not the first time they had sent us such a letter. This was the last thing I needed to see today. I headed back to the apartment.

I'm not sure which one of my companions met me upon my arrival, *Merlot* or *Martini and Rossi*. We sat down together as I resumed the daunting task of reading through the mail. There was once a time in what seemed like not such a distant past that I would have set any mail of this nature aside for Fred to deal with. However with more and more on my plate these days, this was just another one of those daunting tasks I had to assume. Fred had always taken care of our taxes. Like most of our contractual documents, all I ever had to do was sign on the bottom line. Fred took care of such matters. So what was up with this and what about these penalties? I was scared to death. This could not have come at a worse time. Tonight would certainly not be one of those scripted dinner conversations. I went into the kitchen and began to prepare dinner.

Not long afterwards Fred came waltzing through the door in his usual upbeat demeanor, calling my name, "Percibol." I greeted him with much less enthusiasm. Sensing my irritation and lack of interest in whatever he was saying to me, he went into the bedroom to wait for me to call him to dinner. Should I go into the room and confront the matter now, or wait until after dinner? I decided to wait. I finished preparing dinner and called Fred to the table, he said grace. The next words out of his mouth were "How was your day?" I could not contain it; it could not wait until after dinner, I could not sit through another scripted dinner. I presented Fred with the letter.

Fred did not appear to be at all surprised by it nor was he concerned about its contents. I asked him what he had planned on doing about it and just how he intended to handle the situation? The letter even indicated that the taxpayers could have their wages garnisheed if these taxes were not paid. I said, "Well last time I looked I was the only one getting a paycheck around here! Are you going to let that happen to me Fred?" That statement infuriated and insulted him. Fred let me know in no uncertain terms that he was well aware of this matter, and that there was nothing for me to be concerned about; he would handle it, period!

This was one time I could not allow the period to end the conversation. I did not drop it. "Sure," I said, "and just how do you plan on doing that?" The more I persisted on knowing just how he planned on dealing with the matter the more defensive he became. The controlling, no nonsense, don't mess with me and my business, man I had married showed up at the dinner table that evening. Fred was not about to allow me to question him or to doubt him. To even suggest that he was not able to take care of the situation angered him to no end. That controlling macho, "I'm in control attitude," only exasperated me more. How dare he hide behind what used to be; how dare he deny the seriousness of the situation? No, we will deal with this, and we will deal with this now! You will not shut the door on this! He became even more defensive and almost hostile towards me. I felt as though I was on trial and I was being made to feel guilty for bringing the matter up. "I will take care of it Gwen." Fred was in denial; he was not willing to accept his limitations and no one knew better than I what those limitations were! He could not take care of it without my help. I needed more of an answer from him and I wanted it now! The tension between us grew. The words being exchanged between us escalated to damaging proportions. What was happening here? We were both out of our element. This scene had never been played out in this union. Before I knew what was happening, I rose from the table, and exclaimed, "After dealing with those damn kids all day I have to come home to more crap. I don't know how much more of this I can take." Fred replied. "You don't have to take anything Gwen, leave now." Before I knew it, the words were out, "No, I have a better idea, why don't you just die now." I ran out of the apartment leaving Fred sitting at the dinner table all alone.

In that instant, I felt as if my life was over. We had never been so unkind, so cruel to one another. If words could kill, I was guilty of committing verbal assassination against my husband. I had immediately been convicted in the courtroom of my very soul. It was the coldest, blackest day or rather night in my life. I walked aimlessly the streets of downtown Detroit. I asked myself, "What am I doing out here?" Where was I going?" I found myself sitting on our favorite stump, the spot where Fred loved to watch the fireworks. As I looked up toward the Millender Center my gaze took me even higher, I looked up toward the heavens. I asked God to please forgive me for allowing the devil to get such a stronghold in my life. How could I have been so cruel to Fred? I knew that Fred was not himself. I knew that Fred would never do anything to deliberately hurt or bring harm to me. I would rather die myself than to ever hurt Fred. Those words had literally pierced my heart and my soul. I would do anything to take those words back, for him to have never heard them. But I could not take them back, they were out there. He heard me say them.

I knew I could not sit out there all night. I got up from that stump and headed back toward the apartment. But I didn't go straight home, I made a detour. I stopped off in the hotel lounge. I took a seat in the corner of the lounge and waited for my cohort Merlot to join me. Those words just kept echoing over and over in my mind and deep within my spirit. They were almost haunting, like a ghost from the past. Where had I heard them before?

Suddenly, like a rushing wind it all came back to me and grabbed so tight to my heart and soul it did not want to turn me loose. I remembered it as though it were yesterday. We had stopped by my mothers' on the way home from church just as we did practically every Sunday. My mother had been having a very difficult time dealing with her aging mother. For so many years I watched those demons of addiction rest, rule and abide in my mother's life. When I heard my mother say to my grandmother, "I wish you would die," I immediately lashed out with an evil tongue. Before leaving my mother on that fateful Sunday she left me with these words, "You just wait, your day will come."

Mother was prophesying to me that day that Fred would one day get old.

The reality of the situation was made manifest in that lounge. I was turning into my mother. I got up from the table and headed straight for the apartment. Not knowing what to expect I asked God to give me strength to face what lay behind that door. I walked into the apartment and went straight to the bedroom where I found Fred sitting there in his 'big chair.' He sat in silence. I stood there and said nothing. I just looked at my husband. He looked so frail, so helpless, so rejected. Again, I wanted to take back those words. I could not bear to see him look so sad from the pain I had caused him that night. I don't think he even realized that I had returned to the apartment. When I finally got up the courage to make my presence known, I said to my husband, "Fred are you all right?" He looked up at me and said, "Yes, Gwen, I'm all right, are you?" I answered, "NO, Fred and I am afraid that I never will be again. I am afraid of what is happening to me to us." He invited me to come into the room. I entered the room with extreme ambivalence. I approached him and took a seat on the side of the bed. The two little words, "I'm sorry," did not seem adequate enough to begin to remedy this situation, but they were all I had at my disposal. "Fred, I'm sorry." I apologized for the words I had spoken to him, I asked him to please forgive me. Fred simply said as he had on every occasion of even the slightest disagreement between us, "Gwen, I am never angry with you."

While I was in the lounge pacifying and assuaging my sorrows, Fred had been sitting there in his 'big chair' talking to God about us. He rose from his 'big chair' and sat on the side of the bed next to me. "I need to talk to you Gwen."

He prefaced his remarks with these infamous words "Gwen, don't interrupt me, until I'm finished." How many times had I heard those words? Whenever I heard those words, I knew the attorney was about to plead his case. "Gwen, I don't know how much more time I have to live. I've lived my life. God has been good to me and you are the best thing that ever happened to me. I can't bear to see you so unhappy. You are still a young woman and I don't want my life to be a burden on you." Upon hearing those words, I rushed to interrupt him but he repeated his instructions to me. "I ask that you not interrupt me." I want you to call my sister Louise, and tell her to come get me. I can live out the rest of my days in Columbus." I sat there in silence, listening to my husband plead for me to abandon him. I could not believe what I was hearing. My heart began to race and the tears filled my eyes. I felt as though my life had ended. I had breached the sanctity of our wedding vows. I had been convicted in the courtroom of my heart and soul and now I found myself sitting in Fred's courtroom of justice. My husband was the defender, the judge, and the jury and he had handed down my sentence, my punishment for this terrible crime I was indeed guilty of committing. My husband was ordering me to throw him away.

When Fred was finally finished pleading his case, I responded to my husband. With tears flooding my eyes, I begged his forgiveness over and over. "Fred I love you and you are not a burden on me." I wanted to take Fred in my arms and cradle him in the bosom of my love, as if he were just my little boy. I loved Fred Persons more than life itself, I needed for him to know and to hold fast to that truth. I let him know that I would not be calling his sister Louise to come and get him. "I am your wife, and I will be here for you, but I need help, Fred, I am afraid of what's happening to me." I asked my husband to pray for me, to pray for us that night. That is exactly what Fred Persons did. We fell on our knees and Fred prayed for us!

Folks, we should never be misled by our own goodness. It matters not how right you are or how well acquainted you are with God. It is easy, almost too easy to stumble and fall. Trouble and evil are ever present realities. They will trip you up and throw you down and attempt to conquer your soul. Trouble will seek to destroy you. Trouble is a universal predicament.

None of us is what God would have us to be. If we say we have no sin, we lie and the truth is not in us. Said the tent maker from Tarsus, "When I try to do good, evil comes to see me. When I try to walk right hidden snares try to entrap me. It matters not how upright you are, the devil is always on your trail. (Dr. William A. Jones)

We got up off our knees, and Fred admonished me as he had so many times over the years to "Trust in God and to keep the faith." I knew then that was the root of my trouble. I had allowed my faith to get low. If I had not allowed my faith level to get so low when trouble came knocking at our door my faith should have greeted trouble at the door and issued trouble its walking papers. But my faith did not meet trouble at the door and these unwelcome intruders were allowed to invade our 'pot of gold'.

Over the years, Fred had taught me how to pray. Fred told me to keep praying about it and to read the blessed book. Not only did he tell me to read the book, he told me what to read. Romans 8 and Hebrews 11:6. Then he left me with his famous last words, "Trust in the Lord with all thy heart; and lean not unto thine own understanding. In all thy ways acknowledge Him, and He will direct thy path." I suppose that is exactly what happens to the spiritually uninitiated. Once the devil is allowed to get a toehold in your life, he can then get a foothold in your life and before you know it he has a stronghold in your life. That was my predicament. My husband was okay, Fred had always been okay. It was Gwen, who needed to strengthen what Rev. Dr. Frederick Sampson referred to as that 'vertical connection'. It was time for me to get okay, to get spiritually reconnected. I needed an antidote for my trouble.

Once again I found my life tormented by that daunting question of "How long?" It was not the depth but rather the duration of my distress and sadness that produced my despair.

For the next few weeks I took my husband's advice. I sought God's intense and personal word for my life. I needed strength for my journey. I needed a WORD from the Lord. I began to search God's words on Comfort, Faith, Guidance, Hope, Joy, Kindness, Love, Patience, Peace, Strength, Truth and Understanding. Like the woman at Jacob's Well, I began taking my pot to the wells each morning. There fresh cool waters of righteousness awaited me and before long, Grace met me at the wells.

I'm not sure when it happened, but it happened. Jesus met me at the wells. The Lord sent grace to get in my pot with trouble. He either fixed the pot for me or He fixed me for the pot. In any case the results were the same, He fixed Gwen for Fred. My life was redefined at the wells or perhaps I should say it was more clearly defined. My single charge in life was to take the very best care of my husband.

After mother got well, she said to me one day, "I don't think anything can come between you and your husband." Mother was right but the dime store shrinks, the nay sayers, the skeptics, the critics, and let's not forget, the player haters would have to think again. I believe the Lord brought me to Fred Persons sixteen years ago for this appointed time. He looked down from eternity and decided the day and time that the two should become one. Fred needed me more than ever and nothing and no one would interfere with that charge. My prayer daily was that God would make me the best wife I can be for Fred.

Grace did for me what He did for the woman at the well. When Jesus met that woman at Jacob's Well, he performed one of the most amazing happenings in the bible. When He got through dealing with her situation, He placed a crown so high above her head, it would take the rest of her life to try and grow tall enough to wear it (An Anatomy of Forgiveness, Dr. William A. Jones). And so it shall be with me. No matter how tall I grow in His grace, there will always be room above where I stand.

Part Two

From Richer to Poorer

I have been young, and now am old:
  yet I have not seen the righteous forsaken,
  nor his seed begging bread

Psalm 37:25

From Richer to Poorer

"If only my money was my money and his money was our money". Most sisters do not look for and expect our knight-in-shining-armor to come riding up on his white horse, whisk us off to a big house in suburbia, become stay-at-home moms and get free tickets to the Oprah Winfrey Show. The fact is, if they are fortunate to even find a husband in these times, too few African-American men (especially if they are just out of the starting gate) have that option available to offer their wives. In today's economy it takes two paychecks just to make ends meet. So for a sister to be able to declare, "my money is my money and his money is our money," probably sounds like the best deal in town. I never expected that my acceptance of Fred's marriage proposal would find that declaration upon my life. I did of course antici-pate that being married to Fred Persons would come with some degree of financial freedom and advantages. But I fully expected to be his helpmate in every sense of the word. Now I suppose some might say it sounds like I married Fred for his money. I must admit there may be a grain of truth to that assertion.

What is that I hear you say, Dr. Phil? "When you marry for money you pay for it every day of your marriage." Dr. Phil is right. The financial freedoms that came along with being married to Fred did come with a cost, but for the record, it had a price tag that did not bankrupt me.

I married a much older man. One with old fashioned ideas and values. Fred Persons embraced the philosophy that regardless of whether a man's wife worked outside of the home, the man should never rely on the wife's income. In other words, Fred did not believe in living beyond the means of his income. Put another way, if his income could not support it, we did not have it.

Fred was indeed the 'king of his castle', and we lived by his golden rules. Fred made the gold, Fred made the rules. Fred was in charge of most things. As he liked to put it, "I pay the note on this pad." Fred did pay all the bills. Although I signed the lease renewal every year, I was never quite sure from year to year just what the note was on this pad. The note on this pad also included our monthly garage fee and our membership to the fitness center. Up until a year or two ago I had never walked inside the management office; I never had a reason to. If there was ever a problem, Fred took care of it. Without compromise the problem would be resolved. Until recently, I never saw the inside of a utility bill; Fred paid them as well.

Fred absolutely loved shopping for food. He would not allow the freezer to get low. Although we did not have a large freezer in the apartment whenever it looked (in his estimation) to be getting low that was his sign to make a bee-line to the store. He kept it well stocked. The same applied to his medicine and spirits cabinets. Better to have it and not need it, than to need it and not have it; that was another one of Fred's philosophies.

Fred preferred for us to grocery shop together and I always kept a list of things on the side of the refrigerator as things got low or as they ran out. It was not unusual for me to come home and find that Fred had replenished that list. He objected whenever I stopped by the store to pick up a few things, "Why couldn't you wait until we went shopping together to buy those things?" How many late night stories have I heard about how much his father loved and took good care of his wife and his family. One of Fred's favorite memories as a boy was that he never came home to an empty house. There was never a single day when he came home that his mother was not there. Another story he often shared was that his father always did the shopping. Fred would say, "Mama cooked what Papa bought home." I suppose the same remained true for us with one exception. I cooked what Fred brought home, only Fred brought home what I needed and what I wanted. I suspected he inherited his love for grocery shopping from his father. Fred did not like for me to spend my money on food for us. That was his responsibility. He could turn any occasion into a major social event, including a trip to the grocery store. The cashier girls loved to see Fred coming. How many people do you know who tip the check-out girl? Fred Persons did and probably only Fred Persons. God was at his best when he made Fred Persons.

Soon after we were married Fred put me on his car insurance policy. The only thing that he did not assume was my car note. So what was there for me to do with 'my money' (hope my grandmother isn't listening)!

I mentioned previously my passion for decorating. I absolutely love to decorate. So one would assume or think, umm, she probably puts all of her money in her house. Not so; nothing could be further from the truth. Soon after the honeymoon period I approached my husband about redoing the apartment, possibly replacing some of the older, dated items, particularly the ones he brought into the marriage. Whenever I even intimated this to Fred, he absolutely would go ballistic. "No, there is nothing wrong with this apartment Gwen. That would just be spending money foolishly (his money). Now since the 'king of the castle' had spoken, or had put his foot down, what was there left for me to do with my money? (hope my grandma is still not listening).

With the exception of the big difference in our ages our views on money were probably the only other big difference between us. Fred had only one credit card to his name. He only used that when we went out of town. Fred did not subscribe to the buy now/pay later ethic. Regardless what it was, if Fred did not have the cash, he did not get it, from food to furs. On the other hand, I was from a different school of thought. I fully subscribed to the buy now/pay later ethic. I was without a doubt my mother's child. Spending money foolishly and wasting money had undoubtedly been linked up to my DNA.

For years, we kept the same outdated TV's, stereo system with the eight track cassette player, that gigantic microwave oven, and all of our combined furniture we brought into our marriage. As long as Fred was in charge we bought precious little, if anything new for the apartment. Fred's old fashioned notions did not allow him to embrace technology either, so we had no VCR's, DVD's, CD's, answering machines, voice mail or caller I.D. on our telephones, cordless phones, cell phones, or computers. I used an old canister style vacuum cleaner of his for the first three years of our marriage. Once it stopped working Fred went out and purchased a brand new upright model for me.

There you have it Dr. Philippians That was one of the first prices I had to pay for marrying for money. I had to sacrifice or forfeit my passion for decorating, a passion that had followed me since those early years at the foot of my dollhouse.

However, do not weep for me. The mourning period did not last forever and my joy did come in the morning, not the next morning, but it did come.

A close first to decorating was my passion for fashion. I loved shopping. I loved buying clothes, shoes, hats, purses, jewelry and.... well I guess you get the point I'm trying to make. I was a clotheshorse! I simply loved to shop. Period!

I'm not sure if this was an inherited DNA footprint or something Jackie instilled in her girls early on. Jackie loved to take her girls shopping. Even under the protests of her mother, Jackie made every effort to see that her girls were the best dressed on the block. She succeeded!

Shortly after we were married I lost a tremendous amount of weight. I was looking good. Fred Persons was the happiest and the proudest man in town. I developed quite a reputation around this town. Fred loved to say "You're the sharpest gal in town."

By now I am sure the answer to the question, "What was there for me to spend my money on" is patently clear. I spent practically every dime I made trying to maintain that reputation. Spending 'my money' foolishly became my mission in life. I had every conceivable credit charge card known to man and woman. Let me call the roll: Bloomingdale's, Neiman Marcus, Jacobson's, Saks Fifth Avenue, J.L. Hudson, Lord and Taylor, and others not so well known, plus a plethora of bank credit cards. I had so many clothes Fred had to have maintenance to come into the apartment and assemble all the necessary hardware to turn what was once a storage room into a closet for the overflow of my coats, hats and clothes. If that was not enough, when the shelves in that newly created closet came tumbling down, Fred found one of those retail display stores and purchased a portable clothes rack for me to hang my clothes. He then had maintenance to reinforce the original shelves with 2x4's to handle the added weight. After it was over, I knew what I had coming.

Not withstanding the fact that 'my money was my money and Fred's money was our money' as a general rule, 'Fred's golden rule' he stayed out of my financial affairs and I was not allowed in his. Fred and only Fred managed 'his money'. The only time Fred saw the inside of my paycheck was during income tax season when he asked for my W2 form. Fred was an ex-internal revenue agent. He had always done our taxes. But whenever he suspected that my spending might be getting out of hand, Fred did not hesitate to sit me down (quite like my grandmother did to mother) for one of his serious lawyer talks. His admonishment was always the same, "Now Gwen, you make good money. Don't spend all of your money on clothes; after all, you can only wear one suit at a time." He never pried into my spending or my savings. Once he had finished his lecture, it was over. He did not run it into the ground. He had put it out there and it was up to me to take heed. Fred never tried to send me off on some kind of guilt trip. But I guess in good conscience, he couldn't. After all, when it came down to spending money on Gwen, Fred carried his share of the weight and guilt. Fred was guilty of aiding and abetting. He was guilty of contributing to the crime of 'keeping Gwen looking good'.

Our affinity or our appreciation for clothes was a two-way street. Fred loved to see me looking good as much as I loved looking good. Fred loved to look his best and I loved seeing him look his best. After all Fred had a reputation for being the sharpest lawyer in downtown Detroit. What a couple! Folks loved to see us together!

If I thought Fred celebrated me throughout the year, Christmas was awesome. Fred had impeccable taste. He spared no expense when he shopped for me. Each year his special girls would ask, "What piece of fur or leather did Fred buy you this year?" Christmas had always been our most favorite time of the year. Long before we were married we discovered our mutual love and enthusiasm for the holidays. Our first Christmas together, Fred gave me a twelve piece place setting of Lenox fine china. He didn't stop there; coupled with the china came a sterling silver champagne bucket and matching goblets. Fred was once an avid golfer. That first year I gave him every conceivable piece of golf paraphernalia I could lay my hands on, twelve in all, one for each of the twelve days of Christmas. Receiving and accepting these gifts was not easy for Fred. Much like Grandma Jones, Fred Persons was a giver not a receiver. So you can imagine presenting him with all of those gifts in front of my family was quite an embarrassment for Fred. He was out done and undone. Fred openly objected all the while he unwrapped his gifts. But deep down in his heart I knew he was thrilled. No one had ever shown him this kind of love and attention. Not only was his heart whistling a happy tune but my heart sang to the rafters too! I knew I had made him happy in spite of his mumblings and grumblings. That tradition continued throughout our courtship, along with the mumblings and grumblings.

The first year we were married, the 'king of the castle' quickly announced another one of his 'golden rules'. I wanted to buy Fred something really special for Christmas. Four years of golf paraphernalia had gotten old. So I asked Fred, "What would you like for Christmas?" He replied, "Don't spend your money on me.

Save your money. Just buy me a nice card. When I suggested that I wanted to buy him a new suit he just about went ballistic. "I have lived all of these years and I have never let any woman buy my clothes and I'm not about to let you start now." For the first two or three years of our marriage, I obeyed or honored my husband's wishes, and stuck to buying him pajamas, robes, more golf 'stuff', or his favorite cologne. What is that I hear in the background? "How's that working for you?" I can tell you, it was not at all fulfilling for me. I wanted and needed to receive the same gratification from giving to Fred, as Fred received from giving to me. Why couldn't I make my husband understand that giving was reciprocal? Dr. Phil, this was the second price I had to pay for marrying for money, but this time the cost was a bit steeper. For you see, I was denied the joy that comes through giving. But once again, do not weep for me for my joy did come one morning.

Our fourth Christmas I decided to throw all caution to the wind. It was time to update Fred's trusty little brownie instamatic camera. Fred absolutely loved that camera and took it everywhere we went. Folks looked forward and expected Fred to be at all the events taking their picture. He loved to take my picture whenever I left the apartment. There were times I never knew where or when to expect the brownie to show up! That Christmas I bought Fred a new camera. Naturally he objected, saying he did not need a new camera; his old camera was perfectly fine. I think he just did not want to learn how to use anything new and different. He found every excuse in the book not to like it. My feelings were crushed, and I was mad, real mad at him! "Why won't you even give yourself a chance to try and see if you like the camera?" I pouted like a little child all day and my pouting paid off. The following day I came home and caught him sitting in his big chair reading the directions. Once he learned how to use it and after the first set of film was developed, I never saw the brownie again. Fred became well acquainted and was developing quite a love affair with his new toy. Seemed like more than ever before (if such a thing is possible), every time I left home it was a Kodak moment. I could not leave home without hearing the words, "Stand there and let me take your picture."

I learned early in our marriage that if you want to see Fred absolutely lose his mind do one of the following, mess with his wife, his health, his law practice, his camera, his golf clubs and last but not least, his clothes. Christmas 1993, I decided to test the waters once again, only this time I knew I would be treading deep waters, but I stepped in anyway. I bought Fred a wrap around hound's tooth top coat. Christmas Eve was the time for gift exchange in the Persons' household. When I presented Fred with his unwrapped gift, he first questioned what was inside of the box. When I finally convinced him to open it, you guessed it! Fred went ballistic! "How many times have I told you, Gwen, I have never allowed any woman to buy my clothes and I'm not about to start now. I do not want you spending your money on me. All I want is a nice card! Take it back!" He meant every word out of his mouth, or so he thought. Fred did not have a monopoly on going ballistic.

When he had finished with his bellyaching. I let him have it with both barrels. "You don't love me, you say you do but you don't really! Why do you persist in denying me the opportunity to show you how much you mean to me? Don't you think that I want and need and yes, deserve to feel the same gratification and joy that comes from giving? Giving is a two-way street. I love you Fred, but you won't let me show it. You keep tying my hands." I then let the dam break. The tears came gushing from my eyes like a river. One of those ugly cries-- nose running, face contorted; I even resurrected the semblance of a panic attack. I knew I had won then. Fred never wanted to witness me having another one of those ever in life again. It had been a little over one year since I had my last real panic attack. That sealed it for me! I could have won an Academy Award that evening. It was indeed a grand performance. That evening Fred agreed to keep the coat.

Although he had agreed to keep the coat the night before, when we got ready for church the next morning, I practically had to beg Fred to wear his new coat. He put the coat on, and tried his best to find all kinds of faults with it. Just like the new camera I had given him a couple of years ago, he tried his best not to like it. Fred had always credited me for my taste in clothes. He would soon learn that shopping for him was no exception. The coat was sharp and as with all of his clothes, Fred wore it well. The coat looked good on Fred; he looked like a million dollars and he knew it! After the Christmas service Fred was gifted with compliments at every turn. When we arrived at Carolyn's for Christmas dinner, the family ranted and raved over how good he looked in that coat. Especially Mama, she was so proud and happy for her baby daughter. Mama knew just how much this meant to me. And believe you me, as vain as my husband was, those compliments did not fall upon deaf ears. Fred loved hearing every bit of it. The immediate days following the holidays found Fred in that coat everyday. He would arrive home every after-noon with a brand new compliment to share. As much as he hated to admit it, someone other than he *could* pick out his clothes. I had sown the seed and the harvest was yet to come!

The third price I had to pay for marrying for money was never redeemable. Before marrying Fred my travels had been limited to sorority conventions. I had hoped that once we were married we would have done much more traveling together. I could not have been more wrong. Our annual Mother's Day trips to Columbus, Ga. were the extent of our travels as husband and wife. The very popular adage 'been there, done that' must have been coined expressly for Fred K. Persons. When I arrived on the scene, Fred Persons had had it all and had done it all! At that juncture in his life, Fred had very little interest in traveling. However, he always encouraged me to do more traveling, even without him. But like most everything, if we didn't do it together, I got very little enjoyment out of it. Consequently, besides the Delta conventions, I've only added one cruise and a trip to Mexico to my travel resume. However, each time I have traveled without Fred, he always paid for my airline ticket. "Keep your money in your pocket and enjoy yourself." Sisters, now how's that for "my money is my money and his money is our money?"

Fred often said he regretted that he did not meet me earlier, so that he could have put me in that white house on Lincolnshire in Palmer Woods. Knowing full well, that he never wanted to be a homeowner again in life, Fred would lovingly say to me, "Who knows, the Lord can still bless me again and I will buy you that house you've always wanted." All Fred ever wanted to do was to make Gwen happy.

Allow me to backup Fred had all the material trappings in life, but he often told me he never knew love and genuine happiness until he married me. And he let me know every night, "God has been good to me, and you are the best thing that ever happened to me." Sisters, hearing those words every night is more precious than gold. God was at his best when he made Fred K. Persons.

You'll recall my saying that one of the things that would cause Fred to go ballistic was to interfere or to 'mess' with his law practice. Consequently, his law practice and any discussion of such, was off limits. Therefore, when he came to tell me of his decision to close down his office in the Book Building, the news came as quite a surprise to me. Fred felt that the monthly over-head expenses were becoming a noose around his neck, particularly with the decline in the number of cases he was currently handling. His work load had decreased substantially. Fred felt it was time to move his practice home and go into semi retirement. He justified his decision by saying, besides, "More money for me to spend on you."

In 1997, Fred did close down his law office, moving forty years of practice into our apartment. I walked into the apartment one afternoon and there it was in the foyer, in the dining room, in the living room, boxes and boxes filled with forty years of Fred's blood, sweat, tears and genuine passion for the practice of law.

Although Fred never showed any outward signs of regret, remorse or sorrow at the closing of his law practice, I knew this had to have been one of the saddest days in his life. I knew it was one of mine. I had to figure out where we were going to put forty years of his life.

For the next two years, Fred continued the practice of law out of the apartment. He was accepting fewer and fewer private cases. Time was bringing him in. The bulk of his work was coming from court appointed assignments. This proved to be a pretty good arrangement for him. Judges whom he had known over the years were assigning him cases regularly. The hassles of private practice were behind him. This was not such a bad deal for him; after all, all Fred wanted to do was 'keep his feet wet'.

Several years after the Malice Green killing in Detroit, the after effects of this allegedly racially motivated case were evidenced throughout Wayne County. Recorders Court was particularly affected. Case assignments and methods of payment to the attorneys took on an entirely new complexion. That 'walk in the park' was virtually over. The ensuing years found his assignments getting fewer and farther between. A dam had definitely been put in his cash flow, and the results were coming home to roost!

Our weekly Friday night rituals at Joe Muer were getting fewer and fewer. It wasn't unusual for us to find ourselves sitting at home on Friday night, eating carry-outs from Bennigan's or some other near by restaurant. No 'doot aboot it' Fred had spoiled me! I silently pouted through these dinners and blamed him for this. I felt cheated, betrayed! How could we end up like this, sitting home on Friday night? After all we had an audience waiting on us out there! We must not disappoint our fans. People expected and looked forward to the Persons being at Joe Muer on Friday night. I had money; well at least I had credit cards. Do you think he would allow me to take us to dinner? You guessed it. If he could not afford it, we did not do it. "Pay your bills Gwen, you don't need to charge another thing."

Our last visit to Joe Muer had been on January 12th 1997, when we celebrated our ninth anniversary. Eight months later this once bustling establishment, a cornerstone in the city of Detroit, closed its door. While we had already mourned its death in our lives months ago, the entire City now joined us in our grief. I often said that Fred Persons willed the closing of Joe Muer Restaurant. If the doors to Joe Muer had remained opened, Fred's pride could not have handled it. Fred got too much enjoyment from taking me there on Friday night. What a tragic, tragic loss! Joe Muer was gone forever. It would be sorely missed in this town especially by Fred and Gwen Persons!

Those ritualistic trips to the grocery store were becoming less frequent. My mini stops by the grocery store were being met with fewer objections. In fact, I think he deliberately pretended not to notice. As hard as it was for Fred, I think Fred was accepting the fact that he could no longer carry the load alone. However, his pride would still not allow him to ask for my help. In the ensuing months I would later realize that perhaps it was not just his pride interfering with his acceptance of the changes taking place in his life.

Sometime in 1998 I found the utility bills among my stack of mail. I don't know if Fred brought the mail up on that day and deliberately left these bills for me, or whether I brought the mail up and set them aside for him and he just ignored them.

Does it sound like some kind of cat and mouse game? In either case, I opened them and to my surprise there were 'shut-off notices' inside. How could this be, 'shut-off' notices', in Fred Persons name? Had he just forgotten to pay them or was this his way of asking for my help? In any case, I did not make a big deal out of it, I just paid them. From that month onward and with no word spoken between us, I had inherited the utility bills.

I was totally unprepared for what awaited me when I walked into the dining room, on the first Saturday in July 1998. Fred sat at the table with such a deflated look upon his face; I knew something terrible must have been bothering him. When Fred said to me "Baby I am going to need some money for the rent this month." I just about went ballistic (but this was no act). Fred had never asked me for so much as a dime in all the years we have been married. Money to pay the rent? I could hardly believe what I was hearing. I lashed out at my husband, "Why did you wait until the last minute to spring this on me?" In retrospect, I should have been like the man whose faith in God was so strong, that whenever he approached the Master in prayer his posture was simply this, "Lord the answer is yes. Now Lord, what's the question?" When Fred came to me for money, I should have simply asked, "What do you need?" That was not at all my posture. I didn't react quite like the helpmate I had once pleaded him to allow me to be to him. I was not so gracious to my husband's request. I reacted like a selfish, spoiled brat. "You picked a fine time to ask me for money. You do realize that in two weeks I will be going to the Delta convention in New Orleans." After I was finished with my tirade, Fred very calmly assured me with these words, "I'll have it back to you before your trip Gwen." With those words spoken to me I was reminded that I was still growing in God's grace.

A few days into the week, I'm not quite sure which day it was; Fred came home with that little dance in his step. I recognized it right away. Fred had made some 'bread' today. One of Fred's greatest joys and the one that gave him the greatest pride, was being the breadwinner, around his pad, and then spending that 'bread' on Gwen. He couldn't wait to say to me, "Write down what you need from the store." I obeyed my husband's instructions and went into the kitchen to survey the cupboards. When I was finished off we went but not before making one stop.

Fred Persons believed in the blessed book; he believed every word in the book. Therefore, when we left the house, Fred drove straight over to St. Stephen A.M.E. Church. [Why could he not wait until Sunday morning? For the answer to that question I invite you to read it for yourself. It can be found in Malachi 3:10

and Ecclesiastes 3:13] and from there to the market. As we went up and down each aisle, Fred kept constantly reminding me, "Don't scrimp, get whatever you need now." Once we were back home and had the groceries put away, Fred handed me the cash he had borrowed. He was in his glory.

The following week as I prepared for my trip to New Orleans, Fred surprised me with some unexpected spending money for my trip. When I returned from New Orleans, Fred was waiting for me as I stepped off the runway. I did not have to wait for him, I did not have to look for him. As always, he was there waiting for me. I did not know that that would be my last Delta Convention, and that would also be the last time Fred would be waiting for me as I stepped off the runway.

By the end of the summer 1998, Fred's 1982 Imperial decided to die. My, how Fred loved that car. He tried to hang on to that car as long as he could. It was the last year Chrysler made the Imperial.

I pleaded with Fred to let me help him get it fixed. His pride and his sense of practicality would not hear of it. "I don't need a car anymore Gwen, anyway, where do I go without you?"

We can make it with one car." When he finally made up in his mind that he was not going to put money into fixing his car rather than getting rid of it Fred parked it on the top level of the Millender Center garage, and there it stayed for nearly two years.

I suppose I should not have been too surprised by what happened next. When it was time to renew the auto insurance that year, Fred had quite naturally dropped the Imperial from the policy, consequently leaving only one car to be insured; mine. Guess who inherited the car insurance that year? Just another something extra added to my plate that was already beginning to overflow. When I went to Fred, Fred wasted no time gently reminding me, "Now Gwen, you make good money, stop spending so much on clothes." I had no defense; he was right! With a draught in the land' why was I still buying more clothes? I had a closet full of clothes with the price tags still handing on them. The more that was piled onto my plate, the more money I spent on me! I was still spending my money foolishly.

When Fred got the pictures developed from New Orleans, I could hardly believe my eyes. When did I put on all this weight? I sat down and pulled out some earlier photos of me. When did that sharp chick disappear? I honestly did not recognize myself in those pictures. I looked awful. I was disgusted. And why had Fred silently stood by and allowed me get so out of control. He used to be my worst or best critic! I had to do something about all of the weight! Did I have what I knew it would take to commit to returning to the Weight Watchers Program? One thing I could begin to do, was to get back in the gym. If nothing else, it was a good stress buster. Lord knows I needed to find a healthier way to relieve some of the stress.

Seldom if ever, did I go to the gym on the weekends, but I woke up on this particular Saturday, feeling pretty good about my decision to get back into my routine. I headed down to the fitness center. I did not recognize the person behind the desk and she apparently did not recognize me because she asked to see my membership card. Membership card?, I thought to myself. When have I ever been asked for one of those? I did not have one to show her. She informed me that I would not be able to use the facilities without proof of membership. Did she know to whom she was speaking? I headed back upstairs. I was embarrassed, to say the least. I rushed to tell Fred what had just happened to me. When I finished telling him the story, my knight-in-shining-armor left the apartment. When he returned, he informed me that I was to return to the gym. I asked Fred what happened. "I took care of it," was all that he said. I had no doubt that he would take care of the situation.

When I returned to the gym, I was met with a boatload of apologies. By the time she got through apologizing to me, I almost felt sorry for her. Even though I was not there to witness the carnage, I knew he gave her hell to pay. I could almost feel her pain. I was sure it was not just due to her treatment of me and

Fred's complaints to management, but it was not long after that incident the young lady was relieved of her duties in the fitness center. I later learned that she had over stepped her bounds on other occasions as well.

The year had been one hell of a roller coaster ride for me financially. Only two weeks left before the opening of school, or at least that was what I was counting on. This was contract year for the Detroit Federation of Teachers and the last thing I needed was a strike. But that was exactly what I got in the fall of 1998. More stress. My dependency on self-prescribed remedies was becoming more apparent. When I turned to Fred his best advice to me was "Gwen, keep the faith." I tried to make the best of it, so I decided to pump up my exercise routine. By the time the strike ended I was looking and feeling pretty good about myself.

After returning to work I initiated a 5:30a.m work-out schedule.

A couple of weeks into my early morning work-out routine, Gradine, the morning receptionist, politely asked if I knew that my membership had expired? I replied,"I was unaware of it. Fred had always taken care of it." So why was I surprised. I was not going to make it an issue. I was more than willing to sacrifice some of my foolish spending in order to keep my gym membership current. I would now be paying my membership fee to the fitness center out of "my money."

I was seriously beginning to wonder about Fred. Was Fred beginning to have lapses in memory? Or was he consciously avoiding, denying the realties in his life? Had my 'King of our Castle' turned into the 'King of Denial? It would have been so much easier on me if Fred had just come to terms with the reality of his situation. We needed to renegotiate this contract. But no, Fred Persons was too proud. He was still holding onto his manhood, and more importantly to hope; the hope that things would reverse themselves. That this was just a temporary setback, that he would be back in the driver's seat once again!

By Christmas 1998, for whatever reason, Fred had lost a tremendous amount of weight. I decided to replenish his wardrobe. This was the first year in all the years we had been married that Fred had not come to me and asked, "Baby, is there anything special you want for Christmas?" Sometimes I think this was just a ploy he used to throw me off; he would always gift me with something far beyond what I may have requested.

Fred was a man of strong conviction and as much as it must have hurt him, if he didn't have the 'bread' he didn't buy it. I knew he did not have the bread that year. Christmas Eve I came home with not just two suits, but three suits. Two for him and one for me. I don't know how much of it was my own pride, for what would I tell his' special girls' when they asked "What piece of fur or leather did Fred give you this year?" Or how much of it was my love for my husband? I only knew I did not want him to wake up on Christmas morning and not have a gift for me under the tree. I brought a beautiful red trimmed fur suit, for me from Fred.

Little did I know that Fred had brought my gift weeks ago. Nothing that I could have wrapped and put under that tree, could have compared to what was waiting for me on Christmas morning.

The card read:
For You Sweetheart

I don't know what I ever did without you,
Before I ever saw your gentle smile,
Before I ever had you here to turn to,
To laugh with, and to talk with for a while
I don't know what I ever did without you,
Before I had you always by my side,
Before you ever warmed my heart with kindness,
Before you ever filled my heart with pride
I don't know what I ever did without you,
For you've become a part of me somehow,

And since I've had you here to love--
And to love me-
I know I couldn't do without you now

Merry Christmas
With All My Love

The new year found Fred spending more and more of his days at home. His work load was scarce, to say the least. Before I left home each morning, Fred would faithfully, ask, "Is there anything you want me to do for you today?" Fred needed to be needed. He needed to feel useful. I became very creative. I could always come up with something that just had to be done while I was at work. After running my errands, Fred spent the remainder of the day sitting in the lobby waiting for me to return home.

With the exception of the rent, the new year found me paying practically all of the bills around this pad. Sisters, does it sound like I'm whistling a different tune these days? Let's try this one on for size, "my money is our money, his money is our money". Sometime during the month of June came another financial hit! It was close to the end of the school year. I had been to the gym that morning and running a bit behind my schedule. When I got to the gate to exit the garage, my access card did not release the bar to let my car out of the garage. I found myself on the inside of the office. I learned that our monthly parking fee had not been paid; in fact, it had not been paid in over three months. I used their phone and called up stairs and explained the situation to Fred who immediately came down and resolved the problem. I was allowed to exit the garage. The situation gnawed at me throughout the day. How disconcerting.

Is Fred losing it? How much more of it can I take? The end of the school year was at hand. It had been an exceptionally warm day for the month of June. It was definitely time for school to be over. My nerves were on edge and I had just about come unglued. I was emotionally spent. When I arrived back to the

Millender Center that afternoon Fred was not sitting in his usual spot I headed straight to the apartment. When I opened the door I immediately felt the heat. It was stifling hot in there not a bit of air. I checked the A.C. it was turned completely off. I then checked all of the windows they were shut tight. Had Fred been in this apartment with this oppressive heat and no air all day or had he closed the windows and forgot to turn on the air before leaving? I was really beginning to get concerned about him. That gnawing question returned. Is Fred losing it?

I could not bear to stay in this Turkish sauna a minute longer. I turned the A.C. on high and headed back down to the lobby. I retrieved the mail and took a seat in Fred's favorite spot.

What the heat and the kids had not accomplished, what I found in the mailbox pushed me right over the edge. A letter from the IRS. My eyes could hardly believe and my mind could not comprehend what I was reading in this letter. To top things off, this was apparently not the first of such a letter to be mailed to us. What about these penalties! Garnishment, what does that mean?

In all the years I've worked for the board, I've never had to work one summer. Even before I became Mrs. Fred K. Persons, I never had to work in the summer. I had always depended on my income tax return to get me through the summer. From the sound of this letter, we would or I would not be getting a refund this year. Not only would we not be getting a refund this year, we owed Uncle Sam and we owed him 'big time'!!

Trouble entered our lives that day by way of a letter. We were at a crossroads in our marriage. Our marriage vows 'for richer for poorer,' now read 'from richer to poorer'. Fred prayed for us that night. Fred encouraged me to read the blessed book and to keep the faith.

I shadow boxed with trouble and weariness all summer. Fred had stopped going to the golf course. The travesty that was allowed to take place in Recorders Court became even more evident during the summer of 1999. I did not have much disposable income that summer. My trips to the golf course were few. I was watching my pennies closely. I stuck close to home and Fred stuck close to me. I needed an escape, I needed an antidote for my troubles. How would I ever survive these long, hot summer days? I took my husband's advice. I began to read the blessed book. I started an intense search through the scriptures for God's personal word for my life. I woke every day reading my Bible. Fred would often walk into the room and query, "Baby, God's not calling you to preach is He?" As the weeks passed and the Word entered my spirit, I was quickly uncovering an antidote for my trouble. A prescription for coping, medication through meditation.

That summer God gave me another writing assignment. On Saturday June 17, 1999, I received the following note from my soror, Cathy Smith.

Dear Soror Gwen,
Recall, I told you that you/we did not know of God's plans for you. It appears that you are to become a talented writer. Thanks for my book on Forgiveness.

Before retiring for bed that evening, I told Fred of my plans to write a book. We knelt to say our prayers and when we got up off our knees Fred took hold of my hand and said these words to me, "Write your book."

The following evening when we tuned into the Bethany Hour, Dr. Jones preached a sermon entitled, *Fresh Water from Old Wells,* I now had the title for my second book. Not only did I borrow the title of my book from that sermon, the opening song from that sermon became my theme song for the summer of 1999. "Jesus is a Rock in Weary Land." I spent the remainder of the summer at the wells searching God's personal word for my life. I don't know exactly when it happened, but I do know what happened and how it happened. Before the summer was over, grace paid me a visit.

The fall of 1999 I suspect that Fred had finally accepted that his days in court were just about over. But knowing Fred as well as I did and his faith in God, he was not going out without a fight. Another one of Fred's favorite sayings was "I'd rather wear out than rust out." Fred was counting on that last 'big win.' I guess you could call it his 'swan song' (from the Well of Faith, II Timothy 4:7). That fall, I unexpectedly found myself in a brand new 2000 Cadillac and Christmas 1999 found me with more unexpected blessings. Fred came home one afternoon, shouting to the rafters, "Perci, Persobal." I had seen the signs often enough over the years. Fred had made 'some bread' and apparently lots of it! Fred handed it all over to me, mercy me! "Merry Christmas, go spend it on yourself." I practically redecorated our apartment. I replaced Fred's eight track component stereo set with a new stereo system. I purchased a new dining room set. I bought new art work, I was on a mission and nothing could stop me now and by virtue of God's intervention, not even Fred Persons tried to stop me. My joy did come one morning. My passion for decorating had been resurrected.

God had been good to Fred. We were at the dawn of the New Millennium. The New Millennium redefined the modus operandi in the Persons household. The first thing on Fred's agenda for the New Year was to have one of those lawyer talks with me. One of those, "Don't interrupt me until I'm finished talks." A discussion, by all accounts, we should have had months ago. When the discussion concluded, the contract had been renegotiated, Fred had literally dethroned himself. (from the Well of Truth, John 8:32) The "King of the Castle" had stepped down from his royal throne. The golden rules had been rewritten. Fred admitted and had accepted the fact that he could no longer handle things. He confessed that he no longer had the physical energy nor the mental stamina that it took. He turned everything over to me. Fred was entrusting me to manage our lives or rather 'our money'.

The Queen of the castle now sat upon her royal throne. Fred Persons, the royal ruler of the roost, would now be ruled by the royal hen. Fred was leaning and depending on God and on me. My what an awesome responsibility!

I had to proceed with extreme caution and care, but I was more than ready for the challenge. I had been to the wells and grace had entered our pot. I was prepared to give Fred the best that I had. I would not disappoint God or Fred. My daily affirmation became, "God, make me the best wife you would have me to be for Fred". (from the Well of Faith, St. Matthew 6:30)

The rules were rewritten around this pad and I helped to rewrite them! New rules for us to live by and live we did. I was determined we would not do and be without. For the first time since our marriage I taught summer school in both, 2000 and 2001. Also, in the summer of 2001, I was hired as a mentor for Marygrove College. These extras allowed me to continue my passion for decorating and to the delight of my heart, enabled me to rekindle Fred's love for fine dining. We were back on the restaurant circuit. I knew grace was fully operating (from the Well of Joy, Nehemiah 8:10) for Fred was more than appreciative and readily accepted my support without his infamous mumblings and grumblings.

I was determined to see to it that Fred Persons wanted and needed for nothing. I tried to anticipate his needs even before he knew what they were. I fed him, I clothed him, I took him wherever he had or needed to go. Fred may have given up his crown, but he was still my king, he would always be the 'king of this castle.'

For the last two years of Fred's life, all he had to do was to sit back and enjoy the ride. But far above the joy I tried to give to him, my joy was even richer. I was the one doing the driving for him. I was finally able to give back to my earthly king a portion of what he had so freely given to me all those years. (from the Well of Joy, Isaiah12:3)

Now, sisters, let's back this train up to where we started, first it was 'my money is my money and his money is our money', next 'my money is our money and his money is our money', then it was 'my money is our money and his money is my money, in the end it was all our money. Sisters, we have played this happy tune, this little ditty, if you will, three different ways. To me they all sound rather trite. Why, you may ask? Because that is not how the story ends. There exists a tuning problem with these little ditties; they are all out of tune. They are out of tune because they are out of the will of God. Sisters, it's tune-up time, if you please. It is time for some prescriptive preaching, a prescription for preservation.

Fred Persons knew that to be good for God, to be good for others, and to be good for oneself, you must be in tune. Fred stayed in tune. Fred loved to read the blessed book. He'd been reading the book all of his life. Not only did Fred believe the book, he believed in the efficacy of the book. Fred started bringing the Lord the tenth at the age of seven. Another one of Fred's favorite quips was, "I dare you to try Him." Try Him, stretch out on His promises. Folks, if you begin to make your deposits in the bank of eternity early and often, then you too can declare with Fred K. Persons, "I have been young and now am old; yet I have not seen the righteous forsaken, nor his seed begging bread."

P.S.

IT ALL BELONGS TO HIM! IT IS ALL HIS!

106 Gwendolyn D. Persons

Part Three

From Health to Sickness

When Jesus heard that, he said,
this sickness is not unto death,
but for the glory of God, that the Son of God
might be glorified.

St. John 11:4

108 Gwendolyn D. Persons

From Health to Sickness

Some of my most cherished moments are of the intimacies we shared in our bedroom. Not unlike most married couples Fred and I shared our most intimate moments in the bed. Perhaps unlike most married couples, however, were the verbal discourses we shared each night before falling off to sleep that have served to unite our hearts and souls. Oh, how Fred loved to take a backward look down memory lane. Of particular fondness to his heart and to my ears were the stories he shared with me of his childhood years in Columbus, GA. Over the years, I do believe that Fred shared with me just about every detail of his childhood-- from his first faith lesson at the age of seven to his graduation day from Spencer High School at age fifteen.

All of the stories Fred shared with me during our nightly discourses were documented and supported each year when we made our annual Mother's Day visit to Columbus. His sisters loved to tell me about their childhood memories of their big brother Fred. Louise's favorite story was of the time she broke her leg and Fred carried her everywhere she had to go. Of course, I loved hearing his mother share her favorite memories of her 'boy.' Mrs. Persons often told me that Fred was double promoted not once, but twice; the first time in the kindergarten and then again in the first grade. She even said that the teachers wanted to double promote him a third time, but she would not allow it. It was obvious early on that the good Lord had put more on the inside of his head than on the outside. The kids at school kept him reminded of that fact when they mocked him regularly with those infamous words, "Fred, Fred cabbage patch head." Wish I had been around then, I would have had their heads for calling 'my baby' such names. But I'm sure Fred did not need anyone to fight his battles. That's probably when he first authored his now famous line, "If you see me fighting the bear, help the bear." In spite of their intended cruelty, their mocking did not compromise Fred's self esteem. If anything, it probably gave him more self confidence. Fred held cherished memories of both his parents. As a lad, Fred told me he never entered his home and his mother was not there. Fred's father was the head of his household; Fred would say to me, "Papa took good care of his family."

I loved hearing all of Fred's bedtime stories, but one of my favorites was the story he told of his chickens. Each time a chicken would die Fred would give it a proper burial in his backyard. He would summon family and friends to participate. Fred always said, "I wished the Lord had called me to preach. But he never did."

Another one of Fred's favorite recollections was leaving home at the age of sixteen with one suitcase in hand, headed north to Atlanta, Georgia. The son of a Methodist preacher, his father was sending his son to enroll in Morris Brown, a Methodist College. However, upon arriving on campus Fred disobeyed his father's instructions, walked across the street and enrolled in Morehouse College, a Baptist school. Fred kept this secret from his father his entire freshman year. From his first day on campus, Fred championed and lived up to the Morehouse motto, "You can tell a Morehouse man, but you can't tell him anything." Alpha Phi Alpha Fraternity probably gave him one of his first opportunities to live up to that motto. As a pledge, Fred was asked to shovel coal on Homecoming night. He told his big brothers where to shove it and took himself off line, an eternal Sphinx. That night Fred Persons not only became a Morehouse man, he became his own man, through and through. Enrolling in Morehouse College was without a doubt one of the proudest decisions Fred ever made for himself.

There are so many more cherished bedtime stories such as these. But as hard as I've tried, I find it rather strange that I am unable to recall Fred ever telling me of any kind of childhood diseases or illnesses. I cannot even think of or recall one account of Fred being sick as told by him, his sisters, or his mother. My archives record no record of the measles, the chicken pox, the mumps, polio, a broken leg; nothing resembling childhood sickness is listed.

In fact my memory bank only held two deposits recorded in its ledger concerning his health issues as a full grown man. The first entry was that of a war injury. Fred often spoke of how he lay prostrate on a military bed for sixteen months due to an injury to his knee. The injury resulted in a permanent metal knee cap placed on his left knee. That knee has affectionately been referred to by me as Fred's 'fat knee' and one of my favorite parts of Fred's anatomy. How often have we lain in the bed and played our own version of the *Mating Game*. One of my favorite questions to Fred was, "Can you name your spouse's favorite part of your anatomy?" I could never decide what the correct response should be; his bald head, his thumb (especially when he wore his knit gloves in the winter) or his 'fat knee'. I loved him from head to toe, but there was something magnetic about parts of his anatomy. Let me not digress. Getting back to those recorded health issues, the only other recording was that of his walk with asthma. I am not exactly sure just how many years he suffered with asthma, but what I am sure of, is that he always gave God the glory for curing him of this illness. Fred had often said to me "The Lord just took it from me." That had been his testimony. I think that is referred to as divine intervention or is it divine providence?

Divine health had been precisely how I had referred to Fred's health. Unlike most of his contemporaries, Fred only had to take one pill a day, no two, one for hypertension and the other an over the counter self-prescribed multi vitamin. Both of these he took religiously each morning with his glass of orange juice. I never had to visit my husband one day in the hospital. Again, unlike most of Fred's contemporaries, Fred did not suffer with arthritis, bursitis, glaucoma, cataracts, hearing loss, hip/knee replacements, back problems or diabetes. He very seldom if ever complained of even the slightest headache. For a man in his winter season Fred Persons was in great shape. Walking is often credited for paying huge dividends in one's health and adding years to one's life. If that is a fact, then Fred Persons was our poster boy. It was a well known fact in downtown Detroit that Fred Persons loved to walk. Fred spent many years walking all over downtown Detroit. At the age of seventy nine Fred was still playing eighteen holes of golf without a cart. Ask why the Nomads were in such great shape? They walked! Fred was in great physical shape!

I cannot recall one day during our marriage that Fred stayed home from the office or from court due to a cold, the flu, or just being under the weather. Fred was very vigilant about his health. He made regular and sometimes irregular trips to his doctor's office. Fred enjoyed a personal relationship with Dr. Harcourt Harris, a relationship that allowed him to run in and out of Dr. Harris's office at will and unannounced. It's a little something Fred liked to refer to as a professional courtesy. I am sure the fact they were club members didn't hurt either. As a result of that relationship Dr. Harris had no compunction in referring to Fred as an 'old fart.' According to Fred, Dr. Harris always concluded his annual examination of Fred's prostate, with the words, "Your prostate is normal for an 'old fart'." I suppose the last time Fred heard that reassuring pronouncement was somewhere back in 1997. That was the year Dr. Harcourt Harris closed his medical practice in Detroit and retired south. This privileged doctor/patient relationship that Fred had come to rely on and expected had come to an unexpected end. For the first time in his adult life Fred was without medical attention.

During the summer of 1997, Fred had his first bout with gout. He woke up one morning with this debilitating and excruciating pain. He was at a loss as to what to do. I drove my husband to the emergency room at Harper Hospital. Once seen by the emergency room doctor, Fred was diagnosed with gout, a condition caused by the build up of uric acid, causing swelling and pain in the joints. We were advised of the foods to avoid and how to treat this condition. The emergency room physician advised Fred to follow up this condition with his private doctor. On the way home we stopped and had the prescriptions filled. Gout has often been referred to as the rich man's disease. Ironically, it made its debut in Fred's life after his run with the good life was beginning to coast. Over the next two years, we had repeat performances of this same scenario. Gout kept showing up!

In was in the fall of that same year, somewhere around October, Fred started to experience what he described as a rapid or an accelerated heart beat. It was then that Fred had his first contact with the doctor who had taken over Dr. Harcourt Harris's medical practice. Incidentally this doctor shared the same name, Dr. Harris. This would eventually prove to be the only thing they shared.

I refer to it as a contact and not an appointment, because knowing my husband as well as I did, I would not be at all surprised if Fred just showed up and expected to be seen by the 'good doctor.' Fred never discussed this visit with me, but something had transpired that did not sit right with Fred. This was a man much Fred's and Dr. Harcourt's junior so perhaps they just did not click. Or did the doctor reveal something to Fred that he did not agree with? Then again, it would not be a far stretch of the imagination to assume that Fred was kept waiting too long before he was seen by the good doctor. Patience had never been one of Fred's strong suits. Whatever the reason, Fred divorced himself from the relationship before it ever had a chance to wed. Fred did not return to his office.

Weeks later and still concerned about his heart palpitations and still in need of medical attention, Fred sought advice from Jim Stephens. Jim was a good friend, a member of our church. Before retiring a year or two back, Jim had been chief administrator of the Veteran's Administration Hospital in Allen Park. As an honorably discharged veteran and at no cost to him, Jim convinced Fred that he should not hesitate to take full advantage of this newly constructed state-of-the-art medical complex. Jim even offered to go with Fred to get the process underway. To make the deal even more attractive, this new facility had been built in the shadows of downtown Detroit.

In the weeks that followed, Fred remained pretty tight lipped about the outcome of his visits to the hospital. He never involved me in the process. All the information to follow came to my attention months later. According to that information (medical records from the VA) Fred had his first appointment with Dr. Matta on December 3, 1997. Dr. Matta *reported that Fred had gone to a private M.D. for a physical and was told that he had an abnormal EKG. The private physician ordered more diagnostic workups Medical records indicate that the patient then decided to come to VAMC.*

Fred's initial visit with Dr. Matta further reported no complaints of dizziness or chest pains, just a fluctuating heart rate while sleeping that had been happening on a daily basis since October 1997. There were no other complaints reported on this first visit. Lungs were reported to be clear. Although his appetite was also reported to be good, records indicated that Fred expressed some concerns in regards to his weight loss. Dr. Matta ordered another EKG. The results revealed normal sinus rhythm, nonspecific T wave abnormality and abnormal EKG. Fred's next appointment was scheduled for December 8, 1997 for a cardiac evaluation, at the Non invasive cardio Holter Monitoring Clinic.

Fred returned home from that visit wearing a heart monitor. For the first time, he readily shared his concerns about his irregular heart beats and his visits to the VA hospital. Fred told me that he was to wear this heart monitor for a week and maintain a diary.

Fred did not maintain a dairy as requested.

On December 17 when he returned to the hospital, the Holter report (heart monitor) summary yielded the following impressions and findings. *The basic mechanism was Sinus Rhythm 65 to 121 bpm and an average of 95 bpm. There were frequent premature ventri-cular complexes of various morphologies. There were occasionally supra-ventricular ectopic complexes. There were no pauses.* He was given a prescription for a diuretic. Fred's next appointment with Dr. Matta was scheduled for December 22, 1997.

The day before this appointment, I received a phone call from Dr. Matta. Doctor Matta asked me if Fred had discussed his visits to the VA with me. I informed him that the only thing he had discussed with me was his concern regarding his irregular heart beats and the heart monitor which he was required to wear. Dr. Matta asked if I had observed any irregularities in Fred's sleeping habits. I reported to the doctor that I have observed Fred sitting up at night at least once or twice a week. When asked if I had observed any sweating or coughing associated with this behavior, I reported none. He then continued by sharing with me the results of Fred's prostate examination. Dr. Matta told me that Fred did indeed have an enlarged prostate, but this was not a real concern for a man his age. Dr. Matta added that additional testing would probably be recommended. Before concluding the conversation, Dr. Matta informed me that Fred had an appointment the next day. He then posed the following heart wrenching question to me, "Why is it that a man Mr. Persons' age meets all of his appointments alone?" Just the fact that the doctor had to ask that question pierced my heart. I informed the doctor that it was my husband's choice. "Dr. Matta, if my husband only asked I would have been with him at every appointment. He said he understood and thanked me for the information. I thanked him for the phone call. I never spoke to Dr. Matta after that day.

That evening when Fred arrived home, I told him about the phone call from Dr. Matta. It did not take long for Fred to show his irritation toward the doctor. He was not at all pleased to hear that the doctor had been discussing him with me! "Why did he call you?" Sensing his irritability, I clearly did not want to irritate him further. I did not want to give him reason for divorcing himself from yet another doctor, I never mentioned the complete disclosure of my conversation with Dr. Matta. I simply said to my husband, "Fred, he was merely concerned as to why you were always alone for your appointments." I had to let Fred know I was there for him to take as good of care of him as he had taken care of me. I asked Fred if he wanted me to go with him for next appointment. Of course he declined my offer. I then asked the question "Fred, are you keeping anything from me?" He assured me he was not. The words were not spoken between us, but his message to me was clear nonetheless, "If you see me fighting the bear, help the bear." Fred had no intention of discussing this with me. I was wise enough to know when to hold them and when to fold them. The subject was closed.

The next day, Fred kept his appointment with Dr. Matta. As a result of that visit the medical records document the following report. *The blood work revealed Fred's PSA was reported to be elevated, 10.65, as a result, Dr. Matta made an appointment for Fred to be seen by an urologist at the VA. That appointment was scheduled for January 9, 1998.*

The urologist also reports *the actual PSA to be 10.65 and the predicted, 7.8. No nodule was felt on the examination. The prostate was enlarged measuring approximately 65 GM. No apparent or obvious hypoechoic area or lesion was demonstrated. A total of six random biopsy passes were done. Fred was reported to have done well.* The next appointment was scheduled for January 21, 1998.

One month into the new year Fred still had not discussed with me the results or the reasons for his regular visits to the V.A. He never tried to keep the appointments a secret; he was just not forthcoming with the results. Fred was obviously quite impressed with the massiveness of the structure and the efficiency, or rather as he preferred to put it, the professionalism in which it was run. Fred returned from his visits as excited as a kid with a new toy. He returned home as though he had been at some sort of grand social gala. Fred even got excited about taking public transportation to the hospital. But of course, that's Fred K. Persons, he had an uncanny knack for turning an ordinary situation into a major happening. Fred's fun-loving spirit was infectious. I'm certain that anyone at that hospital who had the slightest contact with him was drawn to his presence. No one could be around Fred Persons very long and not feel his presence. Fred met no strangers.

According to the medical records, it was at this appointment that Dr. Matta scheduled Fred for a biopsy, the date, January 29, 1998. Fred kept the appointment and was scheduled to return to Dr. Matta in two months.

Two months passed and Fred returned to the clinic on March 23, 1998 at 1:00 pm. Dr, Matta writes the following. "Fred *Persons a 78 year old African-American male. Came for biopsy results. Informed patient about biopsy being positive for cancer. Patient does not want to believe that he has prostate cancer. He believes that this is false. I had called him and told him that I have something important to tell him about the biopsy results - one month ago, however, the patient waited until his scheduled appointment to come in, he said he wanted to talk to me in person. I explained to patient about prostate cancer and treatment options. Patient is upset and does not want to see urologist or prostate cancer specialist at this time. He says he may change his mind later and agree to see them. I believe patient is competent and he does not want to inform his family. So I respect his wishes. RTC 1 month.*

Fred's Final Diagnosis, from the VA was dated April 6, 1998.
A. Pro static biopsies. right side: Pro static adenocarinoma, Gleason's score 6 (3+3), involving approximately 10% of total tissue submitted Glandular atrophy B. Pro static biopsies, left side: Pro static left side: Pro static adenocarcinoma, Gleason's score 7 (3+4), involving 20% of the tissue submitted Glandular atrophy.

The verdict was in. Fred had prostate cancer.

I imagine when most men learn that they have prostate cancer, they usually seek help. Well, who ever accused Fred Persons of being like most men? Fred never returned to Veteran's Hospital and he never discussed any of this with me. Just like the disease itself Fred remained silent on the subject.

For the next several months I sat by and watched the man I married change right before my very eyes. Fred had slowed down considerably. He appeared to be getting weak and feeble both physically and mentally. He seemed to be losing interest in just about everything he once enjoyed so much. However, if Fred was ever in any type of pain or discomfort, he never once complained or mentioned it, at least not to me. Another translation to that all too familiar one-liner "If you see me fighting the bear, help the bear" was this, 'don't stick your nose or your mouth where they were uninvited.' Consequently to satisfy my inquiring mind, I learned to employ the use of my other sense (hearing) to keep me informed.

One evening the phone rang. It was Jim on the other end. We picked up the phone at the same time. When I hung up my end I stealthily headed for the bedroom door. I stood outside of the door and listened to his end of the conversation. As dishonest as it may have felt, I had convinced myself that it was the right thing to do. I told myself "Fred has been keeping something from me." I heard him say to Jim he was certain that the doctor had given him 'this thing'. 'This thing?' What could he be referring to? Fred continued by saying he was going to sue the doctor. It sounded as though Fred was trying to build a case and he wanted Jim's support or at least his approval.

During the summer of that same year (1998), Fred suddenly appeared exuberant, as if he had a tiger by the tail, much like the man I had married. Nothing gave Fred greater pleasure than winning 'a big one' and making some bread. Still not giving total disclosure to his implied meaning Fred would often announce to me, "Gwen, I'm working on a 'big one.' Whatever 'this thing' was, Fred was obviously hoping to cash in on it. I don't know if Fred was in a complete and total state of denial or if the thought of winning what may be his final 'big one', his swan song, if you please, consumed and clouded his ability to think and see clearly. Knowing Fred as well as I did, it was probably the latter. Fred just wanted to win one more for Gwen. Throughout the remainder of the year, Fred continued to lose weight. I was aware that his visits to the VA stopped months ago. Finally one evening I asked my husband, "Fred is there a medical reason why you're losing so much weight?" Immediately he became defensive and accused me of not feeding him the proper foods. This was the last thing I expected from him. Was this some sort of defense mechanism? Or was senility creeping in on him? I knew perfectly well that the only change that had occurred in his (our) eating habits was the closing of Joe Muer restaurant. The grief that we both suffered as a result of that loss was enough to cause temporary weight loss in both of us. However, I did not argue with my husband. I felt so badly for my Fred. I could hardly contain my emotions and I felt the tears welling up in my eyes. "Fred are you keeping anything from me? Please do not shut me out. Is there anything you need for me to do for you?" I pleaded with Fred, "Please allow me to take as good of care of you as you have taken care of me. Fred you are not allowing me to be the type of helpmate God intended for me to be to you." Fred assured me that I was the best helpmate he could have ever hoped for and that he would never keep anything from me.

I solicited my mother's help. Each Sunday after church Mama would prepare some of Fred's favorite meals. During the week, I made sure Fred had some kind of dessert after dinner. Nothing seemed to help. To no avail, the weight simply did not return.

There was another one of those overheard phone conversations that summer. I eavesdropped on a call Fred had with Sam Gardner. Fred was apparently trying to cash in on 'this thing' he thought the doctor had given him. For the next year, Fred put on a great masquerade. He never discussed his health or even hinted that there was anything wrong with him. The one thing he continued to do however, was to accuse me of not feeding him the proper food. But, thank God, heaven did not let this big lie live forever either.

Divine intervention.........

Of all the unforeseen, sickness was the least intrusive visitor. Sickness appeared in the form of cancer, a cancer that is described as silent. Sickness made its debut, or coming out if you will, on Thursday evening, September 23, 1999. It was an evening not unlike any other. We had finished dinner. Fred cleaned the kitchen and I retreated to my usual spot to do whatever would keep me busy for the remainder of the evening. Only minutes into the evening, Fred joined me. He entered the room with these words, "Gwen, stop what you're doing, I want to discuss something with you." How many times over the years had he prefixed a discussion with those ominous words. He continued, "Don't interrupt me until I'm finished." I knew then it had to be something mighty serious. So I fastened my seat belt and braced myself. Straight forwardness had always been one of his strong suits. Fred had always believed and practiced the philosophy, "The only way to say it is just to say it." That philosophy was uncompromisingly applied to the things he wanted to bring forth and open up for discussion. That night was no exception. He did not stumble. He did not stutter. He laid it all on the line. "Gwen, I have prostate cancer." Fred confessed it all that evening. He told me he was given this diagnosis in January 1998, twenty months ago. He said that when he was first given this diagnosis he did not believe the doctor. Fred felt that he had been misdiagnosed. Fred said that he believed the doctor had given him *this thing*. An "Aha moment" if ever there was one. He admitted to me that evening that he had called on Jim Stephens to assist him in his pursuit against the hospital. He did not stop there. He confessed that he had gone as far as contacting Sam Gardner's office. Another "Aha Moment." So that was the *big one* he had been working on all summer. I obeyed my husband, I did not interrupt him. Fred had apparently done some research on prostate cancer. He described to me his symptoms and the progression of prostate cancer. He informed me that if prostate cancer spreads, the most common initial site was the bone and pelvic lymph nodes. Once it had attacked the bones, it had reached the final stages. Fred continued by describing the severity of pain he had been experiencing over the past two days. Fred had localized the pain in his pelvic and hip area. "I've given this considerable thought Gwen. I do not want any treatment. I do not want chemotherapy. I do not want to put you through that debilitating treatment. I asked you a few weeks ago if you would call my sister Louise to come and get me. Would you do that for me now?" I was speechless and not because I had been given instructions not to talk. If I thought I felt helpless all of these months, I felt completely paralyzed at that moment. I was bewildered! I was frightened and scared out of my wits. I knew something was wrong with Fred all of these months, but not this! Doctor Matta had assured me that an enlarged prostate was common for a man Fred's age. What had I thought was wrong all these months? Just hearing the word cancer for the first time frightened me. Not the "BIG C."

I must have been in a state of shock at that moment. "Gwen, the Lord only promised three score and ten, that's seventy. God has been good to me. I'm eighty years old. He has given me ten bonus years and you're the best thing that ever happened to me." Hearing him confess all of this he sounded so defeated, so final, it was as though he was preparing to check out of here tomorrow.

Was that Fred Persons, the brilliant criminal defense attorney? How could he have been in such denial all of these months? Why had he allowed all of this time to pass, time that could have prolonged his life. Fred's health, my health had always been a top priority of his. Why had he given up on his health, his life, on me, on us? Fred had always been a private person, his own man, strong and fiercely independent, a born fighter. He was a man with unyielding faith in God. Where was his fight now? And more importantly, where was his faith?

Fred concluded by telling me that he had spoken to Rev. Huggins earlier that afternoon. He told Rev. Huggins of his plans to have this discussion with me tonight. He said that he asked Rev. Huggins to stand by in case I needed to speak to him. Well, at that moment I wasn't sure what I needed. All I knew was that I must have experienced every human emotion known to man or wife. I was afraid, I was angry, I was resentful, I was hurt. I felt betrayed, and yes, once again, I felt my husband had abandoned me.

What does all of this mean? I wanted it to not be so. Fred looked so helpless and I was helpless to help him. I wanted to take Fred into my arms and love him back to wellness. Instead, I fell apart and cried like his baby. Still trying to take good care of me, Fred held me in his arms and as natural as breathing, said to me, "Gwen, keep the faith and trust in God." (from the Well of Understanding, Proverbs 3:5)

The next morning when I arrived at work I assembled my sorors together, Deborah, Delores and Pat. We sat in the library and I shared the news with them. We held hands and they prayed with me. In the midst of my tears they comforted me with the words "Everything will be all right, Gwen." I returned to my office. I called Fred to check on him. He said he was feeling okay, but I did not believe him. I asked him if he needed for me to come home. Fred promised that he would call me if he needed me. I hung up the phone. I desperately needed to talk to someone whose *vertical connection* was secure. I needed to talk to someone who I knew could get a prayer through. I called Soror Clara Crowell. Clara was saddened by the news, for she loved Fred and Fred was crazy about Clara. Clara knew how much Fred loved good preaching. She invited us to come to Tabernacle Baptist Church that evening for the final night of their Christian Education Week. Dr. John Borders had been the speaker all week. I told her that if Fred was feeling up to it, we would certainly be there. When I got off the phone with Clara, I called Fred back and asked him if he felt up to going to Tab that evening. Without question or hesitation, he asked "Are you kidding, try and stop me." I hung up the phone. I knew I could make it through the rest of the day. (from the Well of Hope, Psalm 31:24)

As soon as I got home from work I called Sheila, my oldest friend with the news. Sheila inquired as to what I planned to do? When I explained to her that Fred did not want radiation or chemotherapy, she suggested the holistic approach. I had no answers for her at that moment. I told her we were on our way to Tabernacle for the evening, but I would call her tomorrow.

Service was scheduled to begin at 7:00 pm. Fred had always been punctual (to a fault). However, this particular evening it was obvious that he was in a great deal of pain and was having difficulty preparing himself to leave the apartment. As expert as he had tried to be at camouflaging his discomfort, he could not conceal it from me. I suggested that we stay home. He was not having it. Fred insisted that he was okay and that we were going. We slowly made our way to the garage. It was difficult for Fred to put one foot in front of the other. I felt my husband's pain. Had he been right last night? Had the cancer spread to his bones? When we arrived at the church we were unable to find parking nearby. The closest parking spot available was two blocks from the church. I begged Fred to allow me to drive him back to the church and let him out while I parked the car. Pain notwithstanding, Fred was very clear! "Absolutely not, you are not going to walk not even one block in the dark all alone, I'm not helpless Gwen. Wherever you park this car, I can walk back to the church with you." I knew there was no point in arguing with Fred. At times he can be so pig headed, so stubborn, and this was one of those times! I obeyed my husband. I found a parking spot about three blocks from the church. We got out and I held onto Fred's arm (as a mother would her child) and helped him get to the church. With every step he made I continued to feel his pain. I felt so sorry for my husband that night, and once again I felt helpless to do anything for him. We made our way to the church and were able to be seated before the service started. The church was packed. This had been our first opportunity to hear Dr. Borders. There was no mistake about it, Clara was absolutely right. Fred was in store for some real good preaching tonight. I think he must have forgotten all about his pain while he was there. It had been a moving worship experience. The Word had been spoken. It was now time to leave. There was nothing else needing to be said other than the benediction. However, it was a well known fact that Dr. Frederick Sampson loved to preach on top of the preacher (bless his heart). Therefore, when he got up to close out the service, I counted on him preaching another sermon. I took this opportunity to excuse myself to the ladies room. I disobeyed my husband that night and left the church and went to get the car alone. There was no way I was letting Fred walk back to the car. The security guards were present and I safely made my way to the car and drove back to the church. I double parked the car, left my flashers blinking and went back into the church to get my husband. Service was just letting out. I found Fred where I had left him sitting. I held onto his arm and escorted him out of the church to his waiting carriage. Needless to say he was not at all pleased with what I had done. At that moment Fred was filled with something and it wasn't the Holy Spirit. Once inside the car Fred went ballistic. I tried to assure him that I was perfectly safe. "Fred, nothing happened to me; besides there were security guards patrolling the area and there were others leaving the church at the same time. I was not out here all alone." No amount of reassurance comforted him. He was livid. "Gwen if something were to happen to you, and I'm right here, how do you think I'd feel? I could never live with myself." He was not about to let me forget who wore the pants in this family. The devil tried to make me angry with my husband for being so bullheaded. But the devil was a liar that night. I had the presence of mind to know that my husband was not angry with me. If anything Fred was angry with himself for growing old and sick. He meant exactly what he had said; he could never live with himself if he felt he had allowed something to happen to me! Fred was only reacting out of his love and concern for me. As always and forever, Fred was only trying to take good care of his baby. If I thought Rev. Sampson had preached on top of the preacher that evening, my husband had them both beat. Fred Persons pontificated the entire drive home and well into the night. I allowed my husband to 'get his preach on' that night. (from the Well of Understanding, Proverbs 14:29)

Saturday morning still found Fred in much discomfort. I pleaded with him to let me take him to the emergency room. He said, "No." His bullheadedness and stubbornness did not look as though they were going on holiday anytime soon. He could be absolutely infuriating. (from the Well of Faith, James 1:3)

I went into my closet and prayed. When I came out of my closet I was still feeling afraid. I did what all children do when they are afraid. I called my mother. Between the tears and the fears, I managed to get the words out of my mouth. "Mama, Fred has cancer." For the first time in my life, I heard my mother pray and she was praying for her baby daughter. Mama offered to come down and help me get Fred to the hospital. I told Mama that he was refusing to go and that I was going to my Weight Watchers class and when I got back home I would try to convince Fred to let me take him to the emergency room. "I'll give you a call when I get back home."

I left Fred in bed and went to class. My oldest sister, Judy was in class for the first time. After class we stood in the parking lot; I gave Judy the bad news. "Oh baby, I'm so sorry." Judy promised me that Fred would be just fine. Together, but in separate cars, we drove to the market. When we finished our grocery shopping, Judy kissed me goodbye and said she would be praying for us.

When I returned home, I immediately went into the bedroom and found Fred still in the bed. I knew things had reached crisis proportion. Fred Persons was not one for lying in bed all day. "Fred, how are you feeling?" "I'm doing fine. I'm just lying here thinking how good God has been to me." I knew he was not telling me the truth. I said to him, "Fred, don't you think we ought go to the hospital?" "I'll let you know Gwen." I was furious with him. He was still tying my hands. I left him lying in bed and went into the kitchen to prepare lunch (from the Well of Patience, James 1:4). When I returned to the room with his lunch Fred reminded me that he was not an invalid, and that he could come to the table. "Gwen please do not dote over me." He got up out of bed and attempted to put weight on his foot, but he could not, the pain was just that intense. He asked for the broom and tried to make a makeshift walking stick. I assisted him into the bathroom and then back to bed. He didn't object to not going to the table. Fred requested that I move the wastebasket closer to the side of the bed in case he had to use it as a urinal later. I honored his request. I then walked out of the room, leaving his food on the nightstand. I was clearly very annoyed with him at this point.

I needed someone to talk to. The most obvious candidate was Soror Elaine. Elaine had lost her husband, Joe, to prostate cancer two years ago. I called and related everything to Elaine as it had unfolded since Thursday evening. Elaine asked me a plethora of questions. Of utmost concern to Elaine was Fred's ability to eliminate his urine. "Gwen, does Fred experience difficulty urinating? Does Fred urinate frequently, especially at night? Was there blood in his urine?" Elaine was also concerned about pain. She asked me, "Was Fred experiencing pain in his back, hips or pelvic area?" With some careful thought and reflection, after Elaine finished asking her questions I attempted to answer them the best I could. I first explained to her that Fred's bathroom is off limits to me when it is in use. His bathroom served two purposes one physical and medicinal in nature and the other more spiritual or meditative in nature. In either case when in use Fred always closed the door behind him. Elaine shared with me the progression of her husband's cancer and how she eventually had to take over Joe's medical care.

Elaine asked me if I thought Fred would talk to her. I did not have to give any thought to that question. If Fred had inkling that

I had been discussing his health with anyone, he would go ballistic! I told Elaine how much I appreciated her offer and support, but I knew Fred would not cooperate. Before hanging up the phone, Elaine said to me "Gwen, that does not sound like prostate cancer to me. It just does not progress like that." Elaine could not believe Fred had been diagnosed over a year ago! She strongly urged me to get Fred to a doctor right away. Elaine offered to get back with me with the names of some of the doctors who treated Joe.

I was utterly amazed at her courage and strength. I wondered if I would have what it would take to do the same for Fred. After all Fred had always been the one taking care of me. I guess somehow I thought it would always be that way. (from the Well of Guidance, Psalm 32:8)

Elaine's personal experience with prostate cancer was she-roic! Elaine lost Joe to cancer in January 1997. I hung up the phone and called Chris Phillips, a dear, dear friend of ours. Chris had known Fred well before I came into his life. Just about one year ago, her husband Phil had been diagnosed with prostate cancer, too. After hearing the news about Fred, Chris was shocked to hear how long Fred had been aware of his diagnosis and to learn he could ever be so neglectful of his health. "Gwen, why has Fred waited until now to tell you?" I reminded Chris of his stubborn side. She assured me that prostate cancer was treatable, depending on how far it had spread. Her genuine concern for Fred, and for me resonated through the phone. Chris urged me to try and see if I could get an appointment with her husband's doctor, Dr. Isaac Powell. Dr. Powell was one of the country's leading prostate cancer specialists and he was a member of her church. Chris offered to intervene on my behalf if I was not successful in making the appointment on my own. "Gwen, Dr. Powell is the best in the field!" I promised Chris that I would call his office first thing Monday morning.

Now let me see who else had been down this road? Who else could advise me? The answer to that question was clear. Soror

Thelma McCrary. Her husband, Mudge, had prostate cancer several years ago. Thelma was just like a sister to Fred. Thelma had always been a no nonsense person. I called Thelma. Thelma was equally as amazed and dismayed with the news, amazed beyond belief that Fred would ignore his health to this extent and dismayed to learn that he would keep such devastating news from me for so long? Thelma was probably just as angry and infuriated with Fred as I had been when I first heard the news. Thelma did not hesitate to give me her best advice, "Gwen you must get Fred to a doctor immediately." She inquired as to who his primary physician was. I told Thelma that Fred did not have one and I explained how his initial contact with the VA had led to the initial diagnosis. Respecting his privacy, I never disclosed to Thelma that Fred believed that the doctor from the VA had given him *this thing* and that he had even tried to bring a law suit against the hospital. I knew Thelma would find that utterly preposterous! Thelma told me her husband's doctor was located in the Fisher Building. She suggested that I give him a call on Monday. I promised her I would give him a call first thing Monday morning. Thelma wanted me to let the doctor know who had referred us. I thanked Thelma for all of her advice and promised to keep her posted.

Fred does not have a host of male friends. A host? Who am I kidding? As a matter of record, Rev. Huggins and Jim Stephens were the closest males in his life. I called Jim. After all Jim was no stranger to the situation. He had been involved from the onset. I repeated the same scenario to Jim. Jim did not try to conceal his involvement. He very candidly told me that Fred had confided in him well over a year ago when he first had concerns about his heart. Jim said that Fred even consulted with him after the cancer diagnosis. He said that it was at that point that Fred swore him to secrecy. "Gwen, Fred never, never wanted you to be worried about him." Jim apologized to me for keeping me in the dark all those months as he had promised Fred. Jim also assured me that he never stopped encouraging Fred to seek further medical attention, even after his fallout with the VA. Needless to say, Fred did not take Jim's advice.

I was relieved to learn of Jim's continual involvement and concern for my husband. I thanked him for being such a good friend to Fred. How well did I know how stubborn and willful Fred could be. I never once let Jim know that I had long since been aware of his initial involvement. I continued to describe Fred's symptoms to him. Jim was inclined to agree with Elaine. As the former director and administrator of the VA Hospital, Jim was a valuable medical resource. After I got through describing Fred's present condition, Jim asked me if Fred was currently taking any kind of medication? "Yes, a diuretic or pressure pill. Jim explained that the diuretic could possibly be a potassium depleting diuretic, which could potentially trigger swelling and pain in the joints. All of the symptoms Jim described fit Fred's current condition. Suddenly it all came together. I had been blind sided by Fred's absolute certain self diagnosis of his cancer. I could not see the forest for the trees. How many times had I been down that road with him in the past? Elaine was most likely correct; those were not the signs of prostate cancer. In fact it was looking more and more like another flare up of gout. I thanked Jim, told him I would keep him posted and that if Fred was not feeling any better in the morning I would be taking Fred to the hospital. Jim was relieved that I was finally made aware of Fred's condition. (from the Well of Joy, Psalm 51:12)

Jim had given me hope.

I made my way back into the bedroom to check on Fred. He was still in the bed. I crawled into bed beside my husband. Fred was in a mood to talk. Fred talked, I listened. Convinced that the cancer had reached its final stages, Fred began to talk in terms of finality. For the first time in our marriage, Fred instructed me where to look for insurance papers and other documents I would need. "Gwen I do not want you to put a whole lot of money in the ground; you have to live after I'm gone." He had always been so wise and practical about his money. Fred said that he hoped the Lord would let him live to see the New Millennium, but if not, he was ready to go home. Fred repeated the Lord's promise "God only promised three score and ten, Gwen. He has kept his promises to me." Fred had always claimed longevity in his life. How many times over the years did he say to me "I'll be around a long time? Mama lived until the age of ninety three." The conversation was more than I could handle. Fred was not practicing what he had always preached to me, "Keep the faith." In every situation Fred had always operated at a faith level that subscribed to the Lord would make a way somehow. Fred walked by faith. He lived by faith. Faith had always been Fred's calling card at the King's dwelling place. So where was his faith now? I asked myself, "Had he lost his faith, or was he dying by his faith?" (from the Well of Faith, Proverbs 3: 6)

I needed an escape from this conversation. The phone offered me the escape I needed. It was security calling. Sheila was in the lobby. I instructed security to allow her to come up to the apartment. I told Fred that Sheila was here. I got out of bed, closed the door behind me and met my friend at the door. Sheila and I sat at the dining room table. We sat momentarily in silence. Then, I proceeded to give her a blow by blow. Sitting there with Sheila, the apartment suddenly felt cold and empty. No one had ever visited our home when Fred was there and they did not experience his presence, his hospitality, his love. His presence was conspicuously absent that afternoon, or said another way his absence conspicuously present. Sheila felt it as well! She sensed my preoccupation. I said to Sheila "Things may not be as dark and final as Fred seems to think, but we still had to begin to deal with it." I reassured her I would call her tomorrow when we returned from the emergency room. I walked Sheila to the door. We hugged each other and said goodbye. (from the Well Hope, Psalm 71:14)

Before returning to the room, I secretly went into Fred's sanctuary and took inventory of his medicine cabinet. I found some very dated prescriptions, some as far back as 1990. I tossed them out. I spotted the bottle for the diuretic he was currently taking. I took it out of the cabinet and read the label. What was it Jim told me to look for? I could not remember. I called Soror Rolanda. Rolanda was a pharmacist, a soror, the daughter of a dear friend, Henrietta Davis. Jim's wife, Betty, Henrietta and I are close friends. In fact over the years we, along with another couple from church, Ralph and Burnie, used to do a lot of things together. I gave Rolanda an abbreviated explanation for my call. I explained to Rolanda what Jim Stephens had suspected in regards to the potassium depleting indicator. Rolanda asked me to look on the bottle for that indicator. Geronimo! There it was! Jim was right! Elaine was right! This pain was not the cancer after all!

I called my mother and gave her the good news. Mother was overjoyed and repeated her offer to come down and assist me in getting Fred out of the bed in the morning. I promised to call in the morning if I needed her assistance. I did not call anyone else that night. Before retiring I prayed for the strength I would need to face whatever I had to meet in the morning. I prayed that the Lord would have compassion and help us. (from the Well of Strength, Psalm 46:1). I returned to the room and crawled back into bed next to Fred. Fred resumed his instructions to me as to his final will and testament.

Sunday morning, September 26, 1999, was more than a struggle for me, but with the Lord's help I did manage to get Fred dressed and down to the car. Once inside the hospital, it was down hill all the way. After Fred was examined by the emergency room physician, the diagnosis was quick and painless. Arthritic gout and water on the knee was the source of his severe pain and the reason Fred was so certain that the cancer had settled in the bone. I explained to the emergency room doctor the sequence of events leading us there that morning. The doctor asked why Fred had not sought treatment for the cancer? I did not feel the need to repeat the sequence of events to the emergency room doctor. So I offered no explanation. He assured us that my husband's self diagnosis was incorrect; the pain he was experiencing was not a direct result of the cancer, but that we should not hesitate to follow up on the diagnosis from the VA. The doctor also wanted Fred to see his primary physician the next day to follow up on the gout. I could not believe the next thing out of his mouth! "Tomorrow have his doctor to drain the water off of his knee which was the source of much of his pain." That day I went ballistic! "Doctor, my husband does not have a primary care physician and he needs immediate relief from this pain." I insisted that it be done right then and there. Within seconds the procedure was completed. The doctor wrote out the prescriptions and sent us on our way. I knew the routine from there. We left the hospital headed for the pharmacy. While waiting on the pharmacist to fill the prescriptions I shopped around for anything else that I thought might give Fred some relief; included was a jar of *Icy Hot* ointment, the blue stuff. Once the prescriptions were filled, I took my husband back home.

Grace met us at the door ....

Once Fred was settled into his 'big chair' I immediately started to administer the meds to him. Then I said to my husband, "Let's talk." I had enough practice over the years. I started off the conversation this way, "Don't interrupt me until I'm finished." For once without his infamous mumblings and grumblings my husband obeyed his wife. My first objective was to assure Fred that the pain and discomfort he had been experiencing this weekend was merely symptomatic of a flare-up of his gout. Furthermore, I told him that I believed that the sequences as they have unfolded over the weekend were nothing less than divine intervention. "I believe it was the Lord's plan to reveal the truth to me. Honey, now that the cat is out of the bag, we have to deal with this thing."

I reminded my husband how closely he stuck by my side when I was going through those anxiety attack episodes. "Fred you were the only attorney in town who would and probably could get away with checking his appointment book first to see if his wife had a doctor's appointment before accepting a court date. "Well, Baby Persons, it's pay back time! I'm taking over from here! I will be on the phone first thing in the morning to get you an appointment to see a doctor."

Attorney Persons did not object. That evening Fred cancelled his instructions to me as to where to find those legal papers. His instruction were replaced with where to locate all of his medical records from the VA. Fred then assigned the task of saving his life to me and the Good Lord, "It's in yours and the Good Lord's hand, Gwen, I'll do whatever you say."

Was it to be that easy?

I left Fred sitting in his big chair while I went into the kitchen to prepare dinner. While out of his sight I took the opportunity to return some of those promised call-backs. I made the calls in this order. First on the list, my mother, Jim Stephens and then Sheila. The message repeated with each call, "The diagnosis is gout, but tomorrow our journey begins." After dinner I continued to return phone calls, still on the call back list, Elaine, Chris and Thelma. Thelma gave me the name of Mudge's doctor. After completing all of my call backs, I called Rev. Huggins for the first time this weekend.

Tonight I took over Fred's KP duties, and then rejoined my husband in our bedroom. I rubbed his fat knee with some blue stuff (Icy Hot). The medication had already begun to take effect. Fred was beginning to feel better. We settled in for the evening and prepared ourselves for more good news from on high. We tuned to the Bethany Hour and for the next little while Dr. Jones continued to lift our spirits and bring light and illumination to what had been a dark place for the past two days.

The message for the hour, "When your faith level is low." It was a message on faith, exactly what Fred needed to hear this evening. The Holy Spirit and Dr. Jones restored my husband's faith and gave Fred a brand new lease on life. That evening Grace paid a visit to our abode. I realized at that moment that I would not be the one taking control of the situation. The Master had gone to work. The Great I AM had gotten busy. The author and finisher of our faith stepped in and took charge. The light of the world brought illumination to a dark situation. Jesus took a look at the situation and said, 'Thou *spirit of unbelief, listen to me! I charge thee on the basis of my absolute authority over all things, I charge thee, come out of Fred Persons. Do it right now, come on out now and stay out*! Suddenly that foul and negative spirit of unbelief seemed to march right on out of Fred. Comfort, Hope and Joy came to us that evening. But above all else, Fred's Faith level moved from low to high.

The Lord *is* a rewarder of them that diligently seek him. What a remarkable change came over Fred. What a transformation! Once again, when it counted most Fred was going to allow his wife to be the helpmate God intended for me to be to him. Looking after and taking good care of my husband was what God had commanded me to do and with His help I was ready for my journey. The prayers of the righteous avail much and my prayers had been answered. (from the Well of Guidance, St. Luke 1:79) My cup of joy runneth over!

It had been a long exhausting weekend; we were both spent. I rubbed his cabbage patch head, Fred said our prayers, and we crawled back into bed. But before closing his eyes and saying good night to me my husband said, "God is good and you are the best thing that ever happened to me."

When I arrived to work Monday morning I cancelled all of my therapy sessions for the morning. I spent the entire morning on the telephone trying to get Fred an appointment. First, I called Thelma to get the name and number of her husband's doctor. I hung up the phone and called right away. I explained the urgency of my situation and also the individual who had referred me. To my dismay, the nurse was unable to accommodate us. She explained that the doctor had stopped taking new referrals months ago. My next call was to Dr. Isaac Powell, the cancer specialist who had treated Chris's husband. Unfortunately the same disappointment met me on the other end of that conversation as well. The earliest possible appointment I could get for Fred was in late October. We did not have the option of waiting several weeks for an appointment. I hung up the phone. At the time, I did not have an internist either. My primary care physician, was Dr. Ethylene Crockett Jones, an Ob/Gyn. Dr. Jones, worked out of Detroit Riverview Hospital. I hesitated for a moment and thought about waiting until that evening to give Elaine a call for the names of the doctors who treated Joe. That lasted for only a moment; I knew time was critical. The Holy Spirit ordered my steps in a different direction. (from the Well of Guidance, Isaiah 58:11)

I called Dr. Jones office and explained the situation to her. Dr. Jones had known Fred since she was a little girl growing up on American Street in Detroit. Fred was a close friend to her father, the late George Crockett Sr. Fred told me stories of how the children, Dr. Jones and her brother, George Crockett Jr., the judge, would be playing on the staircase during his visits to the home. He also spoke very highly of their mother, the acclaimed no nonsense baby doctor, the late Dr. Ethylene Crockett, who enjoyed an outstanding, distinguished career as one of the first African-American female doctors in the city of Detroit. Dr. Jones extended her concern and sent her regards to Fred. She then gave me the name of an internist, Dr. Tah, on staff at Detroit Riverview Hospital. I thanked her for her assistance and immediately called and got an appointment for Fred. Our appointment was scheduled for the very next day, Tuesday, September 28, 1999, at 1:00 p.m. (from the Well of Hope, Lamentations 3:26)

I called Fred to check up on him and to tell him that I had scheduled a doctor's appointment for tomorrow. He simply replied, "I'll be ready." I spent what was left of the morning sharing the good news with my Sorors, Deborah, Delores and Pat. I serviced my students in the afternoon.

When I arrived home from work that afternoon, Fred did have a new lease on life. He exhibited practically no sign of discomfort. He seemed to have made a miraculous recovery. Fred was feeling and acting much like himself. The medication and the Holy Spirit were working with Fred. After dinner Fred felt well enough to resume his KP duties. I retreated to my quarters and made some calls. I called my mother, Chris, Elaine and Thelma with an updated report. A few minutes later, Fred walked into the room, and handed me all his medical records from the VA. He repeated the exact words he had spoken to me on Saturday night, "It's in yours and the Lord's hands Gwen, I'll do whatever you tell me to do."

That evening things in the Persons' household were back to normal and it felt good. (from the Well of Peace, St. John 14:27) Fred settled into his big chair for the evening to watch a World Series game. I resumed my phone calls. My last call was to Louise. That evening I told Louise that her big brother Fred, had prostate cancer.

Our journey begins..........

Beginning this journey would prove to be the biggest mountain I have had to climb in all of my life. I prayed that the Lord would continue to direct my path. (from the Well of Faith, St. Matthew 17:20) The Holy Spirit reminded me who was in control, the battle was not mine, but the Lord, mighty in battle, and that the battle was His, not mine.

The following day when I awoke I felt equipped for our journey. That morning before I left for work I reminded my husband that I would only be working half the day. "I will be back to pick you up at noon." He said he would be sitting in the lobby waiting. When I arrived to pick Fred up he was not sitting in the lobby, he was waiting at the front door, ready, willing and eager to get this journey started. That positive, upbeat spirit was all over him that day. With medical records in hand we arrived at Detroit Riverview Hospital for our initial appointment with Dr. Tah.

We signed in and I completed filling out the necessary paperwork for Fred and together we returned them along with my Blue Cross Card and Fred's Medicaid Part 2 card. We then took a seat. While we waited, my husband asked the question "How much is this going to cost you, Gwen?" I never expected such a question. Cost me? I responded to my husband's query. "Nothing Fred." I assured my husband it would all be covered under my medical insurance. And what Blue Cross does not cover your Medicaid Part 2 would. "Are you sure Gwen?" "Yes Fred, I am sure." Fred looked as though the weight of the world had been lifted from him. While sitting in that waiting room, it was revealed to me why Fred had delayed treatment for all of those months. He was concerned about the cost? Had he just not wanted to burden me with the medical cost? Was Fred just trying to protect and look out for me? I had hoped not at the expense of his own life! We would have this discussion later. We had not been kept waiting long when the nurse called Fred to the back. I followed. She took his vitals, his temp, his BP and his weight. Just in that brief span the nurse knew his profession, his age, and how much he cared for that ol' piece of chick (that would be me). The nurse was in stitches. After she composed herself she ushered us into an examining room to wait for the good doctor.

When the doctor entered, I had mixed reactions. She was female, that was good! She was reasonably young, that was better! She was African-American, that was the absolute best! Fred loved women, especially fine, young women of the African-American variety. The doctor had it all going on for her, except for one thing. Fred's definition of fine was not synonymous with fat. Dr. Tah was a healthy sister.

Dr. Tah introduced herself. She presented herself as a very warm, poised, efficient professional. She didn't beat around the bush. She posed the query "Who wants to start?" I started the ball rolling by explaining the sequence of the past weekend. I further apprised her of Fred's initial contact with the VA and the fact that he was diagnosed with prostate cancer nearly two years ago, but had elected not to seek treatment. Fred interrupted with these words "Doctor I'm here because I love this 'ol piece of chick' and this is what she wants me to do!" Fred gave just a partial testimony of God's goodness in his life. "Doctor, I'm eighty years old. The Lord has been good to me." Dr. Tah did not want to believe Fred was eighty years old! "Mr. Persons, you're not eighty years old! You're right; God has been good to you!" After hearing Fred's praise and testimony, the good doctor reciprocated and gave her own praise report of God's goodness in her life. "You are indeed blessed to have this ol' piece of chick' for a wife." They continued to have church right there in the good doctor's office. That cemented the relationship. Anyone who testifies to the goodness of the Lord was all right with Fred Persons. In addition, the good doctor carried a sense of humor which more than made up for anything else she may have been lacking or carrying. She had quite an engaging charm. They were two of a kind. Little did Dr. Tah know, but she was in like Flynn. Fred very humbly and willingly submitted himself to her care. I took this as a good sign that Fred was concerned about his health, and for the first time in months Fred mentioned his rapid heart beat. He also called to her attention his excessive weight loss.

I was then asked to step out of the room while she gave Fred the routine digital examination. When I returned Dr. Tah confirmed that Fred did indeed have an enlarged gland. She wanted Fred to see an urologist right away. She left the room to set up the appointment. Fred said to me "I like her. Thanks, you're the best thing that ever happened to me." Dr. Tah returned. "Your appointment with Dr. Maitland is Monday, October 4, 1999 at 2:00pm. Showing as much efficiency and professionalism as ever before Fred whipped out his little appointment book and entered all of the information just the way I had seen him do for me. Dr. Tah then directed us to the lab for serum PSA blood work. In addition, we had to go over to the hospital and make appointments for a CT scan, a bone scan and an echo cardiogram. These appointments were scheduled for 8:00

am respectively, Wednesday October 6, and Thursday, October 7. I was also instructed to pick up the x-ray film of Fred's bone scan and the biopsy report from Veteran's Hospital. The urologist would be needing them. There is a saying that goes something like this, "The journey of a thousand miles begins with the first step." Our journey had only just begun; together we had taken our first step. That evening after dinner I sat down and carefully went over all of Fred's reports from the VA.

I had five days in front of me to learn as much as I could about prostate cancer. I had never heard of a PSA, and quite frankly I was not even sure if I knew where the gland was located. At the time we did not have a computer at home and my experience with computers on the job had been rather limited. I had never been on the Internet either. I did not have a clue as to how to go online. The following day with the help of Soror Delores Allman, media specialist and Soror Deborah Sinclair, staff coordinator, I got a crash course in technology. They taught me how to get online and how to use a search engine. For the next two days I stayed after work for my intense internet training. I went to http://www.prostrcision.com. The information on prostate cancer was out there! I learned that PSA stands for, prostate specific antigen. The PSA is a large protein produced only by prostate cells, normal or cancerous, and not by any other cell in the body. Fred was right, if prostate cancer cells spread (metastasize) the most common initial site for spread is to bone and pelvic lymph nodes. The PSA test is a simple blood test that can be performed in almost any doctor's office or laboratory. All men should get a PSA test. The American Cancer Society recommends that starting at age 50, men should have a PSA test each year. For those men whose father or brother had prostate cancer, as well as all African-American men, PSA testing should begin at age 40. Before PSA test became available in 1987, most men diagnosed with prostate cancer were not curable. Prior to the development of PSA, detection of prostate cancer was by digital rectal exam or by the development of symptoms related to cancer, such as urinary obstruction or bone pain from spread of the cancer. An elevation of PSA can be found before almost any other detection method for prostate cancer. However, other diseases of the prostate, besides cancer, can produce an abnormal PSA level. Therefore, an ultrasound examination with needle biopsy of the prostate gland is usually done if an elevated PSA is found. The probability of prostate cancer cure is directly related to the pretreatment PSA. In all series; screening may help men detect cancer while it is most curable.

My search yielded voluminous information. I printed out the information and systematically organized it into a loose leaf binder. My searches took me from cause to treatment options. I was officially enrolled in Prostate Cancer 101. I spent my evenings reading and rereading the information until I felt comfortable with this newly acquired knowledge. As I read, I took copious notes and formulated questions to ask the doctors who would be treating Fred. I was on a mission to fulfill my one and only objective, to take good care of Fred and to be as good a wife to Fred that the Good Lord would have for me to be. I wanted to become empowered with the knowledge that would save my husband's life. Ironically, in addition to the vast amount of information I found on the Internet the September 14, edition of the Michigan Chronicle, ran an extensive article on prostate cancer. The article featured the most recent work of one of the countries leading physician's in the study of prostate cancer, who was Dr. Isaac Powell (Phil's doctor). The article reported Dr. Powell's effective means of treating this type of cancer at the Barbara Ann Karmanos Cancer Institute. This article could not have been more timely. The more I read and the more I learned about this cancer, the more empowered I became. I was becoming fiercely energized and driven to gain all the knowledge that I could about this disease. Each time I read an encouraging piece of information I tried to get Fred to read it. I wanted him to be actively involved in this process too. "Fred, read this and let me know what you think." He would always promise to read it later. "Leave it, I'll read it later." He meant it when he said "It is in yours and the Lord's hands."

Thursday night, September 30, 1999, somewhere around 10:00 p.m., I lay in bed and without any prior warning my heart suddenly began to accelerate. The feeling was not quite the same as those old familiar panic attacks, but the feeling was just as unsettling. My heart was beating out of control. Lord, please don't let this begin again, not at such a critical time in Fred's life! He needs me now! I had prayed that those attacks would never return, not just for my sake, but for Fred's as well. I never wanted to put him through that again. I could not continue to lie in that bed. Fred was no longer driving. How will we get to the hospital? I called my sister Judy, who lived minutes away. Judy had been released from the hospital only days ago for a routine heart procedure herself. She came right away and drove us to the emergency room at Detroit Riverview Hospital. I ordered her to go right back home. I told Judy that we would call a taxi to take us back home. We literally had to wait hours before a doctor finally saw me. I told the attending physician my concerns. Upon his examination he found nothing wrong. The EKG read normal. My blood pressure was normal. My temperature was normal. All of my vital signs checked out okay, just the way it was seven years ago. No conclusive diagnosis was ever made for those attacks either. The emergency room doctor diagnosed my symptoms as being stress induced. I suppose under the current circumstances that was an accurate and reasonable diagnosis. The doctor suggested that I follow-up with a visit to my doctor, wrote out a prescription for a tranquilizer and released me to go back home. We stood on Jefferson Ave. at 1:00 a.m. and hailed a taxi back to the Millender Center.

The following week I had to make certain nothing was seriously wrong with me. What if something were to happen to me? Who would take care of Fred? I made an appointment to see a heart specialist in the Detroit Medical Center. The echo-cardiogram read normal. Over the next couple of weeks I took the medication only when I felt anxious. I did not intend on becoming dependent on tranquilizers. The need eventually went away (from the Well of Faith, 1 Corinthians 16:13).

It was during the 1999-2000 school year that the Detroit Board of Education slapped some ridiculous penalties or sanctions on usage of employee sick bank. A restricted or limited number of sick days would be allocated for each employee during the school year. If those days were exceeded, the employee would automatically forfeit any pay raise for the coming school year. It was still early in the school year and I had already freely dipped into my sick bank. A well meaning co-worker reminded me of the new rule. I didn't stutter. "Whatever it takes, coming to work late, leaving work early, not coming at all, no pay raise, no job. Whatever it would take, I would make the sacrifices for Fred." The sanction was never carried out; as a matter of fact it was lifted the following year.

On Monday, October 4, I left work early, and drove home to pick up Fred for our appointment with the urologist. He was not standing in the door way of the Millender Center waiting for me. I parked the car and went up to the apartment. He was not there either. Where in the world could he be? Had he forgotten about our appointment? I got back into the car and drove to look for him. I found my husband a few blocks from the apartment. Fred had been in court all day! I did not ask any questions. He must be feeling pretty good. I was delighted to hear the news (we sure could use the bread). Fred got into the car and I drove my husband to the doctor's office.

A urologist is a doctor who specializes in diseases of the urinary tract. He entered the examining room and we made our introductions. Dr. Maitland was a young African-American man. The doctor inquired as to Fred's medical care and the name of his attending physician. Once I gave the doctor Fred's history we learned that he attended the same medical school as the young Dr. Harris who had replaced Dr. Harcourt Harris. He inquired as to the reason Fred did not continue his medical care under the practice of the new Dr. Harris. Fred was slow to respond. How well I knew my husband. As a result of this question I sensed a bit of irritation from Fred. Unlike the female gender, the brothers had a rough row to hoe with Fred K. We can't afford to get off on the wrong foot with this doctor. I prayed, "Please don't stay there too long. Let's just move on. Change the subject and change it now!"(from the Well of Patience, 1 Timothy 6:11)

The Holy Spirit took charge. Fred repeated his same pro-nouncement to Dr. Maitland, "I'm here because I love this ol' piece of chick. Dr. I'm eighty years old. The Lord had been good to me." The reason for our visit had been temporarily suspended. The subject had been changed. Dr. Maitland was awe-stricken to learn of Fred's age and began to sing the same praise refrain. "Mr. Persons you certainly don't look like you're eighty years old. God has been good to you and he's blessed you with a wonderful wife." It was now his turn to give praise and testimony. Fred inquired as to the good doctor's church affiliation. We learned that his wife grew up in St. Stephen A.M.E. Church. That knowledge consummated the relationship. Fred was ready to rock and roll with the good doctor.

The visit could best be described as one that was consultative in nature. Dr. Maitland clearly outlined the next steps and briefly discussed some of the possible treatment options. However, he conclusively admitted that due to Fred's age he was not likely to be a candidate for surgery.

He explained to us that in addition to today's digital rectal exam in order for him to determine the stage of Fred's cancer and to recommend the best treatment options, he would need the biopsy report from the VA, as well as the most recent bone and CAT scans taken at Detroit Riverview. As soon as the words were out of his mouth, I handed the doctor all of the reports and film from the VA. As the doctor and I continued to talk, Fred sat there in silence. When he thought we were about done discussing him, Fred said to the doctor, "I did not know my wife was so brilliant." I could clearly see that they both were genuinely impressed by my

Fresh Water From Old Wells 143

level of knowledge and efficiency. "Mr. Persons, you are indeed a lucky man, with a wife like yours, you are in good hands." Fred concurred with the doctor, but he attached an addendum to that statement "Doc, luck had nothing to do with it! God is good!"

Dr. Maitland had passed the faith test. Fred left there extolling the virtues and singing the praises of this young African-American 'professional.' Our next appointment with Dr. Maitland was scheduled for Monday, October 18, 1999.

On Wednesday, October 6, I took Fred to Detroit Riverview for his scheduled bone and CAT scan appointments. The following day we returned to the hospital for the echo cardiogram. Both of these appointments had been scheduled for 8:00 in the morning.

When we returned to Dr. Tah's office on Tuesday, October 12, the results of the blood work indicated elevated levels of the protein. Fred's PSA was reported to be 15.0. To Dr. Tah's amazement, after nearly two years since the initial diagnosis, and without any treatment whatsoever, Fred's PSA had only gone from 10.65 to 15.0. Praise God! Once again divine intervention had worked another miracle in Fred Persons' life. My research indicated a PSA at this level, the chances that the cancer cells were confined only within the prostate gland itself was 25%. A PSA of over 20.0 almost all men have cancer cells outside of the prostate. Dr. Maitland would give us these results when we returned to his office on October 18.

In the meantime, I had two other concerns for Dr. Tah today. First, I pointed out the swelling in Fred's feet. Dr. Tah suggested this may be related to his heart. Upon review of the echo cardiogram however, she saw no reason for alarm. Although she did however advise that Fred elevate his feet as much as possible. My second concern was his weight loss. Dr. Tah discussed nutrition and a diet menu to promote a healthy prostate. She strongly encouraged a reduction in fat intake and suggested that we add Ensure, a food supplement to Fred's diet.

Over the next five days I got back on-line. I searched the Internet for treatment options for prostate cancer. The method selected to treat prostate cancer depends on its stage, speed of growth, the age and general health of the patient. Depending on the stage of the cancer, prostate cancer can be treated by one or more of the following methods. Surgery, radiation therapy, radioactive seed implantation, hormone therapy, chemotherapy and 'watchful waiting', also called expectant therapy. At that juncture we did not know what stage Fred's cancer was in. However, we had already been told that due to his age, Fred would not be a candidate for a radical prostatectomy.

Monday, October 18, we returned to Dr. Maitland's office. All of the reports had been delivered to his office, the CAT scan, bone scan biopsy and lab work. When we entered the examination room, the doctor did not hesitate to give Fred his praise report. "Mr. Persons, I have some good news for you. You are indeed a blessed man. Two years out, and an elevated PSA and no intervention, the cancer has not metastasized and spread outside the gland to the bone" (Fred's initial suspicion). Dr. Maitland echoed the same amazement as Dr. Tah. Fred gave God all the glory. "God is good."

Having said that, Dr. Maitland proceeded to give us the next steps. He discussed treatment options in depth. "Here are your options, 1) do nothing, 2) internal radiation, 3) external radiation or 4) hormone therapy. I felt like a well informed consumer. I had done my homework. I was able to ask intelligent questions regarding the best treatment options for my husband. Dr. Maitland could not help but recognize and comment on how informed about this disease I was. "Mr. Person's you are very fortunate to having such a devoted wife. I wish all of my patient's took this level of advocacy with their own health." Fred looked at me and then said to the doctor, "A little knowledge is dangerous, but Doc, I don't know what I'd do without this 'ol piece of chick."

This experience taught me just how vitally important it is to be your own best advocate and to be directly involved in your own treatment process. Before leaving his office, we were taken into another room to view a video on treatment options. Dr. Maitland gave us more literature to take home and read. Our instructions were to read over the information carefully, <u>together</u> and make up our own minds. When we returned to his office on October 23, he would give us his recommendation.

We left the office rejoicing and praising God. With this good news, it was time for a Hallelujah Praise Fest. It was celebration time. I surprised Fred and took him out to dinner. (from the Well of Joy, Psalm 30:5) It had been weeks since we had dinner out. That evening we dined at Carl's Chop House.

Decisions, decisions, decisions. I prayed. I asked God to give me demonstration and direction that would lead us to the right choice of treatment. (from the Well of Guidance, Psalm 32:8).

My evenings for the remainder of that week were spent reading about the different treatment options and telephoning folks with progress reports. I was feeling good and so proud of myself. It felt just good being able to take care of Fred. He needed me and I was and would be here for him!

On my lunch hour Tuesday afternoon I called Soror Clara to give her Fred's praise report. During our conversation, Clara asked if I had thought about having Fred speak to Dr. Sampson. Dr. Sampson was a cancer survivor. He had been on the battle-field for the past four or five years. Not only was Dr. Sampson a survivor, he was a spokesperson and leading advocate in the city of Detroit on prostate cancer among African American men.

I took Clara's advice and called the church. I introduced myself to Ms. Lee, the secretary, and explained the reason for my call. Fred Persons was no stranger to Dr. Frederick Sampson or to Tabernacle Missionary Baptist Church or to Ms. Lee.

Fred and Doc not only shared a connection in the church house, but also the courthouse. Dr. Sampson was indeed a community activist in the city of Detroit. He spent many days in the City County building, (Fred's favorite hang out). It was there their friendship took root. Whenever we were in attendance at

Tabernacle for Sunday morning worship service, Dr. Sampson would always acknowledge the *lawyer* from around the block, St. Stephen A.M.E. He would jokingly add, "The lawyer's membership is around the corner, but I think he claims membership at Tab." St. Stephen A.M.E. and Tabernacle are both part of the Westside Ministerial Alliance. Each year the Alliance comes together for both the Good Friday and Thanksgiving Services. And let's not forget to mention, we never missed being in the house at Tab, whenever Dr. William Jones was in town. When Clara had her house blessing in 1996, Dr. Sampson was there to perform the blessing. Before the ceremony, Dr. Sampson recognized the steward from St. Stephen A.M.E. Church and asked that Fred say a prayer before the blessing. When the Conerway's celebrated their 50th wedding anniversary, Dr. Sampson was there to bless the auspicious occasion. We were privileged to be among the invited guests. Indeed, Fred Persons was no stranger to Fred Sampson.

The secretary gave me an appointment for 2:00 p.m., on Friday October 22, 1999, the day before we were to return to the urologist. Once again the Great I AM had interceded on our behalf. The timing could not have been more perfect. I hung up the phone and called Fred right away. No answer. When he arrived home that afternoon, I told him that we had another appointment. "With whom this time, Gwen?" I immediately sensed a bit or annoyance in his voice. Fred was a very private person and had never tolerated me discussing him with others. I promptly answered my husband, "This one is with Rev. Sampson."

Assuming that the appointment was one of a spiritual nature (which I'm sure it will turn out to be, how can it not seeing who it was with?) Fred asked "Why didn't you first discuss this with me?" I explained or reminded Fred of Dr. Sampson's own personal challenges with prostate cancer and that Clara suggested that we ought to give him a call." Some people, not many, could do no wrong in Fred's book. Clara Crowell and Fred Sampson were two of those shining stars. In a state of excited anticipation (as only Fred K. had a way of displaying) he ordered me to "Make the appointment." "I already did Fred; the appointment is for Friday October 22."

I began to notice that Fred had picked up his work pace. It looked as if he had started to accept more assignments. It seemed to be doing him good, he was back to his old self, and that made me very happy. My research also suggested that a positive attitude plays a huge role in the healing and treatment process of cancer patients. If that is the case then the battle has been won, Fred K. wrote the book on positive attitude.

As the weeks passed, it was clear that I was carrying all the weight in this decision making process. What a hoot, not only was I carrying all the weight figuratively, but literally as well. It seemed that my efforts to support Fred's nutritional needs and increase his weight gain benefited him not. I was the only one putting the weight on around here. I was getting heavier and heavier. Was I subconsciously eating my way through this challenge?

After much deliberation and meditation, I had narrowed our treatment options down to two choices, external radiation and seed implants. With the external beam radiation therapy the rays are delivered by machine and radiation is given in brief sessions. The procedure is painless and lasts for just a few minutes. Radiation therapy can cause a variety of side effects. Most of these are minor and disappear after therapy stops. In brachytherapy or seeds, the rays come from tiny, radioactive seeds inserted directly into the prostate. The seeds are too small to be felt by the patient and do not cause any discomfort. The seeds give off rays and remain active for weeks, months, or up to a year, and can remain safely in place for the rest of a person's life. The amount of time that the seeds remain radioactive depends on the dose and what type of radioactive material is used. I tried to encourage Fred to read some of the literature and be involved. I am leaning toward external radiation.

When we arrived at the church, we went into the church office. Ms. Lee, the secretary, recognized Fred and welcomed us to Tab. She immediately picked up the phone and announced our arrival. We were not kept waiting long. Rev. Sampson soon appeared and escorted us into his study. Once behind closed doors he greeted us as if we were his old friends and members of his congregation. Over the years, whenever I saw Rev. Sampson, outside of the church, (whether with Fred or alone), Doc would call me the lawyer's 'angel on furlough'. I loved it and that day was no exception.

Before we got to the heart of the matter, Fred Sampson and Fred Persons had solved the state of things in this world's present order. Rev. Sampson then began to chronicle his history with prostate cancer. He talked about the urgency of African-American men getting tested early and the role he played as an advocate in the city of Detroit for early detection of prostate cancer. He very candidly discussed his operation and the subsequent treatments that he had to undergo, his remissions as well as the recurrences. It was then our turn, or should I say Fred's turn to talk. Fred, the one who had taken a back seat, a passive role during this entire process, took over the conversation. He did not hesitate to credit me for getting him to this point. "This was all my wife's idea to come here today." I reminded Fred whose idea it really was. Fred expounded on the goodness of the Lord and how blessed he was to have this 'ol piece of chick'. "I don't know what I would do without her." Most of Fred's remarks had little to do with the reasons we were there.

When I felt that he had testified sufficiently, it was time for me to bring Doc up to snuff. I butted in. I proceeded to give him a very descriptive report of the sequence of events over these past weeks which incidentally began to unfold the night we were there for Dr. Borders final service during Christian Education Week. When Rev. Sampson learned just how long Fred had had cancer, (and not sought medical intervention) and that it had not spread outside of the gland itself, Rev. Sampson just about shouted to the rafters. He credited that miracle to Fred's vertical connection. It was my turn to speak again. "Rev. Sampson, I have done quite a bit of reading regarding treatment options for my husband. Tomorrow when we return to the urologist we are expected to give him our decision."

When all of the evidence was presented Rev. Sampson gave us his best recommendation. Without much deliberation or reservation, Rev Sampson advised external radiation as the best treatment option for Fred. (from the Well of Guidance, Psalm 37:23) My prayers had been answered, the Lord had indeed led us there that day. The Lord had given us clear direction and demonstration (from the Well of Patience, Revelations 2:2). "When two or more are gathered in my name, there I shall be also." The three of us were in agreement. The following day we would give Dr. Maitland our decision.

As I got up to leave the study Rev. Sampson once again acknowledged me as 'Fred's Angel on Furlough." He concluded his remarks with these words, "Girl, you ought to write a book. Think of how many other wives are going through it. You could be an a source of knowledge and encouragement for other wives facing prostate cancer." I turned to Rev. Sampson but before I could get the words out of my mouth my husband rushed to say," She is. Doc, she's the best thing that ever happened to me."

Rev. Sampson then excused me from his study and escorted me into the sanctuary. He left me there while he returned to his study to speak to Fred privately. A few minutes later, the two men joined me in the sanctuary. Rev. Sampson led us in prayer at the altar. After he finished praying for us, Rev. Sampson gave us a brief history about the wood carving positioned in front of the altar. He told us that his daughter brought it back from a trip to the Holy Land. Fred Sampson bade us Godspeed and asked that we keep him informed of our journey. We promised to do just as he asked. We thanked him for taking time out of his busy schedule to meet with us. Rev. Sampson left us with these words "God bless your hearts." I will be forever thankful to the giant preacher on Beechwood and Milford with the giant heart. "God Bless his heart, too!"

This had been a blessed afternoon. It was just what the Good Lord ordered for Fred. If I thought Rev. Jones had given Fred a new lease on life a few weeks back, that day, Rev. Sampson had given Fred the deed of ownership. If Fred had wings he would have flown. Instead, when we got to the car he insisted on driving. This was the first time since we had gotten the 2000 Cadillac that he expressed any desire to get behind the wheel. I requested that we go by Mama's. Fred drove straight to Mama's, and gave her our praise report. Our visit was brief. Mama was very proud of her baby daughter and so happy for her son-in-law. I promised to call tomorrow after we left the doctor's. (from the Well of Joy, 1 John 1:4) It was a Friday night. We both felt we deserved a night out. How we longed for our favorite spot to dine on Gratiot and Vernor. We went back to Carl's Chop House.

The following day we returned to the urologist office. Dr. Maitland dispensed with the small talk. "Have you had a chance to read the information I gave to you?" "Yes, and in addition to that we met with Rev. Sampson on yesterday." Dr. Maitland was quite familiar with this preacher and his connection with prostate cancer throughout this city. He was pleased and impressed that we had the wherewithal to make that contact. Dr. Maitland proceeded to give us his best recommendation. But first he wanted to hear from us.

I took the liberty to speak on our behalf. "Dr. Maitland, as a result of yesterday's visit our minds are made up. We have decided on external radiation for my husband." The doctor smiled, his smile spoke for itself, this was clearly his choice as well. Dr. Maitland concurred with our decision and gave us his reasons for supporting external radiation. He then explained the benefits and the side effects that we could possibly expect.

My research paid off. I was on a level playing field with the doctor. Dr. Maitland applauded us on our team effort and commented again on my advocacy on behalf of my husband.

The next specialist in the pecking order would be with an oncologist. Dr Maitland scheduled that appointment with a Dr. Frazier at Grace Hospital for Thursday, November 11, 1999. We spent the remainder of the weekend celebrating the good news. Fred was indeed his old self that weekend! And what a weekend it was!

On Friday evening, November 12, 1999, St. Stephen A.M.E. church would be celebrating its 80th anniversary. Without Fred's knowledge he had been selected to be honored for his fifty years of stewardship on the Steward Board. During one of my phone conversations with Sheila I mentioned the celebration to her and intimated that I was thinking about inviting family and friends to share the occasion with us. I went as far as saying "I would love to invite his sisters, Louise, Joyce and Frances to join us." Fred had not seen his sisters since his mother's home going five years ago. I don't think Joyce had been to Detroit in over forty years and Louise does not fly. I doubt if they'll come." Sheila responded, "Call them, let them make up their own minds."

Sunday evening I called Louise. I gave her the progress and praise report. Before hanging up the phone, I told Louise about the upcoming 80th Anniversary of our church. I gave her all the details and asked if the three of them would consider coming. Louise was pleased to hear the positive news. I asked her a second time about coming, she merely gave one of her sweet expressions "We'll see, baby." Louise did promise to discuss it with Joyce and Frances and get back with me. After hanging up the phone I started making more phone calls, inviting Fred's Harem of Honey's and my family to be a part of this special recognition. I was not able to celebrate Fred's 80th birthday earlier in the year. This will be the perfect substitute.

All of my research strongly recommended that the patient always seek a second opinion. What better place to have that done than the Barbara Ann Karmanos Cancer Center. The following day I called the center and made an appointment. I was instructed to bring all of Fred's medical records and his films from both the

VA Hospital and Detroit Riverview Hospital. We were given an appointment for Tuesday, November 2, 1999 with an oncologist by the name of Dr. Hassian. Coincidently, this second opinion was scheduled nine days ahead of the appointment with Dr. Frazier. When I told Fred that I made this appointment, he did not see the necessity for a second opinion. Fred was quite comfortable with the state of things as they were. He was ready to move forward with the plans Dr. Maitland had set in motion. I assured him this was not in anyway conflicting with Dr. Maitland's course of action. I appealed to Fred's sense of professionalism. "As in any profession, Fred, it does not hurt to get a second opinion, now does it?" I got no argument out of him. Fred very cooperatively opened his appointment book and entered the date.

When we arrived at the Karmanos Center we were greeted by a civilian volunteer. The gentleman was quite cordial and he escorted us to the appointment desk where we signed in and were asked to have a seat and fill out some forms. I completed all of the paper work and took them to the desk. I then returned and took a seat next to my husband. Within a few minutes, the same volunteer escorted us to another section of the center, a rather large waiting room.

While sitting in that waiting room I looked over at my husband. Fred appeared to be preoccupied and exhibited much less enthusiasm than he had shown in recent weeks. I asked Fred if he was all right? He said that he was and reminded me, "Gwen it is in your hands and the Good Lord's Hands."

I kept looking at my watch, thirty minutes or more had passed, we still had not been called. We had a 1:00 o'clock appointment that afternoon with Dr. Tah. It was looking like there would be no work for me that day.

We met with Dr. Hassian, an oncologist. All of Fred's medical records had been forwarded as requested by the center. She discussed at length the location of the cancer and her recommended treatment option for Fred. For the most part, Dr. Hassian seemed to be in agreement with Dr. Maitland. Although there was this one difference, Dr. Hassian also suggested hormone therapy as an additional treatment option. I found this rather curious. Fred's cancer was in stage T2; hormone treatment was usually recommended when the cancer had spread outside the pelvic area. When I said that to Dr. Hassian, she explained that at this stage of the cancer, hormone replacement would be advised in order to reduce the size of the tumor. Knowing the side effects of hormone therapy, particularly the hot flashes, I felt this would be too confusing to Fred at his age. I rejected this option.

Dr. Hassain reiterated at this point, it was just that, an option. She then excused me from the room while she examined Fred. When I reentered the room Dr. Hassian commented on the apparent love and commitment between us. She reminded us of how important that ingredient was for the cancer patient's recovery. Our final decision would be made after we met with Dr. Frazier.

We took off for our 1:00 appointment with Dr. Tah. If I may borrow Dr. Sampson's description of me, these past few weeks, Dr. Tah had been our *angel on furlough* sent straight from heaven. Every step that we had made had been in divine order. I related the progress we had made to that point, and our decision to seek a second opinion. Dr. Tah was more than pleased with our progress and strongly concurred with our decision to seek a second opinion. Today's appointment was of a routine nature. Not much change in his weight. I mentioned to Dr. Tah that Fred's skin was beginning to look very dry and scaly. Dr. Tah wanted Fred to see a nutritionist. As for the dry skin, she wrote us a prescription for a face cream. There was no mention of his heart on this visit. Fred was pleased, and I was too! The praises had gone up and the blessings had come showering down upon us (from the Well of Joy, Job 29:3). Little did we know that would be the last time we would see our angel on furlough.

Sunday evening, November 7, Louise phoned to say that she and Joyce would be coming. They would be arriving on

Thursday, November 11 around 1:00 p.m. The same day of our appointment at Grace Hospital. I suggested to Louise that they get the shuttle bus from the airport. The shuttle would bring them right to the Millender Center or at least to the Courtyard Marriott. I would meet them and bring them over to the apartment. I spent the remainder of the week calling folks to remind them. The party was on!

Thursday, November 11, 1999, Veteran's Day, we kept our 8:30 a.m. appointment with Dr. Frazier, the oncologist at Grace Hospital. When we arrived, there were others waiting ahead of us. We soon learned that most of them were there to receive their radiation treatment. Of all the mornings for such a thing to happen, there was a malfunction with the equipment. All radiation appointments had to be delayed. Even though we were not scheduled for radiation therapy, this problem caused a delay with our scheduled appointment as well. When we finally met with Dr. Frazier, he immediately presented as a very personable and engaging fellow. Deja vu! The order of the conversation repeats almost exactly for yet a third time. Stage of cancer, prognosis and treatment options. But he did not stop there. Dr. Frazier fully explained how radiation treats or reduces the tumor. Radiation therapy uses high-energy rays to kill prostate cancer cells, shrink tumors, or prevent cancer cells from dividing and spreading. It is nearly impossible to direct these rays at the cancer cells. Dr. Frazier further explained that the radiation may damage both cancer cells and healthy cells nearby. Therefore, a process called simulation would have to be done before treatment could begin. Simulation is a process involving special x-ray pictures that are used to plan radiation treatment so that the area to be treated is precisely located and marked for treatment. The doses are usually small and spread out over a period of time, usually one session each weekday for several weeks. This allows the healthy cells to recover and survive, while the cancer cells eventually die. Dr. Frazier also mentioned hormone therapy in combination with external radiation therapy. The consultation was thorough. He was explicit. Dr. Frazier's professionalism. was no match for his charm and wit. I was sure Fred's mind was made up. Dr. Frazier would be his choice (or so I thought). We left Grace Hospital and headed back downtown.

Once we were comfortably settled in the car, I turned to Fred and asked, "Well what do you think Fred?" I was so sure that Dr. Frazier's charm and professionalism had won Fred over. I was surprised to hear his answer. "Gwen, you make the decision, I'm just ready to get it started."

Location, location, location. I had vowed weeks ago that I would do whatever it took to get Fred through this, even at the risk of job reprisals. I would be with him every step of this journey. But as noble as I may have sounded, practicality weighed in on my decision. Fred stopped driving alone months ago and besides, we were now down to only one car. In addition, I was no longer doing much if any freeway driving. How would I possibly get Fred to Grace Hospital every day? The choice was clear! Fred would receive his radiation therapy at The Barbara Ann Karmanos Center. And more important than location, the Barbara Ann Karmanos Center was the leading and most highly recognized cancer center in Michigan. I called Dr. Hassian's office and gave her our decision. When I hung up the phone we had another appointment. That one was with an oncologist for 2:00 p.m., on November 17, 1999.

In honor of Veteran's Day, there was no school in the afternoon.

I had a 1:00 p.m. hair appointment. Fred still had no idea that he was going to be honored the following evening. Neither did he have an inkling his sisters would be arriving later that afternoon!
The reunion with his sister's that weekend was nothing less than a gift from heaven. The surprise at the banquet paled sorely to his sisters visit to Detroit. It had been five years since they had been together. I was sure Fred's health played a big part in getting them to Detroit. If I was not mistaken, that was only Louise's second time flying (Louise will do anything for her big brother,

Fred). I could not have been happier for the three of them. Before leaving, Louise said that once radiation started, if I needed her, she would come back to Detroit. There is no sweeter person under heaven, than Louise Dawkins.

I left work early on Wednesday, November 17. I called Sheila Ward, my supervisor to report my absence that afternoon from the monthly department meeting. I drove home, picked up Fred. We headed to the Barbara Ann Karmanos Center for the second time that month. Our appointment was with Dr. Chuba, a radiation oncologist. A radiation oncologist is a doctor who specializes in using radiation to treat cancer. The purpose of the appointment was to prepare Fred's body for treatment using the simulation process. This process had been very thoroughly explained to us when we met with Dr. Frazier. The nurse stressed the importance of not washing the area that had been marked for treatment. The marks must not be washed off until all of his treatment was over. The results of the simulation would determine how much radiation would be needed and how many treatments would be needed. Dr. Chuba assured us once the treatment began, he would be following Fred's progress on a weekly basis monitoring his response to treatment and his overall well-being. Dr. Chuba would revise the plan if needed. He outlined the time frame expected for the duration of the treatment. Radiation therapy usually is given five times a week for up to eight weeks or for forty days. Weekend rest breaks allow normal cells to recover.

Scheduling Fred's first treatment was the next step. The literature that was given to us indicated that the clinic hours were from 8:00 a.m. to 5:30 p.m. I also read that transportation was provided by a limited number of volunteer drivers. I was so hoping that an evening appointment would be available so that I could accompany my husband to his appointments. It was not. The only available time slot was 2:00 in the afternoon.

There was no shortage of bedside manner with this doctor either. What a character. He had a wonderful sense of humor and what charisma. He had it all, looks too! How blessed we had been; the doctors have all been more than professional. It certainly made my job easier. Fred Persons can be a pistol when he wants to be! Dr. Chuba's nurse was just as charming, and she was no slouch either, very tall and attractive, (Fred's kinda gal) the three of them will make a winning team.

Fred's first treatment was scheduled for Monday, November 29, 1999. When I inquired about an alternate time, it was explained that if that was our preference we would have to wait until a patient that was currently in that time slot completes the treatment and we could then be moved. However, since unnecessary delay can lessen the effectiveness of his treatment we must begin right away. We left the Barbara Ann Karmanos Institute and walked over to the Wertz Clinic which would be the exact location where Fred would receive his treatments. Everyone knew Fred Persons never met strangers. He entered the facility and greeted the receptionist like a long lost friend. There we were given a parking permit and an access card that would allow us to enter the designated parking area at each visit. The receptionist showed us how we were to register each day and to watch the monitor and listen for his name to be called. Once Fred's name appeared on the monitor he was to enter the area where the radiation therapy was administered. On Thanksgiving, I announced to the family that Fred would be beginning radiation on the Monday after Thanksgiving. My mother acknowledged my commitment to my husband and said to her baby daughter,"I hope you'll be around if I ever get sick." Mama was so proud of her baby daughter.

When I got to work on Monday, I told Soror Deborah Sinclair that Fred's therapy was scheduled for 2:00 each afternoon. I said that I wanted to be with him each time. Deborah told me not to worry. "Do what you have to do Gwen." I left work early that afternoon. I went home, picked up Fred and we headed to his first treatment. The receptionist greeted Fred by name, "Welcome back Mr. Persons. Are you ready to get started?" One would have thought that the two of them had been friends for years. We checked in and took a seat. Not long afterwards, Fred Persons name appeared on the monitor and his name was called. I followed him to the area where he would receive the radiation. Fred was assisted into the changing room by a nurse and was asked to change into a gown. I was escorted into the control room to watch his first treatment. In the treatment room the radiation therapist used the marks on his skin to locate the treatment area. Fred had to lie down perfectly still during treatment so that the radiation would only go to the area where it was needed. The same area would be treated each time. The therapist had to leave the room before the machine was turned on. The machines used for radiation were very large, and they made noise as they moved around to aim at the treatment area from different angles. Treatment only lasted about five minutes. However, Fred was in the treatment room for about twenty minutes. The treatment was painless. When it was all over I left the control room and returned to the waiting room. Fred dressed and joined me. Fred bid his new found friend goodbye in the same demonstrative way he had entered. This routine repeated itself for the next four days.

The second week of treatment took a different twist. Fred insisted that I did not have to leave work early to get him to the hospital. He said that he could take the bus and get there on his own. I did not like this idea one bit. I suggested that he let me schedule to have the transportation service pick him up from home. He refused saying "I am perfectly capable of getting the bus. It's fun and with my card it only costs a quarter to ride the bus." Monday morning, before leaving for work, I asked Fred again if he was sure he didn't want me to pick him up for his treatment. He was emphatic, "No Gwen, I can get the bus." The king of the castle had spoken. For the first two days it appeared that this might work; until Wednesday. It had been raining all morning. I started calling home around 11:00 o'clock or so, no answer, I continued calling until after noon. Knowing Fred, he had already left for the clinic. Fred was punctual to a fault. If this weather keeps up I would be very concerned about Fred leaving treatment and walking those four or five blocks to get the Woodward bus. I solicited the help of a co-worker, Charles Sanders. Around 1:30 p.m., I asked Soror Sinclair if Charles could leave work, drive my car to the clinic, wait for Fred to come out and drive him home. Fred should be done with his treatment around 2:30. Charles should be back in the building before dismissal. Soror Sinclair gave her permission.

When Charles returned to school, he said that Fred seemed to be a little confused and some what disturbed that someone else was driving his wife's car. Charles had to remind Fred who he was, "Mr. Persons, I work at Butzel with your wife. She did not want you to have to take the bus home in this weather." Fred replied, "That 'ol piece of chick, wait 'til she gets home."

Charles took my husband home and made it back to school before dismissal. He assured me that he was able to put Fred's mind at ease. Charles said he thought that was a good move on my part. "Mrs. Persons you are a good woman."

That evening I pleaded with Fred again "Fred, please let me arrange the transportation service pick you up for the remainder of your treatments." "Absolutely not." He was having no parts of such an arrangement. "I can get the bus Gwen, it only costs me a quarter to ride the bus." I think the fact that it only cost him a quarter to ride the bus fascinated him more than anything. I did not want to stifle his enthusiasm or strip him of his independence. Fred took the bus to the clinic each afternoon. He never complained once about anything.

This routine repeated itself through the third week of treatment. On the last day of treatment during the third week, the weather took a severe turn for the worse. Again, I left work early that afternoon. When I arrived at the clinic Fred was still there. As it turned out, this happened to have been the day that Fred met with Dr. Chuba regarding his progress. Dr. Chuba invited me to join them. It was quite apparent that the two of them had developed quite a rapport. Dr. Chuba inquired as to any significant changes that I may have observed in my husband over these past few weeks. "I am still very concerned about his appetite doctor." The only thing Fred has not lost an appetite for are sweets and they don't seem to be making a difference with his weight either. Fred also had a concern of his own. He complained to the doctor about his inability to hold his urine. For weeks now, whenever we went out, his incontinence interfered. Quite frankly, on more than one occasion, I had almost wished he had stayed behind. Fred was even beginning to exhibit lots of impatience with this himself. Dr. Chuba explained that was not at all unusual. He wrote Fred a prescription for Flomax. Dr. Chuba stressed the importance of not losing too much weight during radiation treatment. "Mr. Persons try to eat at least three meals a day if possible. It is vitally important to maintain a healthy weight. He set up an appointment for us to meet with a dietician. My final concern was of a personal nature. "Dr. can we still fool around during treatment?" Dr. Chuba laughed. "At his age?" Seriously, folks you have no reason to fear intimacy." The only impact radiation would have in this area would be of fatigue. The radiation may cause your husband to feel more tired than usual." If this occurs, Dr. Chuba advised Fred to limit his activities during the day and use his leisure time in a restful way. He further suggested that Fred get more sleep at night. Dr. Chuba signed off by offering to write Fred a prescription for Viagra. Fred just about went ballistic. "I don't need Viagra and I'm not taking it."

As we were preparing ourselves to leave, the nurse gave us some good news. "Beginning next week we will be having a patient coming off a 7:00a.m. time slot. Interested?" I was not aware that there was such an early slot! Before Fred could say anything I jumped at it, "Yes, we would love to." This would be perfect for me Christmas vacation would begin that week. I would be home so I would be able to take Fred and stay with him during his treatment. Fred never opened his mouth, at least not then.

Over the weekend I explained to Fred why I moved his treatment time to 7:00 a.m. Fred did not hesitate to express his concern about getting there so early in the morning. "Why so early Gwen?" Fred thought that he would be on his own that time of the morning. "Fred, now that the weather is beginning to change I don't want you catching the bus. This time frame would allow me to take you and remain there until the treatment is over and I can drive you back home." "How will you ever make it to work on time Gwen?" I reminded Fred I would do whatever I needed to do for him. Besides I am on vacation all next week." I assured him that once I returned to work it would all work itself out. (from the Well of Faith, Hebrews 11:1) My husband held me and said, "I don't know what I would do without you."

The weather did turn frightful that week! But in spite of the weather, I was able to gauge the amount of time it would take each morning in order for me to get Fred to his appointment, drive him back home and get to work on time. It would be tight, but I would manage. The Lord had already worked it all out.

The next day I had planned a small dinner party and there was still much that had to be done. In addition to shopping for the party, Fred desperately needed a hair cut. It had been weeks since his last one and I needed to find a creative way of telling him that without offending him. After leaving treatment that morning I wanted to take Fred back home before heading to the market. I did not want his incontinence to interfere with my agenda. He insisted on going along with me. Consequently, I limited my shopping to the meat market only. After we left the market, I asked Fred if he would mind if we stopped by Spencer's to see if he could fit him in for a hair cut? "Gwen I don't need a hair cut, and I don't need my wife deciding when I should get one!" Why that's a fine how do you do for all I have done for him. I did not say it out loud, but I sure thought it, "unappreciative ol fart." Unlike me, Fred did not hold his peace, "I can decide when I need a haircut." (from the Well of Comfort, Job:10:20) The weather was getting worse by the minute. If it keeps up, we would be snowed in for the rest of the week. "Please Fred, let's stop by the barber shop while we are out today." I reminded Fred of my dinner party tomorrow evening. I was beginning to get annoyed by his willfulness and stubbornness. I had yet another private thought, "You need me for everything." (from the Well of Love, Ephesians 5:33) I reminded him of the deal he had made to me "Gwen it is in the Lord's and your hands." Was this not part of the deal? I ignored his mumblings and grumblings. I took a chance and drove to the barbershop. Spencer, his barber was able to take him right away. Whether he was willing to admit it or not, Fred had to have felt better. I knew one thing for sure, he looked better. That hair cut took ten years off of his looks. We left the barber shop in near blizzard conditions and headed for home. It had been a long day. When we arrived back home, Fred was exhausted. He did not need any encouragement from me, he went straight to bed. There he stayed for the rest of the day. That was the beginning of the fatigue Dr. Chuba had warned us about.

I woke up early the next morning and headed for the market to complete my shopping for the evening dinner party. When I got back home Fred was still in the bed. I put up the groceries and tidied up the apartment. Over the years, whenever we got ready to entertain, Fred would always insist or practically beg me to let him hire someone to come in to do the cooking and the cleaning for me. Fred Person's philosophy, "If you can't do it right, don't do it all." Fred never liked seeing me work too hard! As a matter of record Fred would not hang around the apartment when I started to clean it. With the exception of one, maybe two times, I had always prepared things myself. Fred soon learned that I did know how to do things right and I much preferred to do them myself! Preparing to entertain friends and loved ones never seemed like work; it was simply a labor of love.

Our guests for the evening included Rev. Huggins and Martha, the Conerway's and Rev. Sampson. I believe the saying goes something like this, "You don't miss your water until your well runs dry." I so longed to hear those considerate words from my husband, "Baby let me hire someone to help you." Preparing for this party was proving to be a real challenge. It literally proved to be a *labor* of love. Fred finally got out of bed and joined me in the kitchen. He insisted on helping me get ready. "Baby is there anything you need for me to do?"

"No Fred just get your rest and look good." Those were the same instructions he had always wanted me to obey whenever we entertained. After putting the apartment in order I spent the biggest portion of the day in the kitchen. As to be expected, at the last minute, I discovered that there still remained some things I needed from the store. Unwilling to risk asking Fred to jump in the car and go get them for me, I stopped in the middle of what I was doing and went back to the store. Time was moving forward and there still remained a couple of dishes I wanted to prepare. To top off my duties for the evening, I had to be the chauffeur for the Conerway's. Little Henry had to work, so he would not be able to bring his folks down. How in heavens name was I to handle Levy and her wheel-chair all by myself? (from the Well of Strength, II Corinthians 12:9) Lord, I'm depending on Your Word this evening. You said "I'll never leave you or forsake you."

Back home, oops! I still needed red tapers for the table. I asked Fred if he felt like walking over to the Ren Cen to Hall-mark's to pick up the candles? Fred enthusiastically accepted this charge; he was thrilled to have finally been asked to participate on my program that evening regardless of how menial the task may have been. Fred's memory was beginning to take unannounced holidays. I had to begin leaving Fred friendly reminders. I left him a note on the table and took off to get Henry and Levy.

When I got to the Conerway's to my surprise and relief Levy was not in her chair. She said she felt that she could manage without it for the evening. Getting them back downtown was not as challenging as I had first anticipated. The Lord kept his pro-mise. He did not leave me alone. When we arrived back to the apartment I parked the car in front of the building and escorted

Levy and Henry into the building. As expected Fred was sitting in the lobby waiting for us. I left the three of them in the lobby while I went to park the car.

Getting Levy from the outer lobby into the main lobby however, did prove to be somewhat of a challenge even with Fred's assistance. It became evident to Fred right away what the situation required. Fred asked security to call Mrs. Morris's apartment. Mrs. Morris and Fred had become the official Millender Center greeters, if you will. They spent a big portion of their day together sitting in the lobby greeting the residents as they came and went. Incidentally, Mrs. Morris used a wheelchair. Fred explained the circumstances to Mrs. Morris and she was more than happy to allow us to borrow her chair for the evening. We got Levy up to the apartment without a hitch. My knight-in-shining-armor had put the wheels in motion for what was sure to be a delightful evening. A message awaited us upon our return. It was from Rev. Sampson. Unfortunately he would not be able to join us this evening. What a disappointment! Still with an hour or so in front of me before the expected arrival of the Huggins, I was ready to pick up where I had left off. Or so I thought. I looked for the red candles. I did not see them! "Fred did you forget to go get my candles?" Fred very nonchalantly said he had forgotten. No apology followed. Only these words, "What do you need candles for anyway Gwen? You don't need to burn candles." Fred had never been in favor of me burning candles. But how dare he make this decision for me. I had worked hard planning for the evening and I wanted my red candles! It was too late for me to go myself; everything was closed. Fred knew how anal I could be about certain things and this was one of them. I was angry with him and I showed it! I disrespected and dishonored my husband and in the presence of all people, Levy Conerway!!

"I don't believe this. All that I have had to do today to get ready for this party and I asked you to do me one small favor. And you could not even do that! He did not respond to my tirades, but I knew I had embarrassed my husband in front of our guests. Fred excused himself. "Gwen I'll go to the lobby and wait for Harold Huggins," he said.

The minute he closed the door I felt convicted. I just said to myself earlier in the day, that Fred Persons never wanted to see me work too hard. Fred would have given his eye teeth that day if he could have had someone come in there and do all that had to be done. Furthermore, had he been up to the task he would have run all my errands, too. And as far as driving across town to get the Conerway's never in a billion years would he have allowed it. It would have had to be over his dead body. All that Fred would have wanted his queen to do would have been to look good. That's the way Fred Persons would have done things! I knew that if Fred could turn back the hands of time he would. But that was then and this was now.

So why had I allowed the absence of two lousy candle sticks to spoil our evening. The Holy Spirit and that look from Levy whipped me into shape! Without saying a word, Levy looked at me in a way that only Levy Conerway could do! I knew Fred did the best that he could these days! Fred did not deserve to be treated that way! Lord, I need a double dose of your grace and forgiveness. (from the Well of Understanding, Daniel 12:10)

I excused myself and went down to the lobby to find my husband. I apologized to Fred. "I'm sorry for the way I behaved upstairs, I love you Baby Persons." Fred had already dropped it. "I love you, too, Gwen. Now go back upstairs with your guests, I'll wait here for Harold Huggins." I obeyed my husband. God was at his best when he made Fred K. Persons!

Levy said exactly what I expected her to say, "Did you kiss and make up?" I assured her that is exactly what I did. "You better be nice to my friend." That had always been her way of saying we had her blessings. The Huggins and Fred were not far behind me. Of course the evening was not the same without 'Doc'. Fred gave our guest a blow by blow account of his radiation treatments and made it sound like a party of sorts. But that was Fred Persons' M.O; nothing got, nor kept him down! Fred never stopped singing my praises the entire evening. Little Henry phoned to say he would be coming to pick up his folks. That was certainly music to my ears, it had been a very long and exhausting day. But it was worth every bit of it! All of my labor did prove to be nothing less than a labor of love.

The weekend Fred confessed he had cancer, his only wish was that God let him see the New Millennium. God granted Fred his wish. God had been good to Fred K. Persons. The New Millennium was here. Monday, January 3, 2000, my first day back to work after the holidays, also marked our sixth week of treatment. As a rule, I got up at 5:30 a.m. each morning and went to the gym to work out before going to work. Generally, I'd spend from forty-five minutes to an hour in the gym. With this new schedule my visits to the gym had to be put on hold. Remember the sacrifices I said I was willing to make in order to see Fred through this? Well, this was one of them.

Winter had officially arrived. The mornings were dark, still and cold. We left home each morning at 6:30 a.m. and would arrive at the clinic around 6:45a.m. After entering the parking lot each morning, I would drive directly to the main entrance and let Fred out at the door. Then I would park the car and walk back to the main entrance. The first time I did this Fred went ballistic. "I don't like you walking out there by yourself in the dark! "Why can't I walk back with you after you park the car?" This was one time it did not matter what Fred Persons did or did not like. I was not about to let him walk that far in the cold.

Once inside, we generally had to wait ten minutes or maybe less before his name appeared on the monitor. We saw the same people every morning. It did not take Fred long before he had everyone there laughing, talking and praising God. I sat in the waiting area while Fred received his treatment. The entire process only lasted about thirty minutes. By 7:30 a.m. we were headed out of the door. His mumblings and grumblings resumed, "Why can't I walk with you to the car Gwen?" If I did not feel that Fred was up to making the walk before he had the treatment I was not about to let him to take that walk immediately after the treatment! So each morning I'd say to my husband, "Wait here Perci, while I go get the car."

I developed a functional routine that seemed to work for both of us. I'd stop at the same newspaper stand on Woodward Avenue and buy the morning *Free Press* on the way home. Once I got Fred back home, I did not have to worry about him trying to get downstairs (at least that was my plan for him). I would then put on a pot of coffee, fix Fred a little something to eat and give him his medication. Once I got him situated, I took off for work. Throughout the day, I'd call to check on him and remind him to eat some lunch. "Don't wait until I get home before you eat again, Fred." He always promised that he would.

As sure as the sun rises in the east and sets in the west, two things remained constant during his final two weeks of treatment. The first was his daily objections to being dropped off at the door each morning and me walking back alone. The other constant, was my objective to take good care of Baby Persons.

I suppose the challenges of that dinner party was my prelude to what lay ahead of us for the next two years. Our journey had only just begun. But Fred had taught me to keep the faith and to trust in God. With God's grace, there would be no doubt about it'; we were going to be all right!

I didn't know how long Fred would be with me, but I made a vow to God, to Fred and to myself. For the rest of Fred's life, I would dedicate my life to his! Fred K. Persons was still my knight-in-shining-armor, and I was not about to let him ever forget it! (from the Well of Love, I Corinthians 13:13)

Part Four

From Older to Old

The steps of a good man are ordered by the Lord:
and He delighteth in his way

Psalm 37:23

170 Gwendolyn D. Persons

From Older to Old

I married a man thirty-one years my senior. At the time, I suspect or more accurately, I know many folks(especially the skeptics, critics and nay sayers) accused me of marrying an 'old' man. Nothing could have been further from the truth. Fred was not an old man when I married him. But as I approach this chapter of my book I find myself asking the following question. When did Fred get old?

"I don't know quite how to define 'old folks.' In yesteryear, the categories of age were more clearly defined. You had children, young people, adults, the middle age and 'old folks.' Five categories, five stages in the life process. At some point along the way, transition was made from middle age to old age. And it wasn't at some specific age. Some folks got old earlier than others. I don't know how it happened, perhaps one just drifted into it. But it happened. But nowadays, with so many positive ways to preserve youth and vitality, the distinctions can be difficult to determine. Some folks go to any length to give the appearance of looking younger than their actual years. Then, there are those who very readily accept the change and just seem to grow old gracefully." (Old Folks, Dr. William A. Jones)

When did Fred get old? Fred had always subscribed to the belief that age is nothing more than a number and that you are only as old as you feel. Of all the unexpected and uninvited intruders into our lives, old age was without question the most difficult for me to adjust to. I had accepted and made the necessary adjustments to accommodate for the financial reversals that had beset us. I always remained prayerful and hopeful that divine intervention and medical intervention would heal Fred's body from his sickness. But with this intruder, no amount of prayer would or could turn back the hands of time. There was nothing that I could do about it. I could not keep old age at bay. It just kept right on coming at me! Age, particularly old age is the sponsor of many moods.

It was with this uninvited intruder that I not only needed to ask the Spirit's permission to do a little transposing and to change the order of things, I also needed the Spirit's permission to play this tune in a different key. The Spirit granted me that permission. The vow 'For better for worse' was now re-defined or more clearly defined in this union. "For better for worse" now read from "older to old."

I may not have been sure of when, but I did know what. I knew what happened to Fred when he grew old. Fred's interest did change. For years Fred had a reputation for being the sharpest lawyer in downtown Detroit. Whenever you saw Fred, he was dressed to kill. Fred was unique in his style of dress, always that white shirt and white tie. Fred had more white shirts and ties than the law allowed. He would have them laundered regularly; he never ran out Fred's philosophy, "It is better to have it and not need it, than to need it and not have it." Fred was a gentleman and his style of dress made a statement as to who he was. Fred always, always, wore a hat. Whether he was going to the church house, the courthouse, clubhouse or to your house Fred wore a hat for every occasion.

Appearance and style were important to Fred Persons. Style and grace were Fred Persons' calling card. But when transition was made from old to older, Fred seemed to lose all interest in style and dress. Fred was perfectly satisfied and content to make do with what he had. One way I tried to keep old age at bay was by secretly going into his closet and discarding all of his outdated clothes, shoes and hats. Motivated by my own selfish needs and without Fred's consent, I began replacing his wardrobe with new 'stuff.' I bought Fred new suits, new coats, new shoes, new hats.

The scenario repeated for the next year an a half. I bought Fred whatever I felt he should have, or more accurately stated, whatever I wanted him to have. Not only did Fred seem to lose interest in his own appearance, but his critical analysis and observations of my appearance were also waning. It was almost as if I had disappeared before his very eyes.

My efforts did not stop there. I began to remove every vestige of old age that surrounded me. I was cursed with a curse. Out with the old and in with the new. Not even these attempts could turn back the hands of time. What was even worse, these changes did not seem to make one iota of difference to Fred. He was totally unaffected by all of these external and temporal changes I was making in his life. Fred's mumblings and grumblings toward my spending were even silenced during this period. He was at peace and his soul was at rest. It was Gwen, the spiritually uninitiated, whose spirit was broken and whose soul was restless!

I'm still wrestling with the question *when*? Did the cause bring about the effect, or did the effect bring about the cause? Did closing down his law practice and going into semi retirement, and eventually giving up his law practice all together, advance the aging process? Or did the incessant movement of time naturally force Fred to give these things up? Is that when it happened? Perhaps I will never have a clear understanding to that question.

Years and years of dining out on Friday nights once meant so much to Fred, to us. But when he made the transition from older to old, he was perfectly content being home on Friday night. I tried hard to keep Fred current, but he had no interest in learning anything new. He even stopped reading the daily paper. Each evening at the dinner table without fail, he would repeat the same mundane questions. "Gwen what is dot com?" or "Gwen what is the Internet?" Just as I would begin to make a stab at explaining them to him. He would rush to say, "That's okay, I really don't want to know." I had so hoped I would be able to get Fred interested in learning how to use the computer. I thought that it might give him something to do during the day while I was working. Fred never even learned how to turn it on. Same with the cell phone, the cordless phone, and voice mail. I went as far as programming his own mailbox and message on the voice mail, "Press 2 if this call is for Attorney Persons." Fred never bothered to learn how to retrieve messages. I would say to him, "What if I have an emergency and I need to leave you a message on the voicemail. You need to know how to retrieve them." As important as that was, Fred never bothered to learn. With each passing morning, noon and night there was a growing void coming between us. It was getting harder and harder to relate to my husband.

On the weekends, Fred used to love to stack the pillows in the middle of the living room floor, fix himself a scotch sour and listen to his music. He loved all kinds of music; jazz, gospel, the classics, opera, and had quite an extensive collection of each. The year I replaced his record player with a new stereo system, he refused to learn how to operate it. I felt guilty, almost as though I had robbed him of his music. I would have to make a conscious and deliberate effort at initiating Saturday evening music parties for us. Whenever I would initiate these special weekend parties, Fred always showed as much enthusiasm and enjoyment as ever. Fred never stopped loving his music, he just did not want to learn anything new.

Our first Christmas together I taught Fred how to play scrabble. Competitive by nature he absolutely loved the game. All throughout our courtship and for many years after we were married we would spend hours at our dining room table playing scrabble. I guess one could say we had our own private scrabble parties/tournaments. But when old age made it's appearance Fred lost all interest in the game. I practically had to beg him to play. This was just another one of those voids that stood between us.

An avid sports enthusiast, Fred Persons spent every leisure moment at home in his big chair watching sporting events. I was very concerned for my husband the evening I had to encourage him to watch the football game. On more than one occasion, I walked into the bedroom and the television was turned off. When I asked Fred why he was not watching the game, he would simply say "I'm just sitting here thinking how good God has been to me," and to that declaration without fail he would add "You're the best thing that ever happened to me."

Fred had always been a very proud man in every sense of the word *man*. He never wanted to have to ask his wife for anything. Once his prize possession went from its labor to its reward, Fred even seemed to lose all interest in driving. He parked his 1982 Chrysler Imperial on the top floor of the parking garage. There it stayed for the next eighteen months. Consequently Fred limited his personal travels, including his trips to the golf course. The only time he golfed was when he could go along with me. I'm sure that had much to do with his departure from the game he loved so well. Of course, that was not the only reason he lost interest. Fred was getting old and tired easily.

I recall one Saturday afternoon Fred suggested we go to the driving range, "You need to get loose before you play." We went out to Belle Isle and Fred purchased two buckets of balls, one for himself and one for me. Fred did not hit a dozen of those balls. He simply did not have the energy. I had to hit my balls and his too! That was the last time Fred was on a golf course. That afternoon he bought his clubs into the apartment and parked them behind his big chair. His instructions to me were clear. "And don't you move them." Later that fall I replaced my 1996 Deville with a 2000 DHS. I had so hoped this would get Fred excited about driving again. Fred showed little or no interest in driving that car.

After Fred's radiation treatments, I called to his doctor's attention, the noticeable decay in Fred's teeth, possibly a direct result from the radiation coupled with the fact that he had acquired an insatiable appetite for starlight mints. Dr. Chuba agreed with me and strongly urged Fred to seek dental attention. Right there in the doctor's office, Fred went ballistic. "I can chew my food, that's all I care about, anybody who doesn't like it, too bad. That includes my wife. I don't have much longer to live anyway." Those words infuriated me. Is this the thanks I get for all I have tried to do for him? Dr. Chuba interjected "Mr. Persons your wife is only concerned about your health and she only wants what is best for you. The health of your teeth has a great impact on your overall health. You need to let her make that appointment for you." I wanted to cry, I felt like walking away from him and leaving him to get home the best way he could! (from the Well of Patience, 1 Thessalonians 5:14). His objections continued in the car. I did not deserve nor did I want to hear any of this. (from the Well of Patience, 11 Peter 1:6)

The following Sunday, we sat on my mother's front porch. Totally unsolicited on my part, my mother commented on the appearance of Fred's mouth. She reminded him that he was too sharp for his mouth to be in that shape. My sister agreed with Mama, and then I chimed in with a chorus line of my own. You could not have convinced him otherwise. Fred was sure that this had all been prearranged on my part; he felt I had been discussing him with my family. Fred never cottoned to the notion that I would ever discuss his or our business outside of this marriage. He had always said to me, "Gwen, if you can't bring it to me, take it to the Lord." He did not like the idea one bit! Fred rose to his own defense and put all of us in our place. If ever there was a time those infamous words "If you see me fighting the bear, help the bear," had meaning, it was today. Fred let us know in no uncertain terms he did not need our help. The subject was closed (at least for now).

I just could not understand why Fred no longer cared about his appearance. He used to be so proud, so vain about his appearance. He was still making cameo appearances in court and going to church on Sunday. Fred had not become a recluse by any means! And what about me? Does he not even care how important his appearance was to me? But more importantly, what about his health? For his sake I could not stay silent on the subject. I broached it again during one of our late night discussions. The more I pursued it, the clearer it became to me why he was being so stubborn, so like Fred, if you will. It was not so much that Fred just did not care about his appearance or about his overall health or about me. In fact, the latter to the contrary. As it turned out, all that Fred was concerned about was me. Just like with the cancer, Fred did not want me to spend money on his teeth. "At my age Gwen why spend money on my teeth." (from the Well of Comfort, Job 10:20) Before falling off to sleep that night, grace intervened on my behalf. I was able to assure Fred it would not cost me a dime; that it would all be covered under my dental insurance. The last thing he said to me that night was, "Make the appointment." (from the Well of Understanding, Proverbs 17:27) Although I planned to be with Fred at each of his dental appointments, I selected a dentist with an office in downtown Detroit, the Dr. Golden Dental Center was located on Washington Blvd. right next door to the Book Building (Fred's former office). Our first appointment was for Friday, September 1, 2000.

Fred's waning interest in his appearance was just a portion of what happened to Fred when he made his transition from older to old. Not only did Fred's interest change, but his thinking also got slower and his memory began to diminish. Looking back, this unwanted intruder was probably the first to make it's appearance into our lives. I am totally convinced that the onset of Fred's diminished memory had been gradual. This evidenced itself some time ago by the things that Fred did or more accurately put, the things that he didn't do. For instance, one winter evening Fred was to pick me up from the foot doctor at 6:00 p.m. Fred did not come for me. This was highly unlike my husband. I've never had to wait on Fred; he was always on time (at times to a fault). I waited over thirty minutes, before finally calling home. There was no answer. I had to walk from Washington Blvd. to the Millender Center in the dark. When I got to the Millender Center there he sat. The minute he saw me he jumped all over me, "Where have you been I've been worried sick about you." I could hardly believe what I was hearing! I was incensed!!" Fred you were supposed to pick me up. If something had happened to me, you'd never know it; you're never in the apartment to get the call."

Then, there was the time in 1997, when I returned from Milwaukee, I took the shuttle from the airport to the hotel (attached to the Millender Center). Fred met me at the hotel. When I stepped off the bus, I could have sworn by his delayed reaction that for a brief instant my husband did not recognize his own wife! Admittedly and unashamedly I was glad that he had stopped driving, I was embarrassed by his appearance. Not only was my husband acting like an old man, he actually looked like an old man. (from the Well of St. John 15:10) Then there were all the times I'd ask Fred to run an errand or two for me while I was at work (usually at his request) "Baby is there anything you need for me to do today?" Sometimes he'd remember, other times he'd forget. On such occasions when he'd forget and I'd ask him about it, he'd compensate for his memory loss with these words "What am I your errand boy?" This from the man who practically begged me to give him something to do to fill his day. Fred was also forgetting to give me my phone messages! He would be offended if I questioned him about not giving me my phone messages.

Age is indeed the sponsor of many moods. Fred's personality was beginning to suffer along with his memory loss.I read somewhere that this was referred to as 'mild cognitive impairment.' Coping with this uninvited intruder was not easy. Never in my wildest dreams did I imagine life this way. I never imagined Fred Persons growing old!

There were four significant events that occurred during this transition period. The first took place on August 2, 2000; I turned half a century. Even under the most ideal circumstances, I had never planned for myself nor did I ever expect for Fred to celebrate this day with some elaborate fiftieth birthday celebration. All I ever wanted or needed to make me happy was to be with Fred. I would have been perfectly content celebrating the day alone with my husband at one of Detroit's finest. I waited all day, but Fred never once remembered to say to me, "Happy Birthday, Gwen." I would be less than honest to say it did not bother me, but I did not make a big deal out of it. I simply said to him," Let's order in pizza tonight and celebrate my birthday at home." It was still very early in the afternoon. Fred left the apartment, I assumed to sit in the lobby. When he returned he had a beautiful birthday card for me. I still don't think Fred realized the significance of the day. I was okay with it for all I ever wanted was to be with Fred (from the Well of Understanding, Proverbs 15:17). But that is not the whole story. Allow me to back this train up. The Sunday before my birthday, my mother cooked a special 50th birthday dinner for me. I invited Sheila to join us. I celebrated my 50th birthday with my husband, mother and my dear friend. Now who could have asked for more?

After Fred's radiation treatments were over, he continued under the care of Dr. Chuba for regular and follow-up care. In October 2000, Dr. Chuba announced that he would no longer be maintaining his practice at St. John's Hospital on the east side of Detroit. In the beginning of the New Year, he would be relocating to Macomb County Hospital in Mt. Clemons. To Fred's dismay, this would be our last appointment with Dr. Chuba. Fred hated to see this relationship end, but we both knew it could not be helped. Dr. Chuba assured Fred that practically any internist would be able to monitor his PSA and follow up with his prostate care. Furthermore, since Fred did not have an attending internist, Dr. Chuba strongly urged him to get one. Once again, I was in search for another doctor to treat Fred. My search took me back to where it all began. I went back to Detroit Riverview Hospital. I was referred to a Dr. Nassif. This was the physician who had since taken over Dr. Tah's practice. Our first appointment with Dr. Nassif was scheduled for Wednesday, January 17, 2001.

Our anniversary fell on a Friday night that year, January 12th. We celebrated our thirteenth wedding anniversary at the Rattlesnake. The void that stood between us was growing. Our conversation that evening was so superficial, to say the least. Fred was drifting further and further away from me.

We had our first appointment with Dr. Nassif five days later. The initial contact went well. That conclusion was based solely on how well Fred warmed up to the good doctor. Dr. Nassif gave Fred the routine office examination. Fred's only complaint that day was his incontinence. Dr. Nassif continued Fred on the Flomax as initially prescribed by Dr. Chuba. Up to that day, that was still the only medication Fred was taking. We were scheduled to come back in a month.

With each ensuing day, there was yet another reminder that Fred's memory was failing him. Fred once loved to do the crossword puzzles daily. As a matter of fact, before we were married, we always ended our nightly phone conversations discussing the puzzle and comparing answers. We continued that tradition long into the marriage. Somewhere along the way, I think it was during the newspaper strike, I lost all interest in the crossword puzzle, but not Fred Persons. Fred never did stop buying the paper just so he could do the puzzle. However, during this time I would find the puzzles half completed and on some days untouched. This alarmed me; this was simply not Fred Persons (from the Well of Understanding, Proverbs 16:22).

If there was one thing Fred held on to during this transition it was his KP duty. Although, Fred never once said that he was not up to cleaning the kitchen after dinner, I don't think he would have passed the white glove test. Fred was not getting the kitchen clean like Mr. Wheat called clean. I can't count the times I pulled out a glass, a knife or a fork, only to have to rewash it before using it. I wondered if his eyesight was failing him too, or was Fred just not paying attention, not focused on what he was doing. This scene was all too familiar to me. When Grandma's eye sight began to fail she continued doing some things for herself including washing the dishes. The fact was she just could not see well enough to get them clean. Mama had very little patience and tolerance for most of Grandma's shortcomings, (her many moods) and she never hesitated to remind Grandma of that fact. I would say to Mama "Why do you want to make Grandma feel bad about the dishes, just get another glass out of the cabinet." When my mother's forecast was upon my life, I had to rewind the tape in my own consciousness. Of course, whenever I discovered an unwashed knife, fork, plate put away, it bothered me too! But I never wanted to offend Fred or to cause him any unnecessary shame or embarrassment. I never called it to his attention, I would simply wash it over. I could not rob him of that joy. (from the Well of Patience, Colossians 1:11)

I was able to overlook the unwashed dishes, but the day I found the can of pepper in the refrigerator I knew things were out of order. I knew this behavior definitely bore watching. Was this still a simple case of 'mild cognitive impairment', or had it turned into something more serious?

Fred was not the only one losing focus these days. But in all fairness to Fred, I suppose he was just catching up to me. Over the years, Fred was constantly on me about not being focused. I was always losing or rather, misplacing my keys, my entrance cards, my money. Without fail Fred would be the one to find them for me or have them replaced.

This particular afternoon I had been opening mail after I got home from work. Among the pile of bills, was an envelope with two hundred dollars inside. When I got finished reading and discarding the mail, I took the discarded mail to the trash chute. Later after dinner, something told me to look for the envelope with the money inside. I could not put my hands on it! I frantically searched the apartment for that envelope. It was not to be found. Could I have tossed it out with the discarded mail? After my failed attempts at locating the envelope, I told my knight-in shining-armor what I had done. "Fred I think I threw two hundred dollars down the chute. I expected a verbal reprimand of some sort for not being focused or perhaps words of encouragement such as "It's here somewhere Gwen, I'll help you look for it." But this is not what happened. Without hesitation, Fred immediately got up from his big chair and headed down to the trash room. "Fred where are you going? You'll never find it, besides you wouldn't know what to look for anyway!" My words fell on deaf ears. Fred kept going. I followed him. What I witnessed that night tore me apart. I was not worth a plugged nickel. There he was, Attorney Fred K. Persons, plunging through piles and piles of trash bags trying to recover a measly two hundred dollars. Had he lost it for real? Being a witness to this scene felt like a death sentence. I begged Fred, "Please let's just go back upstairs, I probably misplaced it." Fred was not hearing it, he was bound and determined, Fred was hell bent on coming to my rescue. I regretted that I ever opened my mouth, after all it was only money and not worth this sacrifice. Fred finally gave up the search and we returned to the apartment. My heart ached. Had I lost my knight-in shining-armor?

The following day when I walked through the door, there on the dining room table was two hundred dollars. Fred never said a word said about it, how it got there nor where it came from. I never wanted to intentionally violate Fred's manhood, so I never questioned him as to where the money came from? It would not be a far stretch to accuse Fred of hiring maintenance to search through the trash for that envelope. In any event, I never knew if Fred begged, borrowed or stole the money. But there it was waiting for me! (from the Well of Love, Ephesians 5:28).

I had not lost my knight-in-shining-armor after all. Fred was still the man I married; he had just gotten old. All Fred ever wanted to do was to make Gwen happy. God was at His best when He made Fred K. Persons!

It was at our second appointment with Dr. Nassif when I called the doctor's attention to Fred's declining memory. Fred exploded just like he did the time I first called to Dr. Chuba's attention the condition of his teeth. He interrupted me right in the middle of my sentence. "Dr. there is nothing wrong with my memory, after all at my age some memory loss is expected." He then turned to me and reminded me that he was thirty-one years my senior. Fred assured the doctor that he remembers exactly what he needs to remember. If that ain't the truth! Fred Persons had always remembered exactly what he wanted to remember, the things he deemed were important. Anything less did not clutter the recesses of Fred Persons mind. Unfortunately, I realized this was not the case these days, Fred was no longer in the driver's seat. He was not in control of what entered and exited his memory. Fred may not have agreed, but Fred needed help. Or was it Gwen, the spiritually uninitiated who needed help? (from the Well of Understanding, Proverbs 8:14)

Fred had put me and God in charge months ago. He attempted to renege on that deal when I insisted he needed to see a dentist. Well, he lost that fight and I could not afford to let him win this one either! I broke, I lost it in right in front of Dr. Nassif. And this was no act, this was not one of those staged, attention getting grand performances that I have been known for concocting. The tears were real and they began to stream down my face in veritable rivulets I confessed my most intimate, personal and private feelings and fears in front of Dr. Nassif, a total stranger. I told my husband "I do not know how much more I could handle. Your memory loss is getting the best of me. I do not know who you are anymore and I'm afraid." I also revealed that I was back to having that second and third glass of wine in the evenings. Nothing seems to be helping me to cope anymore. "It matters not how well acquainted you are with God, the devil is always on your trail"(Dr. William A. Jones). I pleaded with my husband to help me! "I need you to let the doctor help us." The doctor asked Fred if he was willing to take a little memory test? It was just that, a simple memory test. Fred's failure was dismal.

Dr. Nassif explained to us that memory loss is not normal in the aging process; Dr. Nassif gave me a checklist, an inventory of sorts to complete concerning Fred's behavior. Once it was completed and scored, Dr. Nassif further discussed some of the signs of Alzheimer's Disease as they appear at the different stages.

Unlike dementia, Alzheimer's disease was a diagnosis of exclusion. In other words, if the patient's brain scans and other lab work rule out loss of brain tissue or other causes for memory loss, then the diagnosis is usually AD. Fred's medical charts showed no indications of either, therefore Dr. Nassif gave us his diagnosis. Fred appeared to be in the initial stages of Alzheimer's.

Dr. Nassif went on to tell us that currently there was no cure for AD, but there were steps that could be taken to make life easier for the patient and the caregiver. Support groups were available to caregivers where they could share coping experiences and get tips on how to care for a loved one with AD. In addition, there were medications available for people with mild to moderate AD. These medications help to maintain levels of important chemicals in the brain, enabling the brain to function better.

The first two treatments made available were Cognex and Aricept. A third treatment, Exelon, was introduced in May 2000. Dr. Nassif recommended that Fred be put on Exelon. The doctor informed us that Exelon was approved for the treatment of mild to moderate Alzheimer's disease. Exelon had been tested in thousands of patient's and had been proven to have a positive effect on overall patient functioning, including activities of daily living, behavior, and cognition. Dr. Nassif stressed to us that A.D was a progressive disease, and it would only get worse with time. The medication would not prevent the progression from occurring, but it would slow it down.

The program starts the patient off by taking 1.5mg twice a day. After two weeks of treatment, the dose may be increased to 3.0 mg twice a day. Subsequent increases of 4.5 and 6.0 twice daily based on the patient's tolerability. February 14, 2001, Fred started taking 1.5 mg. twice a day. Dr. Nassif concluded by emphasizing the importance of taking the medication with meals. The verdict was in. I was handed down my sentence. My husband was in the beginning stage of Alzheimer's. I think this diagnosis frightened me more than getting the news about his cancer two years ago. Another cross to bear! I left the doctor's office with a prescription to cope in my hand. But that was not the only prescription I would receive that day.

Valentines evening I sat my beloved husband down in his big chair. For the second time in our marriage I borrowed a line from his script. "Please don't interrupt me until I'm finished." "Fred what happened to me in the doctor's office today was real. I'm scared. I'm afraid it's trying to come back. I just can't seem to cope anymore. I need you! But I am afraid I am losing you!" I felt like that unhappy soul in Shakespeare's *The Passionate Pilgrim*, "Age I do abhor thee, youth I do adore thee." Fred never appeared to react to my apparent distress, but why should I have expected him to?

Fred Persons was at peace. Fred realized and accepted months ago that 'it was time to be old, to take in sail'. Fred's age was but a 'lusty winter, frosty but kindly'. I'm not sure what magic potion, cure or antidote I was expecting to get from my husband that night. The only thing Fred offered me was the blessed assurance that he would never leave me. He kindly and calmly said, "Gwen, trust in God and keep the faith." That night Fred gave me another prescription for coping. Valentine 2001, my husband sent me back to the wells and that was the best Valentine I could have ever received from my husband.

My journey to the wells became much more frequent with this diagnosis. More than ever before I found myself inviting grace to enter my pot. As the weeks passed, each trip I made to the well made it easier and easier for me to cope with my aging husband. I prayed earnestly, "Lord help me to be the best wife for Fred that you would have for me to be." Fred may have no longer been there for me physically, mentally or even emotionally, but he was always there to give me all the spiritual support I needed.

We met with Dr. Nassif every four weeks. I monitored Fred's response to the Exelon very closely. I adjusted the dosage until I felt Fred had reached an optimal level of functioning, best for him and for me. Fred was now taking two medications daily, Flomax once a day and the Exelon twice a day. I could no longer trust

Fred to eat during the day. Therefore, each morning before leaving for work I prepared Fred's breakfast. Fred seemed to be responding positively to the Exelon at this point.

One evening while looking through one of my favorite catalogs, I ran across the cutest tee-shirt which had these words printed on it, "*I like to walk with Grandpa, his steps are short like mine. He doesn't say "Now hurry up!" He always takes his time. Most people have to hurry, they do not stop and see, I'm glad that God made Grandpa, unrushed and young like me.*"

Fred Persons the 'sharp' attorney, who loved to walk all over downtown Detroit, once stepped high and proud! Now Fred's steps were getting shorter and shorter with each passing day.

I've heard this little quip all of my life, which also aptly described Fred, "Once a man, twice a child." Never had that meant more to me than it did then. Fred seemed to be clinging to me more. He wanted me to take him wherever I had to go. We left the doctor's office one morning and I took Fred back to work with me. He had a ball. I suppose any diversion was a welcome change. Before the school year ended Fred was regularly asking me to take him to work. "Baby can I go to school with you today?"

I did not carry Fred in my womb for nine months, but these past nine months my knight-shining-armor had become just that, Fred Persons had become just my little boy. I promised Fred's mother before she died that I would take good care of her boy. I was determined to keep that promise.

I had my first real scare with AD, in April 2001. Fred had had his partials for over six months. They needed some readjustments. He was scheduled for a 12:00 dental appointment. That same afternoon I also had a 2:00 dental appointment. Somewhere around 10:30 there was a knock at the apartment door. When I opened the door on the other side stood Fred and a security guard, "Mrs. Persons, I found Mr. Persons over in the Renaissance Center, he seemed to be confused, so I offered to walk him home." I was not prepared for this! What was I to do? I took my little boy by the hand and led him into the apartment to his big chair. I tried to jar his memory by asking him a series of questions. At that point nothing seemed to ring a bell. The guard was right, Fred was extremely confused and disoriented. I scolded him for not eating breakfast that morning, "Fred the doctor has told you that you must take your medication with meals." I held his hand and said a prayer, "Lord, this is your child, I offer him unto your hands, I stand on your word. You said You would never leave us nor forsake us. Take care of Fred, take care of us, in Jesus name. Amen." I went into the kitchen to fix him some lunch. When I returned to Fred his mind was still in the same state of confusion. I continued to try to jar his memory. "Fred you have a 12:00 dentist appointment. I could not make him remember that he had an appointment or where the dentist was located. "Fred his office is next to the Book Building." Nothing seemed to be working and time was passing. I explained to Fred that I was going to have to cancel his appointment because I would not have enough time to go with him and still get to my appointment on time. That is what I did. I called and cancelled his appointment and I left my husband, but not alone. I asked the Lord to keep watch over him while I was gone (from the Well of Faith, St. Luke 8:25).

Not only were my prayers heard, they were answered. When I returned from my appointment I was surprised at what I found. Fred's memory had returned to him while I was away. He had his new partials back in his mouth. He had walked over to Dr. Golden's office, picked up his partials and returned home safely. "He may not come when you call, but, he's always on time." (from the Well of Guidance, Proverbs 3:5-6)

My second scare with AD came one evening after dinner. It had been many months since the last time I walked the stairs after dinner. I'm not clear why I decided to resume my walking routine that particular evening. Maybe I just needed an escape, a de-stressor. Walking the stairs was always my time to commune with the Lord. While Fred attended to his KP duties, I headed for the steps. Upon my return to the 32nd floor. Fred was standing outside the apartment door unmistakably vexed to say the least. I said to my husband, "Fred what are you doing out here in the hall?" He replied, "I was on my way to look for you, I was afraid something had happened to you!" If that wasn't enough, he had his gun in his pocket. I was livid! "Fred do you know how absolutely ridiculous you sound? What do you think could have happened to me?" There was no reasoning with him. I could not change his mind. In Fred's mind I had been gone entirely too long and something terrible had happened to me, thus the gun in tow. Needless to say, that encore was short lived. (from the Well of Patience, I Thessalonians 5:14)

Our next trip to the doctor's office was in May. I called to Dr. Nassif's attention a cough that Fred had been experiencing for several days. It was a loose cough that sounded like an ocean roaring on the inside of his chest. It was Fred himself who mentioned the shortness of breath. After listening to Fred's heart and lungs, Dr. Nassif wrote out a prescription for Norvasc and also recommended an over the counter cough medicine, Robitussin.

The third scare with AD happened on Mother's Day 2001. I invited my family for dinner. I was already somewhat anxious about what I had planned to do on that day. A few years back, I made a thoughtless remark to my mother. I recklessly said to my mother, "I wish the Conerway's had been my parents." Mind you now, I was good and grown when I said those thoughtless words to my mother. I was old enough and should have been wise enough to have known better. The words were out of my mouth before I realized it. The damage was instantaneous. I could not harness them and put them back in my mouth. Of course, I did not mean it literally; well perhaps I did mean it forty years ago, while dreaming at the foot of my dollhouse. At the time I said those words, there did not seem like any way I could make a bad situation better. There just seemed like no way I could clean those words up. Another one of Fred's favorite saying went like this, "If you step on my foot it still hurts." To translate, even if you apologize to him for committing an infraction it still doesn't remove the insult. There seemed no good way to repair the damage at that moment. Needless to say, I did not try to make things better at the time.

From that day to Mothers Day 2001, neither one of us ever mentioned those words again. However, I had never forgotten those words and I never forgave myself either. Mother's Day 2001 I planned to apologize to my mother.

The table was set, the food was prepared. I thought I was ready to receive my guests until Fred came into the kitchen and asked me, "Baby, are we having company?" I have been preparing the entire weekend for this and just minutes before my guests were expected to arrive, Fred asked if we are having company? The question threw me for a loop. In my estimation, Fred had been doing so well on the Exelon therapy, or so I thought. There had not been any more scares since the stair incident. I prayed that the AD was not progressing, especially not today!

I walked Fred into the living room and sat him down on the couch. "Fred, today is Mother's Day. I've invited my family for dinner." "He responded, "Who are they?" The question propelled me right into a twilight zone of sorts. I couldn't believe what I was hearing, nor what I was saying to my husband. I was actually identifying my family to my husband, I said, "Mama, Judy, Carolyn, Jimmy, Chrissy, and Keeley." Even after the roll call, Fred still did not give even the slightest glimmer of recognition to those names. Jesus! I sat beside my husband and said a silent prayer for him (from the Well of Understanding, II Timothy 2:7).

Twenty minutes later the telephone rang, it was security. "Mrs. Persons, your mother and sister are in the lobby." "Send them up please." Mama and Carolyn were the first to arrive. The moment they walked through the door Fred recognized them immediately. He greeted them in the manner he always does, "Mommy, sis" as he likes to call them respectively, in his signature style. Fred gave them a big hug and kiss.

"He may not come when you call, but he's always on time." He keeps showing up when I need Him most. Next to arrive was Judy, and finally Jimmy and his family. I told Fred I wanted to say the grace today. But before blessing the table, I asked my mother's forgiveness for those unkind and thoughtless words I had spoken all those years ago. Mother very graciously accepted her baby daughter's apology. Mother's Day 2001, would be the last Mother's day I had my mother with me (from the Well of Peace, A Song of Praise).

I was now an official member of the Exelon Caregivers Partnership. As a member I was able to access the 'member only" resources found on the Alzheimer's Disease.com Web site. In addition, I was now receiving regular support phone calls from Carla, the counselor who had been assigned to me. She kept me abreast and vigilant as to what I could come to expect in the days ahead as the AD progressed. The AD never resulted in Fred's becoming mean spirited or belligerent towards me but his personality did change(many moods). Ever since the cancer, I had to think of creative ways of reminding Fred that it was time for a haircut. Before leaving for work one morning, I asked Fred if he felt like stopping by Spencer's to get a haircut? My creative juices were not flowing on that particular morning. Fred went ballistic, "Gwen, you're not my mother I don't need you to tell me when to get a haircut." I was not up for a debate. The subject was closed, I left for work. When I got to work I called Tony and solicited his support. I said to Tony "If my husband comes into the store(Hot Sam's) today, please encourage him to go get a hair cut. He is looking like an old man."

It was during this same conversation that Tony told me that on more than one occasion when 'counselor' had stopped by the store, he observed that Fred was experiencing a great deal of difficulty with his breathing. He even had to drive him home on one of those occasions. I thanked Tony for the information and made a mental note.

That evening at dinner I asked Fred why he was still taking the cough medicine when the phlegm seemed to have broken in his chest. Fred confessed that he felt that the cough syrup helped his breathing. He stated it this way, "It helps to open up my breathing passages." I accepted his explanation and cataloged it along with the information from Tony; both to be shared on our next visit to Dr. Nassif.

The second most significant event that took place during this period of transition took place on June 19, 2001. I gave Fred an exclusive surprise birthday party. I describe it as 'exclusive' because men were excluded. I summoned a host of Fred's 'Bevy of Beauties' to the apartment to celebrate his 82nd birthday. There was a constant stream of 'Fred's Bevy of Beauties', Fred's Harem of Honey's and 'Fred's Special Girls." Call them what you may, they came! Fred was showered with gifts and lots of love all afternoon and well into the night. Unlike the almost missed dental appointment and Mother's Day just a month ago, Fred quickly bounced back, he was out of the moment only briefly. This particular day, however, his apparent disconnect seemed to linger much longer. Fred had been with me all day, at least physically. We had attended Juanita's mother's funeral that morning. We left there and I drove to the mall to pick up a few things for the party, to quote a phrase from my husband "Better to have it and not need it, than to need it and not have it." When we arrived back to the apartment Fred went straight to his big chair and deposited himself there. I let him rest there for the remainder of the afternoon while I secretly began to prepare for his surprise party. I had arranged for his own "Heaven on earth" or so I thought. I managed to get it all done with no interference from the 'king of the castle.' Once the first guest Inez, arrived I summoned Fred to the living room. There was a spread on the dinning room table fit for a king, my king.

Not unlike my fiftieth birthday a year ago, Fred never seemed to fully engage or comprehend the significance of the day. Fred's mind was not focused on this earthly heaven I had tried to create for him. Fred's mind had always stayed on the Lord, and that day was no exception. His focus was on the eternal heaven. Fred Persons had been preparing to make heaven his home all of his life, and no one, not even I could change that focus now!

It wasn't until late in the evening after most of the guests had gone that Fred seemed to plug in and make a connection. The only remaining guests were Terry and Juanita. Fred had always shared a kindred spirit of sorts with his 'pretty Juanita'. The four of us celebrated well into the night!

The following week I had the pictures developed from the party, the proof was in the pictures, there Fred was, among his Harem of Honey's and a feast fit for a king. He looked totally oblivious and unaffected by what was going on around him that afternoon. Fred's 82nd birthday would be the last birthday celebration with my 'little boy'.

The summer of 2001, Fred's incontinence and his breathing difficulty made it harder and harder for him to get around. Still, Fred counted on and looked forward to going everywhere with me. It was almost as if he did not want to be out of my sight. One of the other things Fred never lost interest or enthusiasm for was grocery shopping. He loved to grocery shop. I came home one afternoon, picked Fred up and off we went. We had not been in the market long before Fred had to find a restroom. Once he rejoined me it was extremely difficult for him to keep up, his steps were so short and he tired so easily. I could feel his pain. Walking through the store was a challenge, but he would not admit to it. I abbreviated my trip and headed for the check-out line. When we got to the check out counter, there was no bagger on duty. Fred, wanting and still needing to be useful and supportive of 'his baby', began to bag the groceries. Fred put all the groceries into the buggy all by himself. The only thing was that Fred forgot to use the bags!

The third significant event that occurred during this transitional period occurred in July 29, 2001. I celebrated another milestone in my life. I had written and published my first book,

God's Got A Word for Delta Women. All summer, my publisher had been sending me the rewrites and corrections. Everything required my final approval. Each time a final revision came in I would rush to share it with Fred. I was on a natural high, my book was almost ready to go to press. It was as plain as the nose on my face, Fred was not 'feeling me' that summer. It was as if I was at this party all alone and there was no one here to dance with me. I quickly discovered that the Lord is never without a witness and there is always a ram in the bush. When I told one of my Chantelle sisters, Beverly Sneed, of my plans to have a 'book blessing' at my church, she insisted that I have a book signing as well. Beverly solicited the help of my two sisters, Judy and Carolyn and they put together one memorable book signing reception on my behalf. Fred was there in body, but once again, he was not with me in the moment. It was as though I was living in the clouds and Fred had taken sail to the sea (Maria Carey). He was not there to share in my joy. (from the Well of Joy, I John 1:4) Out in the parking lot, Fred continued to show signs of not being fully engaged. I'm not sure what had transpired between them before I reached the car, but Juanita held my husband's hand in hers and said, "That's okay Fred, "Once a man, twice a child." Juanita recognized it too and she was absolutely correct. Fred *was* just my 'little boy'.

A week later I was awakened in the middle of the night to a loud unsettling sound. I immediately noticed that Fred was missing from our bed. I found him in the bathroom. Water was everywhere. Fred was bleeding and there was blood on the sink and carpet. I was frightened out of my wits. Fred was standing with one hand stretched to the toilet bowl and using the other hand to hold himself up against the face bowl. "Fred what happened in here? Are you okay?" Before he could answer there was a knock at the door. I left Fred and went to answer the door. It was security. The apartment below had called to report water coming from above into their bathroom. Just how long had he been in there? The security guard followed me into the bathroom and helped me to get Fred back into the bedroom. After he left I helped Fred into a dry pair of pajamas and we got back into bed. I never did get a clear understanding as to what happened that night. The only explanation Fred gave me was "I did not turn on the light and I fell into the face bowl." As long as he was all right so was I! (from the Well of Hope, Romans 12:12)

The next day I was expecting a visit from my mother. When I got up that morning I rushed to pull up the carpet and take it to be laundered. Unlike the cancer, I tried to keep this uninvited intruder close to the vest. With the exception of Carla, the Exelon counselor, I was very limited and guarded with what I exposed to anyone. I never wanted to cause Fred any undue shame and embarrassment. I respected Fred's privacy and therefore I treated this unwanted guest with the utmost privacy. I had the carpet laundered and back down before my mother arrived. (from the Well of Love Ephesians 5:33)

Around the time that the cancer was revealed, I started eavesdropping on Fred's phone conversations. One of the last such conversations was with the son of one of my sorors. This young man was a student at Morehouse. He met Fred the summer of 1999, during the time Richard Swanson passed away. The young man learned at that time that my husband was also a Morehouse man and an attorney. They exchanged phone numbers. Fred got a call from the young man the very next day. I don't know how many of these calls he received while the young man was still in the city, but early that fall the calls resumed. I listened in. Apparently, he was involved in some legal or illegal infraction which required the services of a professional. He was calling Fred on the down low (or at least he thought he was) desperately seeking and expecting Attorney Persons to come to his aid. I could feel the young man's apparent distress and desperation and I so much wanted to call his mother and tell her what was going on and to advise her that Fred was no longer in the position to handle such matters. All of the years we had been married I had never interfered with Fred's legal practice and I

194 Gwendolyn D. Persons

wasn't about to breech that contract at this stage of the game. The young man was on his own. There were very few if any phone conversations to listen in on during those days, but there was still plenty of opportunity for me to eavesdrop (maybe even more). Those days, however, all of Fred's conversations were with God. I will never forget one of those conversations. I overheard my husband saying, "I wonder if Gwen knows how much God loves her?" (from the Well of Love, Jeremiah 31:3)

The summer of 2001 Fred was still accepting assignments.

Just like the Timex watch, Fred takes a lickin' and keeps on tickin'. Fred had always said, "I'd rather wear out than rust out." Fred had to be made to realize that he had already worn out and it is time for him to stop. If he didn't stop soon and very soon I was afraid it would completely wear him out! My other concern was that one of those judges (as much as they may have loved him) would call him into their chambers and request that he not come back into their courtroom. I could not bare for that to happen to him, it would break my heart; Fred had always had so much pride.

It had to have been two of the hottest days of the summer of 2001. That first morning he was scheduled to be in court I insisted on driving him. Fred tried to object. "Gwen, I can walk two blocks." I was not taking no for an answer on that morning. When I dropped Fred off, I asked him to call me when he was ready to come home. Somewhere around 12:00 p.m. I got a call from a clerk in Recorder's Court, saying, "Mrs. Person's, Attorney Persons is ready to be picked up." Thank God he had listened to me and obeyed his wife. I was so pleased that he did not attempt to walk home in that heat. I stopped what I was doing and went to pick up my husband. On the way home, Fred's conversation was jumbled, incoherent. He rambled on and on. My God, I hope he was not like this in court. My worse fears were close at hand. Fred repeated himself three or four times in the course of that short drive back to the apartment. The following day with no discussion between us I drove my husband back to court. On the return ride home however, the conversation was quite different than the day before. Fred was quite clear and lucid about what he was saying to me. That afternoon my husband announced "Baby, I think this will be my last day going to court'." All I could say to Fred was, "Is that a promise?" August 15, 2001, would be a day for the record books in the city of Detroit. It was Attorney Fred K. Persons' last court appearance in downtown Detroit.

After Mama's recovery, she truly did turn into her mother, my grandmother. Mama became very strong and very independent. In September 2000, my mother was diagnosed with breast cancer. Mother never appeared to be at all frightened by this diagnosis. She was a real trooper. She went through her entire radiation treatment alone. Mother never once complained. She put all of her faith and trust in the God. After her treatment ended mother called all of us to her house for a family meeting. Mother did not amass a wealth of material possessions in her lifetime, but she wanted to make her final wishes known to her three girls. It was a sort of last will and testament meeting which none of us wanted to hear.

In the fall 2001, Mama was scheduled for a procedure at Henry Ford Hospital on Friday morning, September 7, 2001. Again, as with the cancer diagnosis, mother refused to ask or depend on her daughters for help; she went alone. However, she knew that after the procedure, the hospital would not release her unless someone was there to drive her home. I did not ask, I told my mother to give me a call at work once she was released and ready to go home and I would come to pick her up. Do you think she did? When Mama was ready to leave the hospital she did not call me. She slipped away and called a taxi to take her home. She called me after she was home.

Thus the fourth life changing or significant event. It was the morning of Saturday, September 8, 2001. I phoned my mother to check on her. Mother just did not sound like herself. She sounded as if she had been crying. I asked my mother if she was all right. I did not like her answer. I hung up the phone, left Fred alone and immediately went to see about my mother. I stood on the porch for what seemed to be an eternity before Mama finally came to the door. Right away I could sense that things were out of order. My mother had been crying and she was in a lot of pain. I asked Mama what was wrong. She said the pain was in her leg. I sat across from my mother and watched her light a cigarette. Within seconds I watched that cigarette fall out of her hand. Mama never even missed it out of her hand. "Mama, do you realize that cigarette just fell out of your hand and on the rug?" My mother looked down and picked it up. Just as I began to inquire about yesterday's procedure, the cigarette fell again! This time I was more than alarmed. Without embarrassing or unduly alarming my mother, I got up and walked over to where mother sat and picked up the fallen cigarette. "Mama you dropped your cigarette again." "I did?" was all she said to me. She then began to cry. "What's wrong mama?" "Do you want me to take you to the emergency room?" Mama did not hesitate, "No, I don't want to go sit there all day." I explained to my mother that she could not stay there alone. "What if you drop a cigarette and set the house on fire?" I called my sister Carolyn and explained the situation to her. I told Carolyn that Mama seems especially confused in her memory, and just did not seem like herself. I told Carolyn that I just did not like what I saw and that I would be taking Mama home with me. "If she does not feel better I will take her to the emergency room." I watched my mother try to dress herself. At the time I attributed it to her pain, but my mother could barely raise her arm over her head to dress herself.

When we got to the apartment I undressed my mother and put her to bed. I went into our room to check on Fred and to apprise him of the situation. I desperately needed my husband's support, his strength and his words of wisdom. That was not what I got. He seemed totally unaffected by what I was saying to him. His lack of concern annoyed me. Did he hear a word I just said to him? I did not get what I went in there for. I went into his bathroom got the icy hot and returned to my mother. Mother was still in a lot of pain. As I rubbed her leg with the blue stuff and mama seemed to be getting some relief from her discomfort. She was able to doze off and take a little nap. While I was sitting at my mother's side, Fred walked into the room. He never acknowledged her presence or asked any questions. He treated my mother's presence as something not out of the ordinary. His body was in the room, but his mind was at sea.

When Mama woke up I asked her if she wanted to take a hot sitz bath? I thought that perhaps this would ease the discomfort in her leg. While mother bathed, I pulled out my medical journal and looked up the symptoms related to this latest diagnosis (sciatica). I then called Nikki's and ordered a pizza for dinner. Fred had been home all day and with little or nothing to do. I took a chance and asked if felt like walking over to Nikki's to pick up the pizza? Fred jumped at the opportunity. After Fred left for the pizza, I went into the bathroom to check on Mama. I felt she had been in the there long enough. When I opened the bathroom door I found my mother crying and unable to get out of the tub. I helped Mama out of the tub and back into the bedroom. I dried her off and put a pair of my pajamas on her. She got back into bed. By this time Fred should have returned with the pizza. Had something happened to him? I was torn. Should I leave my mother and go look for my husband? That is exactly what a did. I left my mother in the bed and went to look for my husband. I found Fred safe and sound at Nikki's still waiting on the pizza. As we walked back to the apartment I found my steps ahead of Fred's. Fred's steps were not fast enough for me I was anxious to get back to my mother's side. I left Fred trailing behind. When I walked into the room my mother was wide awake looking out of the open bedroom window. As she laid in the bed with the fall breeze coming through the open window, mother had a smile upon her face. She commented on how nice it felt lying there. When I heard the door to the apartment open I let out a sigh of relief!

Before eating, Mama sat up in bed and asked for a cigarette. I took a cigarette out of her purse and lit it for her. When I handed Mama the cigarette it instantly fell to the floor just like it had done in her living room. I picked it up and held it to her lips. She took two or three puffs, then put it out in the ashtray. Once Mama started to eat the pizza I knew something was severely wrong. Mama kept dropping the pizza out of her hand, I eventually had to feed it to her. The medical book indicated that a loss of sensation was symptomatic of sciatica. Up to now this is what I had attributed her weakness to. But when her attempts to put her glass to her mouth failed dismally, I became more than alarmed. Mama simply was not able to navigate that glass to her mouth. She kept missing her mouth. My mother had had a stroke. I called Carolyn and told her what I had just observed. Carolyn did not hesitate, "If you think Mama has had a stroke, get her to emergency right now, I'll meet you there." I got my mother dressed and out the door we went. Before leaving the apartment I told Fred I was taking my mother to the emergency room. I told him what my concerns were. The only thing my husband said to me was, "Be careful, and I'll say a prayer." Had he heard a word of what I just said to him? Was this the AD or did his strong faith cause him not to over react? All I know was that I was beside myself and I needed my husband. Mama could barely manage to walk to the elevator. I held her on one side, and she supported herself against the wall on the other. We managed to make it down the elevator and into the car. I can recall the time under the best of circumstances that I could not have left that apartment at night and Fred not be concerned about my safety. In a situation such as this. I needed my husband's support that night and all he could offer me was "Be careful and I'll say a prayer?" I hated what this AD had done to Fred. It had come like a thief in the night and robbed me of my husband. That night I was on my on, or so I thought (from the Well of Strength, Isaiah 35:3).

When I took my mother from her home on that fateful Sunday

afternoon, I never would have imagined that Mama would be leaving her home for the very last time. Mother was admitted into Henry Ford Hospital and remained there eleven days. Not only had my mother had a stroke, but we were to later learn that the cancer had returned. It had metastasized to her liver. During her stay in the hospital the country experienced one of the greatest disasters in history. September 11 found that the AD had advanced. Fred's fragile mind could not grasp or comprehend the enormity of that attack.

The following week mother was released from the hospital and we had to admit her into a nursing home. She stayed in the nursing home for nine days and in Hospice for three days. During this period whenever I when to see about my mother Fred was by my side. My husband had not abandoned me as I had previously thought. We lost Mama on October 2, 2001.

My cousin, Cheryl drove in from Rochester, New York for the funeral. She stayed at the apartment for three days. Fred never quite understood who she was and why she was there. He asked me more than once, "Who is she?"

The family gathered at Mama's house the morning of the funeral. Fred gave me a real scare that morning. He had to use the restroom. His breathing became severely compromised as he tried to climb the stairs. The same scene repeated at the church. After the service Bettye and Burnie had to assist Fred out to the car.

The ensuing days found me desperately needing to connect to my husband.

I needed his emotional support. I needed my best friend. Fred was not there for me.

Two weeks later, Mrs. Bernice Barrington Price passed away. Mrs. Price was like a mother to Fred. Thelma and Hugh were as close as a brother and sister to him. So why then did Fred refuse to attend her home going? I practically pleaded with him to go with me, but Fred just asked that I go for both of us.

How would I ever explain his absence to Thelma? I did not have to explain, Thelma understood.

Fred had always subscribed to the belief that we should never question the mind of God. I can only recall one such time that my husband broke that covenant and fought with God. That was the passing of my dear Soror and friend, Jo Cleta Williams. How many times did he say to me, "I don't understand why He had to call Jo Cleta home." Fred broke the covenant for a second time when Dr. Frederick Sampson was taken from among us. Fred argued with God once again, "Why Fred Sampson?" Dr. Sampson made his transition on October 10, 2001 (They go in three's)

It was a Saturday afternoon. Terri and Juanita had come to the apartment to assist with the condolence cards for Mama. I left Juanita and Fred alone in the living room. When I returned I found them having another one of those moments, a heart to heart if you will. They had both been crying. I was to later learn that Fred told Juanita he was prepared to go home. He just needed to know that Gwen was taking care of herself.

My husband was clinging to me tighter and tighter. Fred did not want me out of his sight. He was now asking me almost daily, "Baby can I go to work with you today?" There was one evening I was scheduled to attend an Academic Games workshop. The workshop was to be held from 6:00-8:00 p.m. at Northwestern High School. When I told Fred that I had to attend a workshop, he just about panicked. He had been alone all day. Fred did not want me to leave him. He practically begged me to let him come along. I tried to explain to him the impracticality of his request. My attempts were unsuccessful. Fred rode along with me. He insisted on sitting outside of the school until I was ready to go back home. "Fred, I will be in there over two hours. You cannot sit out here all that time alone; you must come inside with me." Bless his heart, he tried to assure me he'd be just fine. Although I was not convinced, I honored his directive and I left him in the car while in went into the building. I was not comfortable with him being out there all alone. I was in there all of thirty minutes when I decided to go retrieve my husband and take him back home. I found Fred sitting in the car nursing his crossword puzzle. Fred did not seem at all surprised to see me back so soon. I'm sure to him, thirty minutes was long enough for me to have stayed away from him. I drove my husband back home and deposited him in his big chair. I wished that I could take a leave from my job and stay home with Fred.

Each time I had to go on Colfax, to check on the house, Fred insisted on going with me. There was still much to be done. Of course I knew I could get much more done if I'd been there alone, but Fred always insisted on being there by my side, I suppose for moral support or did he simply not want to be left alone? Whatever the reason he was right there with me.

It had been years since my last panic attack. Why this day I decided to throw all caution to the wind I'm not sure. I took a chance and got on the freeway. That quickly proved to be a bad decision. As soon as I got down there, I could feel it coming on. I tried my darnedest to keep it at bay and ignore it, but it just kept on coming. I had to pull over to the shoulder. I was having a full blown panic attack. Fred recognized the symptoms right away. Without hesitation my husband said to me "Don't panic Gwen, pull over." Fred got out of the car and walked around to the drivers side, "Move over." Fred had not been behind the wheel of a car for over a year or longer. How were his reflexes? This was the height of rush hour traffic, too. Would Fred be able to get us to the next exit? I said a little prayer. Fred got behind the steering wheel and brought us in. (from the Well of Faith, II Corinthians 5:7) Once we were back at street level, I took over. My knight-in-shining-armor rescued me again. All Fred ever wanted to do was to take good care of Gwen.

Before driving to mama's house, Fred asked that I go by the drugstore as he needed a bottle of Robitussin. Fred never left the house without it, not even to sit downstairs in the lobby. I felt so sorry for him, between this breathing problem and his incontinence, it made it so difficult for him to get around. We had not been at mama's long before Fred had to use the restroom. He was not even halfway up the stairs when he called out to me, I ran to see about my husband. Fred could barely catch his breath let alone try and talk. He managed to say, "Give me my medicine." I ran and got the little brown bottle, when I heard my husband say to me, "I don't think I'm going to make it Gwen." I began to panic all over again, but this was not a panic attack! I was scared to death! I could not call 911, there was no working phone in the house and I did not have my cell phone in the car. "Fred, I'm driving you to the emergency room." "No just wait!" Fred took two swigs of the Robitussin and remained there on mama's staircase in absolute silence. I could tell by the look on his face, he too was afraid. "What do you want me to do Fred?" After what seemed to me like an eternity, Fred asked that I help him to the bathroom. I managed to help him into the bathroom, back down the stairs and out to the car. Once we were in the car and his breathing seemed to be stabilizing, I said to him, "This is the last time you'll be coming over here with me." Fred did not respond. By the time we were back home Fred was back to himself. He never mentioned the incident the rest of the evening. Whatever he felt the cough medicine did, it obviously was working for him. I was so thankful he had the presence of mind to have me stop by the drugstore.

Saturday afternoon when I returned from the beauty shop, Fred was sitting in the lobby. When I asked how he was feeling you'd never know that anything bothered him. He was just as upbeat as ever! Fred responded in his signature style, "I'm fine, God is good." Nothing keeps Fred Persons down too long. Hearing those words lightened my apprehensions about the possibility of our attending a concert that evening. I so desperately wanted to keep Fred active and involved in life. Donna, my beautician, had given me two tickets for the St. Charles Church annual concert. I had just about made up my mind that I would not be attending the concert. However seeing Fred in such an upbeat mood, I decided to take advantage of it. Fred loved good preaching and good singing. This may do him a world of good. Also, I did not want to disappoint Tori, my beautician's niece. I knew how much she was looking forward for me being there for her dance performance. The minute the words were out of my mouth, Fred grabbed hold of them and said to me, "Let's go".

Ever since Fred's cancer treatment, wherever we had to go day or night I made sure Fred was dropped off at the door. Even before the onset of his breathing problem I never wanted him to have to do too much walking. Of course he mumbled and grumbled, but as a general rule, Fred complied with my wishes at least during the daylight hours. But sick or well, Fred Persons violently objected to me walking even two feet in the dark, at least not in his presence. That night would be no exception to his rule. I pulled up in front of the church to let Fred out. I requested that he wait for me there while I parked the car. In that instant we were back at Tabernacle Missionary Baptist Church, the year was September 1999. When I requested that my husband get out and wait for me to park the car his exact words to me were the same tonight. "Wherever you park this car, Gwen, I am going with you." However this night it did not end there. I wasn't giving in that easily, not under the current circumstances. I pleaded with my husband, "Please Fred, I will be okay, you do not need to be out here walking, let me drive you back to the front of the church." There was no changing his mind, his mind was made up, my husband was not about to let me walk back to the church without him! We had not made it out of the parking lot when Fred had to stop dead in his tracks. I just about lost all of my patience with him! "Why won't you do as I asked you? I should have known better. We should have just stayed at home." He rebuffed my reproof of him with a counter attack in a style unmistakingly all his own. "Gwen, you're not walking out here alone. If something were to happen to you I'd never forgive my-self. If I die right here tonight, it's my life." Carla had warned me months ago, that this type of mean spiritedness may eventually manifest itself in Fred's personality. Tonight Fred's age was anything but kindly. His words seemed so cruel, so unkind. It was slow going, but we made it across the street. We got to the front of the church and what awaited us appeared as an utterly impossible challenge. The steps to the church were insuperable. I held onto Fred's arm for dear life and prayed with each step we took together. (from the Well of Guidance, A Song of Praise) We had to stop more than once. We made it inside of the church but not without incident. As soon as we got inside the church Fred sat down in the first chair he came to. That unsettling look was back on his face and those foreboding words were on his lips, "Gwen I don't think I can make it." I begged my husband to let me take him back home. Fred took out the little brown bottle. I implored my husband, "Let's go back home Fred." He was bound and determined to stay. When it was time for intermission I did not have to beg or plea with my husband. Fred was ready to leave. I made sure Tori knew that I was there and we left. We left the same way we arrived! One small step at a time. Fred meant every word he had spoken earlier, he did not care if he died right there, he was not letting me walk to the car alone that night. (from the Well of Love, Ephesians 5:28)

The words to this song echoed in my head for the rest of that evening *"Oh, What a Love.... he has for me....that he would give... his life for me.. Jesus went to Calvary to save a wretch like me ..that's love that's love. O what a Love ....he has for me.. that he would give, his life for me."*

We got home and went straight to bed. Not a night has passed since Dr. Sampson's home going, that Fred doesn't ask God why? "Why did God have to take Fred Sampson?" Admittedly, this was starting to annoy me. I loved Dr. Sampson too, but, had he forgotten that I lost someone very dear to me! I was already feeling much guilt. I had been haunted by the words my mother spoke to me Thanksgiving 1999, the day I announced to my family that Fred would be starting radiation therapy. My mother said to her baby daughter, "I hope you'll be around if I ever get sick. I often wonder if Fred had not been ill at the time if I could have taken better care of my mother? "Fred had hardly mentioned Mama at all (from the Well of Understanding, II Timothy 2:7)

Fred did not ask for much, but the one thing he did ask of me, was that I not keep him from church. Fred Persons was temple oriented. God's house had always been Fred's hangout. Fred loved the gates of Zion. He delighted in being present at divinity's dwelling place. When I woke up the next morning, I decided we would not be going to church. I knew what was best for Fred. Fred needed his rest. Besides, I was still silently punishing him from the night before. I punished my little boy that morning and I kept him home from church (from the Well of Comfort, Psalm 69:20).

Sometime that afternoon, the Holy Spirit nudged me, and whipped me back into shape. I had been wrong last night. Fred is not mean spirited nor is he unkind. Fred had always been willful and stubborn. He had always been his own man. All Fred was trying to do last night was exactly what he had always done and that was to take good care of his baby. (from the Well of Understanding, II Timothy 2:7)

When I woke up Monday morning, work was the last place I wanted to be. The weekend had drained me both physically and emotionally. I ignored my body and mind and went to work. Before the morning was over I passed two of the physical therapists in the hall, who quite naturally asked how Fred was doing. I shared the events over the weekend and expounded on those latest breathing episodes he had been having. Before I could finish describing Fred's recent behaviors one of them interrupted me "Gwen it sounds like Fred has fluid on his heart. That can be very serious. Is he on Lasix?" "No," I said. "Gwen you need to call Fred's doctor right away and have him call in a prescription of Lasix to your pharmacist." I took their advice, turned my steps around and headed back into my office and called Dr. Nassif. He was not in the office. I left a call back number.

Sometime that afternoon Dr. Nassif's nurse returned my call. When I explained the nature of my call, she put me on hold. In

206 Gwendolyn D. Persons

just seconds, Dr. Nassif was on the line. I repeated my concerns to him, Dr. Nassif sounded almost astonished when he asked, "Didn't I give your husband a prescription for Lasix the last time he was in the office?" I assured the doctor that he had not! The last prescription given to Fred was for Norvasc. Dr. Nassif said he would not be able to call in the prescription without first seeing Fred. The nurse returned to the phone and gave us an appointment for 1:00 p.m. the next day, Tuesday, November 6, 2001.

This was election day, I only planned to work a half day. But before going in to work, I voted. The 'rocking chair' or 'the cradle.' I voted for experience and went to work. I called home at 11:00 a.m. to tell Fred to expect me shortly. To my surprise Fred answered the phone. He seemed almost anxious to keep the appointment, "I'll be ready." I had always made it a point to remain with Fred in the examining room. This day would be no exception. Fred sat upon the examining table and began to take off his shirt. My eyes were fixated on Fred's bare chest. My poor baby was so weak, so frail, so fragile. My heart ached for my husband and my eyes were saddened by what they beheld. I redirected my attention to the doctor while he examined Fred. I suppose I was trying to read what he possibly was not saying to me. "Doctor, is everything all right with my husband?" Dr. Nassif explained the reason for Fred's shortness of breath. "Mr. Persons does have fluid around his heart, a condition suggestive of congestive heart failure, however, before I can make a definitive diagnosis I would like for Mr. Persons to have an ultra sound."

In my mind, I questioned whether this condition could have had it's onset all those years ago, when Fred first started complaining of those rapid heart palpitations. "Dr. Nassiff, would you advise me to arrange to have my husband seen by a cardiologist?" Dr. Nassif did not feel that was necessary. Of course, he said he could not prevent me from taking Fred to a heart specialist, but he felt the medication he was going to start Fred on would be no different from what a cardiologist would do for him. His answers were just not as reassuring as I expected or needed to hear. I wondered if he was keeping something from me. The appointment to have the ultra sound was set for Monday, November 12. The doctor wanted us back in his office the day after Fred was to have the ultra sound which would be in exactly one week, Tuesday, November 13, 2001. Before leaving the office I mentioned to the doctor Fred's growing dependency on the Robitussin. I expressed my concern that it had become addictive. "Doctor, my husband is convinced that the Robitussin allows him to breathe better." Dr. Nassif reassured me that if Fred felt the Robitussin was helping him to breathe, there was absolutely no harm in him taking it, since the Robitussin was not addictive. I also called to his attention Fred's loss of appetite. As hard as I try I can not get him to see the importance of taking the Exelon with food. There have been several afternoons that I returned from work and found his breakfast in the microwave untouched. Dr. Nassif reminded Fred of the importance of eating regular meals and taking the Exelon with food. If only I could be home with him all day. This was one visit when Fred said very little on his behalf. I stopped on the way home and had the prescriptions for the Lasix and Altace filled. Fred was already taking three meds a day, and now a fourth and a fifth; Flomax, Exelon, Norvasc, Lasix and Altace. I think Fred was getting a bit tired of it all.

Election day had not crossed Fred's mind. But I could not take Fred home without seeing to it that he voted. I drove to the front of the Wayne County Building and illegally parked the car. I walked around to his side of the car, opened the door for Fred and we slowly walked up the steps and into the massive structure. I assisted my husband in the voting process. I knew who would be his choice for mayor, so I helped him to make the one connection on his ballot. He too voted for the 'rocking chair.' That was the only vote we cast! He deposited his ballot and we slowly walked back out to the car hand in hand. To my surprise I had not been ticketed. My heart wept for Fred.

Saturday, November 10, was the Harmonaires concert. I had not mentioned it to Fred. I had decided not to try to get him there that year. I felt it would have been too much for him. I was not punishing him. I was only trying to take good care of my baby boy. This was the first Harmonaires Concert we missed in twenty-four years. When I told Juanita we would not be attending that year, she said she would go in our stead. She is such a dear friend and soror.

All week I struggled with whether I should go ahead and take Fred to a heart specialist. I felt I had made all of the right decisions for him thus far. I could not help wondering if this heart condition had its genesis in 1997.

Did I allow the prostate cancer, the dental concerns, and now the AD to blindside me? Should I have followed up with Fred's heart problem way back then? Would he even have allowed me? Had we waited too late to fix this? That afternoon when I arrived home from work, Fred was not sitting in his usual spot. I took the opportunity to sit with Mrs. Morris before going upstairs and to bring her up to date. Mrs. Morris revealed to me that she, too, had had congestive heart failure for years and that it can be successfully treated with medication. I needed to hear that dear lady's witness on that day.

That year, Veteran's Day fell on a Sunday, consequently it was celebrated on Monday, November 12, 2001. We have always only worked a half day of school on that day. Normally, I would have had my annual mammogram in October. That year however I had to postpone it one month.

My appointment was scheduled for 3:30 p.m. on November 12, 2001. Before leaving for work that morning I reminded Fred that I would be a little late getting back home. I also reminded him that we had to be at the hospital at 7:30 that evening for the ultrasound. Of course, I did not expect for Fred to remember any of this, so I tried calling him back before leaving work to remind him, but there was no answer. Did I really expect to find him at home? Of course there was no point in leaving a message. I needed to take my car in for service as well. I decided to drop the car off first before going for the mammogram. I had to leave my car overnight. I left the dealership with a rental car and headed for my mammogram appointment. It was pretty close to 5:00 p.m. when I arrived home. Just as I expected, I found Fred sitting in the lobby waiting for me. The minute I walked through the door, Fred got up out of his chair and in front of all to hear reprimanded me as if I were a child. "Where have you been, I've been scared to death." Here we go again with this scared to death nonsense! I gently reminded my husband that I had a 3:30 doctor's appointment. As we stepped onto the elevator with other residents on board, Fred's ranting and raving continued, "You could have let me know you were going to be late," then he repeated himself, "I've been scared to death." "Please Fred, don't say it another time," I said as I tried my best to ignore all of his hysterics, at least until we got inside of the apartment. Once inside, I could not hold my peace. I really let him have it with both barrels. "What a public display of humiliation. Did you have to embarrass me in front of everybody. After all I'm not the child in this equation. I told you this morning that I had a doctor's appointment, plus I tried calling you to remind you. Since you never bothered to learn how to use the voice mail, there was no sense in leaving you messages! If you stayed in this apartment sometime, maybe you'd be here to answer the phone. I would hate to really have an emergency and needed to contact you. Maybe I'll have to start leaving you notes." That comment did not go unnoticed. "I am no child and don't you dare treat me like one of your students," he retorted. The argument was on! "Fred did you remember that we have a 7:30 appointment?" "When Gwen?" "This evening Fred." "For what?" "We have to see Dr. Nassif tomorrow and he wants you to have an ultrasound before he sees you." More questions ensued. "Why do I need that? I'm not going."

It had been a long day, I was spent. I was not up, or as the kids say, 'down' for an argument. The devil tried to get me to cave in, to say to my husband, "Fine then we won't go." If we did not have an appointment with Dr. Nassif tomorrow I would have allowed the devil to have his way with me that evening. I would have cancelled that appointment in a New York minute. (from the Well of Patience, James 1:3)

"Fred the doctor wants to get to the bottom of your breathing difficulty. It is important that we keep this appointment." While we were in the middle of this conversation, the telephone rang. It was Pat Nash, a church member and a lifelong friend of the family. "Hi Gwen, I'm just calling to check on Mr. Persons. How is he doing?" What timing? I told Pat we were on our way to the hospital for the ultrasound and I'd get back with her tomorrow. Something transpired while I was on the phone. I suppose grace stirred his pot while I was away from him. When I got off the phone Fred was waiting for me at the door. "Let's go if we're going Gwen."

We still had plenty of time, but always ahead of himself, Fred insisted that we leave right then. He probably thought the sooner we got there, the sooner it would be over and he would be back in his big chair. Nothing could have been further from the truth that evening. We got there early and we left late. Patience was never one of Fred's strong suits and that night was evidence to that fact. He had never liked to be kept waiting for anything. But on that fateful night, I don't think I had ever seen him so restless. Fred never sat down for a minute. He paced the floor the entire time. The wait seemed like it took forever. My patience and nerves were already raw. His pacing got on my last good nerve (from the Well of Patience, James 5:10).

Fred must have made at least two trips to the restroom while we were waiting. The first trip, he got all turned around trying to find his way back, and a nurse had to assist him back to the waiting room. He still did not sit down. Finally, I said to him "Please Fred, try to be patient and sit down. Pacing is not going to make them call you any sooner!" Needless to say, he ignored my suggestion. I could not take it any more; I got up, left him in the waiting room and went for a walk.

I'm not sure how long I stayed but when I returned Fred was not in the waiting room. I asked the attendant at the desk if they had called for my husband. She informed me they had not, perhaps he was in the restroom. That's exactly were he was. Fred had made yet another trip to the restroom. Fred always had a habit of putting his hands in his pants pockets. This would result in raising the back of his suit jacket. He returned from the restroom and continued to pace the floor with his hands in his pockets. Fred walked directly in front of me and I could hardly believe my eyes, the back of his trousers were soiled. Fred had had an accident on himself and apparently was not even aware of it! "Fred do you know you had an accident on yourself?" I scolded him like a mother would her child. Fred told me that he had the accident in the bathroom and had to throw his underwear away. Before he was able to return to the restroom to clean himself up the technician came for him. This was the first appointment in all of these months that I did not go into the examining room with my husband. That night I left him on his own. Once he was in the back with the technician, I walked back out into the hall and down to the main lobby. It was after hours and there was no one around. I should have had a talk with God that night, but instead I sat there all alone and felt sorry for myself.

When I returned, the technician was coming out into the vacant waiting room alone. We were apparently the last patients to remain. I was unmistakingly concerned for Fred and demanded to know, "Where is my husband?" The technician was more than willing to answer my question. Unquestionably irritated himself, he asked me "Are you his wife?" I answered, "Yes." He informed me that Fred kept asking for me the entire time. "He would not be still long enough for me to complete the procedure. Your husband would not cooperate, he was very agitated and came close to becoming hostile toward me. I asked him what did he meant by hostile? Did my husband try to physically harm you?" "No, but he was verbally aggressive and he refused to cooperate." By this time Fred was walking out of the examination room. The technician advised that we explain the situation to the doctor tomorrow and perhaps he could reschedule for another time. The technician had all of my sympathy. I thanked him for his efforts and we left. I said to my husband, "Let's go", and by the way, "Thanks for wasting every body's time this evening."

I purposely walked paces ahead of Fred's short steps leaving him behind to get to the car in the dark the best he could. I got to the car and watched as Fred took tiny little baby steps. He could barely put one foot in front of the other. I should not have left him alone that evening. Fred was afraid and confused. Why did I leave him alone in there? And why had I left him out there all alone now? I'd walked with him every step of the way, why had I abandoned my husband tonight? Fred deserved better than this? Look at him, he needs me now! What was happening to me? The devil had a hold of me and he was not about to turn me loose that night!" Instead of getting out of the car to help my husband, I sat in the car and cried for him and for me. Fred finally made it to the car and we drove home in silence. That was the first night in all of our years of marriage we went to sleep without murmuring a mumbling word between us. We did not even pray together that night! (from the Well of Love, Hosea 14:4)

Fred had always had a short memory for ill will and disharmony. He never allowed himself to stay in that place and if you are around Fred, try as hard as you may, Fred would not let you languish there very long either. I apologized to my husband the next morning. "Fred are you angry with me? I am so sorry for my behavior last night." Fred had always said to me after even the slightest disagreement, "Gwen, I am never angry at you." During the night the Good Lord cast it into the sea of oblivion (from the Well of Love, Psalm 97:10)

We finished breakfast such as it was, and hung around the apartment until time for our 11:00 appointment. We had missed church two Sundays in a row. Last month when Dr. Jones was at Trinity Baptist Church in Pontiac for their Fall Revival we were unable to attend. Soror Susie Binion mailed me the tapes a couple of weeks ago. While we passed the time, I played one of those tapes for Fred, "Rahab, the Harlot." We had church that morning.

I could not see the point in giving the doctor a 'blow by blow' of last evening's events. So, with little or no detail, I simply told Dr. Nassif the procedure would have to be rescheduled. Unfortunately, without the results from the ultra sound, Dr. Nassif was limited in rendering a definitive diagnosis. As with each visit, Dr. Nassif listened to Fred's heart. He walked out of the room and returned with a hand full of free samples. Toprol-XL. More medication!! He wanted me to begin giving Fred one tablet a day. "What is this for?" I couldn't help but wonder if Fred was now being used as some kind of guinea pig. We left there still without a conclusive diagnosis. I made up my mind, then and there, that I would be taking Fred to see a heart specialist!

I decided not to go in to work for the afternoon. Instead I took Fred to Big Boy's where we had lunch. I ordered for him a fish sandwich, fries and a salad. It was more than he could eat. When I got to the register I purchased a banana cream pie for my little boy. Sweets seem to be the only thing that Fred had not lost his appetite for. We got in the rental car to go home. It would not turn over!

I used my cell phone to call Enterprise Car Rental. We must have waited over an hour for the truck to arrive. While waiting Fred needed to use the facilities. The service man arrived while he was inside. Fred came to the car ready to pitch one. He let the driver know that he did not like it one bit that his wife was given such an unreliable car. The driver suggested that if my car was not ready the next day, I should exchange it for another one.

I drove my husband home. Fred deposited himself in his big chair and I was right behind him. Although the hour was still early, I wanted to be close to my husband that evening. I showered in his bathroom and crawled into bed. Fred called it an early evening and crawled in beside me. For the first time in months we talked and talked well into the night. It was like old times. And to my surprise for the first time in weeks Fred did not mention Fred Sampson. I suppose he had finally stopped arguing with God. Before falling off to sleep, the last thing I remember Fred saying to me "Baby, when are you getting your car back?" "Tomorrow Fred."

Before leaving work that day I called to check on my car. It was not ready. When I got home, I never mentioned it to Fred and Fred never asked.

I left work Thursday at lunch time to pick up my car. I called Fred from my cell to let him know I would be picking up my Cadillac. Not surprisingly there was no answer. I decided to surprise him and take him lunch; of this I knew for sure Fred had not eaten anything that morning. The minute I opened the door to the apartment, I sensed something was terribly amiss. The apartment door was unlocked and Fred's wallet along with some of its contents were lying on the floor in the foyer. My alarm was heightened as I approached the bedroom. My senses detected a formidable odor. I rushed to look for Fred. I found him sitting on the side of the bed, undressed. "Baby are you okay? What happened to you Perci? Your wallet was on the floor and the door was unlocked? Sweetheart, did you try to make it to the bathroom and couldn't?"

Fred just said to me, "I don't know Gwen." I cleaned my husband up and put a pair of clean pajamas on him. After cleaning the bathroom carpet I called Soror Deborah Sinclair at school to let her know I would not be returning to work in that afternoon. I gave Fred his lunch and told him I was not going to leave him. I can no longer try and protect Fred. For his sake, it's time to let security and the office know what's happening. At any time they may have a need to contact me during the day. I wish I could be home with Fred all day to watch over him. (from the Well of Love, Ephesians 5:33)

I'm afraid I made a wrong decision about keeping Mama's house. I am in no position, nor do I have the time or the resources to be a landlord. I had enough on my plate. My tenant had been more than patient with me. She had been without hot water for over a month. I had to get over there this weekend to take care of the situation.

Friday night, before retiring, I called Soror Dorothy Tyler to see if she knew of anyone who could install a hot water tank. She recommended her husband's brother. Dorothy said she would contact him and have him to give me a call. Before falling off to sleep, Fred asked what was on my agenda for Saturday. I told him I had to go over to Mama's. Fred asked if he could go along with me in the morning. I replied, "Absolutely not, remember the last time? I will not be over there all day I promise we will do something together when I get back home."

I think Fred had known it for weeks. Fred knew God was coming to take him home and I have no doubt Fred was ready. Fred had been preparing to make heaven his home all of his life. But as prepared as Fred was for this eventuality that we all must face, of this I am also sure; Fred did not want to leave his baby.

Like stars in a dark world, Fred's faith was as fresh as the morning dew. Fred had learned how to lean and depend on Him who holds the world in the palm of His hand. He was rooted and grounded in that faith that moves mountains and goes against logic and brings the impossible to fruition. Fred woke up every morning with his mind stayed on Jesus.

Fred Persons was an old man with fresh faith. Old folks with fresh faith know some things better than others. Fred knew that the Lord's mercies are fresh every morning. Fred knew that he giveth power to the faint and for them that have no might he increaseth strength. Fred knew that he'd never seen the righteous forsaken nor his seed begging bread. He knew that no good thing will the Lord withhold from his own. Fred knew that all things work together for good for them that love the Lord. Fred knew that when you reach your wits end and come to the end of your rope, if you just hold on, the Lord will make a way some how! Fred knew that if you trust and never doubt, He will surely bring you out. He knew that He may not come just when you want him, but he'll be on time. He stayed in tune, he stayed on speaking terms with the Almighty!! During our marriage Fred surrounded me with his love, he supported me with his substance, he enveloped me with his prayers, he encouraged me with his kindnesses. When the days were dark and the nights were long, Fred went to God on bended knees and prayed us through. With that kind of love, faith and trust in God, everything has got to be all right! Surely goodness and mercy **will** follow me all the days of my life and I **will** dwell in the house of the Lord forever!! I thank God for the testimony and witness of Fred K. Persons in my life!!

P.S.
Fred's mother was altogether correct. I **was** blessed with **LOVE**! And what a **Mighty, Mighty Love** it was!!
Fred's love for me was as *fresh water from an old well.*

218 Gwendolyn D. Persons

Part Five

'til Death did We Part

Trust in the Lord with all thy heart
lean not upon thy own understanding, in all thy ways
acknowledge Him and He will direct thy paths.

Proverbs 3:5-6

'til Death did We Part

IF TEARS COULD BUILD A STAIRWAY,
AND MEMORIES A LANE, I'D WALK RIGHT UP TO HEAVEN
AND BRING YOU HOME AGAIN

To My Beloved Fred,

I am so deeply sorry for leaving you here all alone the morning of November 17, 2001. You had practically begged me the night before to take you with me. I had gone over to Mama's house to meet the furnace man. I waited there for him over two hours, but he never came. Anxious to get back home to you, I left. When I arrived back home I was not prepared for what awaited me here. Two residents unfamiliar to me approached me as I got out of my car, "Miss, miss is that your husband who sits in the lobby and wears a hat all of the time?" I reluctantly replied, "Yes, my husband wears a hat." "Get downstairs right away, they're taking him away in the EMS." When I walked out of the elevator and walked into the lobby of the Millender Center, I heard these words, "Wait, wait, his wife is here."

Before I even realized what was happening, I was instantly escorted into the front seat of an EMS unit. I sat along side the driver. I frantically asked the driver "What happened to my husband? Is he all right?" The driver just seemed to ignore me as though I was not even there. I was scared to death. I wanted to be back there where you were. I sat there helpless as I listened to him telephone to Detroit Receiving Hospital to alert them of our arrival. It was clear to me that the driver was quite agitated and annoyed. He had not driven two blocks from the apartment, when he pulled over to the side of the road, stopped the vehicle and walked to the rear of the vehicle. I had no idea what was happening back there. I felt as though I was in a bad dream. My fear intensified with each passing moment. All I could do was to pray for you, "Lord take care of Fred. Please God don't let anything happen to Fred." (from the Well of Faith, I Corinthians 16:13)

When the driver returned to the vehicle he uttered some expletives. I repeated my questions to him, "Sir, is my husband going to be all right? Please tell me what's going on back there with my husband." He told me that there were two unauthorized doctors in the rear treating you and that they were interfering with the EMS technicians ability to do their job. He restarted the vehicle and we were off. I still did not have an answer to my questions. What had happened to you or how you were doing. I knew nothing. At that moment I was not even sure who I was. It all seemed so surreal. I kept pleading "Please God, don't let anything happen to Fred."

When we arrived at the hospital, the technicians put you onto a stretcher. I followed behind. I thought I heard you call my name. I responded, "I'm here Perci." My eyes stayed fixed on you until you were no longer in my sight. Once inside the hospital they rolled you through the emergency doors. I heard my grandmother say, "Gwen, hold to God's unchanging hand." My prayer remained a simple one, "God don't let anything happen to Fred. Please God take care of Fred."

I was escorted into a waiting room where I took a seat in the corner of the room, alone and afraid. At least for a moment, I thought I was alone. No sooner than I sat down I felt a soft touch upon my hand and a sweet sounding voice speaking these comforting words to me, "Mrs. Persons, my name is Shizuka Regard, and as her eyes focused across the room, she identified the other people in the room. This is Dr. Gunn, his wife, Marissa, and Dr. Daher. We live in the Millender Center with you and your husband. We were all with Mr. Persons when he collapsed in the lobby. Dr. Gunn and Dr. Daher immediately started to work on your husband when he passed out. They worked on him until the EMS arrived. They were in the vehicle with Mr. Persons. We did not want him to come alone, so Marrisa and I got in our cars and came to the hospital." She went on to explain that although she had never met me, she had known you since she and her husband moved into the building. "What a wonderful and friendly husband you have, Mrs. Persons. Mr. Persons is such a nice man and just how fond of him I have become." So these were the doctors the technician spoke about. One of the doctors, I'm not sure which one, began to explain the long delay in the response time to the 911 call and the circumstances that found them compelled to assist you. Through my tears and the darkness that surrounded me I somehow managed to thank them for all of their care, concern and apparent love for you. Shortly thereafter, the social worker, I think, and I suppose one of the attending emergency room physicians came into the room and announced that you were gone. "Mrs. Persons, we did everything we could. I'm sorry, but we lost him." "Please God this can't be true. Not my Baby Persons, not Fred. I was numb. This just could not be happening to you. I was not prepared for this day. This can't be real. Why God? Why did it have to happen like this? No chance to say goodbye to you. You were gone! With that announcement, the lights went out in my life.

Mrs. Persons, "Is there anyone we can call to come be with you?" With tears attending my words, I did not have to give it a moments thought. I knew exactly who I needed, who you would want, and who would want to be here with you. I answered, "Yes, my assistant pastor, Rev. Barbara Woodson." I did not have the number on me, I do not even remember giving them an address. All I can recall is that within what seemed like minutes, Barbara was walking through the door. "My precious, precious," is all she said to me as she held me close. "Not Fred K. The Lord has seen fit to take our precious Attorney Persons from us?" Next through those doors appeared someone handing me a plastic bag. I think these are referred to as one's personal affects, followed by these words, "Would you like to see your husband now?" (from the Well of Strength, Isaiah 35:3)

I took hold of Barbara's hand and we were escorted out of the waiting room to where your body lay upon a table. Nothing could have prepared me for that moment. All the life was gone from your earthly tabernacle. Your body was stiff. I had never seen a body in this state before. You were lifeless. You were DEAD. Someone had removed your teeth. Your mouth hung wide open, an empty cavity. I'd never imagined ever seeing you like this. No chance to say goodbye to you. The Lord just came and took you from me. The death angel came like a thief in the night. No chance to tell you one more time how much I love you, for you to hear me say, "I love you Perci'." One last time for me to hear you say "I love that 'ol piece of chick." One last time to hear those words, "God has been good to me and you are the best thing that ever happened to me."

I stood over your dead body and rubbed your 'cabbage patch head.' I asked God again, "Why did He separate us this way?" Barbara held your hand and repeated over and over, "My precious, precious Attorney Persons. My, my, my." I had no words for you, only my tears. The social worker stayed with us. She offered to say a prayer. The three of us joined hands as she prayed. After the prayer, Barbara kissed you and said her goodbyes. It was now my turn to say goodbye to you. Words could not express what I was feeling. I leaned forward to embrace your body, you were cold and lifeless. Nothing lay on that table but a dead body. I knew your soul had left this earthly shell. I kissed and rubbed your "cabbage patch" head again and we turned to leave. At that moment, I felt as dead on the inside as you were. As we were leaving, someone asked where I wanted them to take your body. I instructed them to take you to James Cole Funeral Home on West Grand Blvd.

I held onto Barbara's hand as we made it to her car. I heard you say to me, "Gwen keep the faith." How often had we heard Dr. Jones say, "The word DEAD has to be the most vulgar of all the four letter words." Today I found out just what he meant. Seeing you lying there was the most obscene thing I have ever had to witness in my life. (from the Well of Faith, II Timothy 4:7) Now I must find the strength to plan the hardest thing I will ever have to do in my life. I must go prepare for your home going. Our vows now read 'til death did we part.

November 17, 2001, 3:12 p.m. will be recorded as the day my life changed forever. It was the indeed the day the lights went out in my life. Barbara drove me back to the apartment. I gave her my phone book and she immediately began to make those dreaded phone calls. I have no idea who she called first. I don't even know if I gave her instructions. She just did what needed to be done! It wasn't long before they started to arrive. I'm not sure who arrived first. When Barbara felt that things were sufficiently under control, she said a prayer and left me in good hands.

The calls were made well into the night. I don't remember which calls, if any, I made personally. I am sure that I called Joyce and Louise, but it's not real clear to me what I even said to them. Sheila and Sybil stayed with me that first night. Early Sunday morning, Cynthia and Beverly arrived to prepare for the after church crowd. The Chantelles are all here, but where was Terri? They reminded me that Terri had been here last night. Sunday evening Soror Rose and Iris began writing your obituary.

Monday morning I awoke to the daunting task of planning your funeral. Carolyn, Sheila, Lila and Martha Huggins went with me to the funeral home to make the arrangements. We left there and headed over to the church to meet with Pastor Bowman and Rev. Barbara. While we were still in the study, Sylvia Hollifield called, offered her assistance in anyway she was needed, and of course, that included 'your choir.' I requested two of your favorite songs, *Calvary* and *Great is Thy Faithfulness*. Monday evening, with Rose at the helm, what seemed like a host of sorors were gathered around the dining room table completing your obituary. Over the next three days with the help of family, friends and sorors, the calls were made and the plans were finalized.

The Family hour would be on Wednesday evening, November 23. Your body would lie in state at the funeral home all day, Thanksgiving Day, November 24. Your home going would be Friday, November 25, at St. Stephen A.M.E. Church. Sheila had been with me every day and Juanita every night. They did not leave my side until Tuesday evening, when Judy arrived from Chicago. On Wednesday morning, with the assistance of my brother-in-law, James, Judy's ex, the three of us set off to do the final preparations.

Before leaving the apartment, I realized that there was no way to inform people about this evening's family hour. The announcement would not appear in the paper until tomorrow, Thanksgiving Day, which would be too late. I needed to get the word out today. I immediately went to my computer and printed out some fliers with all of the information. I posted one in the lobby of the Millender Center. I had James drop some off at 36th District Court and some at Recorder's Court.

Judy and I then headed to our first stop, the Detroit Free Press, to drop off the information for the obituary section. Next stop the City County Building, your favorite hang-out. As I approached a security guard and proceeded to explain to him the nature of my visit, I handed him one of the flyers. When he read the flyer he said to me, "No he didn't, not Mr. Persons. Do you know how many years Mr. Persons has been a part of this building?" He offered me his sincere condolences and humbly asked if he could duplicate the flyer and place them strategically throughout the building so that the people that passed through would get the sad news. I granted him permission, thanked him for his kindness and walked out of the building. I was not surprised. You had a reputation around here, everyone knew the City County Building was your favorite hang-out. For over thirty years you made a difference in the lives you touched throughout this city.

Judy pulled up to the door, I got into her car and we headed off to complete our final tasks. Before heading on to what may have been the third or fourth stop on the list, Judy pulled into a gas station. While she got out to pump the gas, I thought to retrieve my voice mail messages. The first two or three messages were calls of condolences. The next message was from a staff writer at the Free Press. I was asked to return the call immediately. I disconnected the voice message and returned the call. She asked a host of questions concerning your military experience, years of practicing law in the city, our marriage etc. etc. Some of the particulars I was unable to answer, but I told her I would look up the information as soon as I arrived back home and that I would call her with information.

One hour later, we were back at the apartment. I looked up the information and returned the call. We both wanted to get our hair done, but the hour was getting late. I called to see about getting us an appointment. Freddie, my beautician told me he could only take one of us. By this time I was spent. These past five days had been a whirlwind. I needed a time-out, some down time, some time alone before this evening. I decided to let Judy have the appointment. I'll wear a 'girlfriend.' Besides, I had purchased a mink hat that afternoon to wear to your home going on Friday.

After Judy left, I found myself alone for the first time since you left me. I fell to my knees and cried out to God! I questioned him over and over again. Why did He allow this to happen to you, to me? Wasn't I taking good care of you? I tried to do my very best! You always said your mother lived until she was ninety four and that you planned to be around here a long time." Why Fred? Why did you have to leave me? What will my life be without you in it? I guess you could say that afternoon I fought with God. (A song of Praise from the Well of Understanding)

I am not sure just how long I laid on your bathroom floor? It seemed like hours before the phone finally rang. I guess God and I needed that time alone. It was the front desk letting me know of the arrival of more friends, Clara and Jennifer. The two of them sat with me for a while. After Clara left, Jennifer stayed and waited with me until Judy returned. Time was moving on, I needed to begin to get dressed for the family hour. As I left the room to get ready I went back into your bathroom and continued my talk to God. I prayed for strength (from the Well of Strength, Philippians 4:13)

James called from his cell phone; he was in the front of the building. Just as I was getting onto the elevator, Judy was arriving back to the apartment. While I waited she ran in, changed her clothes and we met James in the car. Jennifer went home to change her clothes before coming to the family hour.

When we arrived at the funeral home, Sheila was there waiting for me. The two of us walked down the aisle together. I continued to pray for strength (from the Well of Strength, Isaiah 35:3) Seeing your body tonight was nothing like the last time I saw your body. I say your body and not you, because I knew full well where you were tonight. When I approached you, I could hardly describe what I felt. Unlike four days ago when I left you lying on that table in the hospital, tonight was totally different. Tonight you looked like Fred K. When my eyes beheld you, I cannot describe the calm, the peace and the serenity I felt in that moment. You simply looked as if you were sleeping with your finest clothes on. And what a peaceful rest you were in. Sweetheart, you were dressed to kill. I dressed you in your favorite suit and of course your signature white shirt and tie. Juanita helped me to select the perfect combination. You looked like Attorney Fred K. Persons. The best dressed lawyer in this city! That was certainly how you lived and that is how you will be remembered!

Admittedly, I felt much disappointment with the few people who attended the family hour. I expected the chapel to be filled with attendees. I guess that was to be expected considering the time constraint I was operating under. When it was time for us to leave you alone, I was at ease. I knew that you had been transformed. You were now home with your God, the God whom you loved, worshipped and adored. (from the Well Peace, Philippians 4:70) I placed a kiss on your forehead and left you there.

When I woke up on Thanksgiving morning, Judy had already gone out to the news stand and purchased a paper. I immediately turned to the obituary section and there was your face. I could hardly believe that I was actually reading about you in the obituary section. It all seemed so final to me now. It was not a dream. I read the article. I was not pleased with what I read. The writer made my comments about you sound so trite. She used very little of the substantive information I had provided her. I was not impressed. Your life was larger than what was written here. Judy read the article but made little or no comment. Apparently she was not impressed either. So, this past week has not been just a bad dream after all. This was my proof. You were gone and your funeral is tomorrow.

Judy dressed and headed over to Carolyn's to help her prepare for the families first Thanksgiving without Mama. This will be my first Thanksgiving without Mama and without you, help me Holy Spirit. (from the Well of Guidance, Proverbs 3:5-6)

Traditionally, on Thanksgiving, we would have attended church service, left church gone over to Mama's for dinner left there and headed over to the Huggins. Today, I will excuse myself from all three. I called Martha to let her know I will be staying home to wait for your sisters to arrive. I found myself alone for the second time this week. To keep me company, I listened to Bill Jones. He kept me company all afternoon.

In my solitude I found myself back in your bathroom. It seems to be drawing me like a magnet. I suppose I keep coming here because this was the last place your body sat before you dressed last Saturday to go downstairs and wait for me to come back home. How many times this past week have I wished that I could relive that fateful morning over again. If I had only known,

I would not have left you here locked behind this closed door. Never would I have left you here alone Fred. Why was I in such a hurry to leave that morning? I have rewritten the script over and over again. Please forgive me. If I had been here could I have prevented this from happening? Did you have your cough medicine? Could I have gotten you to the hospital quicker? Would it have made a difference? Fred, when you walked out of the apartment on last Saturday, did you know you would not be returning to me? Did you know that the Lord was coming to take you home? Was it God's plan for me to leave that morning without seeing you before I left? Was there something here that He did not want me to see? Something that maybe would have kept me from leaving you alone? Why didn't the furnace man show up at Mama's house? Was it God's plan to keep me away from the apartment and keep me away as long as He did? Why did I return just as they were ready to take you away? Was this all a coincidence or God's plan for us? The questions are endless.

I stayed in your bathroom most of the afternoon. On bended knees I knelt at your toilet. The tears that streamed from my eyes were relentless. My weeping was out of control. My head hung in your toilet. This is the last place you sat your body before leaving this apartment. As unsettling as it may sound your toilet contained the only human remains left of you on this earth. Fred, don't you know that I know what you did behind these closed doors. Here is where you talked to God. Here is where you prayed. You prayed for me, for us, behind these closed doors. Your bathroom is now my sanctuary, your toilet my well. I had another talk with God at the well today.

When I finally got up off the bathroom floor I dressed and went to the funeral home. I needed to be alone with you one last time. When I arrived there was no one there. We were all alone, Fred K. and Gwen Persons, Baby Persons and me.

I suppose folks are with their families today, after all it is Thanksgiving. Lord forgive me, but I was feeling anything but thankful today. I just lost my mommy and now you! What will my life be like without you? For the rest of my life I will hold God to His word. He promised we will see each other again. I expect for you to keep your word too; remember you promised that I would not have to look for you when I get to heaven. Fred, you promised me that you will be that bright shining star waiting for me when I arrive. A few more risings and settings of the sun we will be together again. "Happy Thanksgiving, Baby Persons. I will see you in the morning."

Back at the Millender Center, I found Mrs. Morris sitting alone in the lobby. I wished her a 'Happy Thanksgiving' and came directly to the apartment. I retrieved my messages. There were none. I suppose folks are with family today.

The phone finally rang around 4:30 p.m. Frances was at the hotel. I immediately left to bring Frances back to the apartment. Mrs. Morris was still in the lobby in the same spot the two of you had shared over these past two and a half years. She was alone on Thanksgiving, I'm sure this has been difficult for her as well. I invited her to join us in the apartment. I told Frances that Mrs. Morris sat with you everyday and that she was sitting with you when you made your transition. I let the two of them get better acquainted while I went into the kitchen. Shortly thereafter, there was a knock at the door. Our neighbor, Mr. Needom was on the other side of the door. He had come down to invite me up for Thanksgiving dinner. I explained to him that we were still waiting for the rest of your family to arrive. He then offered to bring the dinner down to us. God has promised that He would never leave me or forsake me. He has already begun to make good on that promise.

Louise, Joyce and Cliff phoned around 7:00 to say that they had arrived. They decided not to come over tonight; they will see me first thing in the morning. I took Mrs. Morris to her apartment and then I walked Frances back to the hotel.

Judy returned from Carolyn's with enough dinner to feed an army. Before the night was over, the Lord sent yet another angel to see about me. My hairdresser's sister phoned to express her condolences; she too is a licensed beautician. When I told her that I was trying to decide what to do with my hair for tomorrow, she offered to come over and do my hair for me. I accepted her offer.

But not to worry Perci. Remember yesterday I bought a new mink hat for back up! As you taught me "Better to have it and not need it, than to need it and not have it." Everything was in order now. I would look and act like Mrs. Fred K. Persons. I promise you will be proud of me tomorrow! Before retiring, I returned to the well. (from the Well of Strength, II Corinthians 12:9)

Friday morning, was finally here. I got up early and started to dress. Judy came into the room several times to check in on me. I assured her I was okay. The family would all gather here and wait for the funeral cars to pick us up and take us to the church. I so much expected and needed Louise to spend some of her time here with me, but you know your sister. She felt she would crowd me out, so she stayed at the hotel with Frances and Joyce. Carolyn came next without Christopher. She said he would meet us at the church. Last to arrive were Jimmy and Chrissy. While we waited for the drivers to arrive we reminisced looking at some old and some not so old pictures of you. It was 10:00 and the car still has not arrived. The family hour was to begin at 10:30 and the funeral at 11:00. The hour is getting late. I know that once they arrived you would give them 'what for.' The phone finally rings it was 10:15 the driver comes up and has prayer with us and we all file out into the hallway, on to the elevator and out into the street. We are ushered into the respective cars. My family is seated in the second car, your sisters ride in the limo with me.

When we arrived at the church Sheila was waiting for us in the vestibule. She positioned herself by my side, I could hear my grandmother say, "Gwen, hold to God's Unchanging Hand." I felt a sense of calm and 'blessed assurance' come over me. It was time for the processional to begin. It was time to prepare to say my final goodbye's. I made my way to the front of the church. Just the way I had left you the night before. You were at peace and at rest. It had only been last month that I said goodbye to Mama in this same place. (from the Well Of Comfort, Psalm 23:4) I did not languish there very long. I viewed your body and took my seat. They started coming down the aisle to pay their final respects. The familiar and the not so familiar faces were all so comforting to me at that moment. I wanted to reach out and hug each and everyone. In spite of the holiday yesterday, you had a full house. It was indeed an honorable testimony to your life and legacy. It was now time for me to pay my final respects. With your Bible and your Moor's medallion in my hand, I arose and went to see you for the last time at least at this level. I placed your Bible and your medallion inside of the casket. I bent over to kiss you, I rubbed your 'cabbage patch head, and said goodbye for the last time. "Fred, I will keep the faith, I will trust in the Lord and we will see each other again. I reminded you of your promise to me, "I expect you to be waiting for me when I arrive. I love you Perci." I turned and took my seat. They closed the casket. It was time for the celebration to begin.

It was not a long drawn out celebration. I know how you detested anything too ceremonial and flowery and showy displays, especially when you are the one on display. The remarks were short but they each spoke volumes to the profundity of your life. I could not have made a better selection of speakers. At some point in the service, Rev. Bowman recognized Mayor Archer in the audience. He invited him to join the clergy in the pulpit. Although not on the program, Mayor Archer was asked to say a few words on your behalf. His words were anything but few. He spoke of the number of years he has known you, not only professionally, but also as his neighbor in Palmer Woods. He spoke very highly of your influence not just in his life, but how over the years you touched and helped shape the careers of so many other young attorneys throughout this city. All of the tributes and remarks recorded the stellar legacy that you will leave behind. Fred your life was a benediction.

Your choir was magnificent. Sylvia and the Harmonaires sang to the Glory of God. You could not have been prouder. But I'm sure you were looking over the balcony of eternity and marveled in their resplendence. They love you and it was evidenced today.

Of course Rev. Huggins delivered the eulogy; you would not have wanted it any other way! It was not an easy task for him. His words reflected your close personal friendship and the mutual love and respect shared between you. I had done a stoic job of holding it together you would have been so proud of me. It was now time for me to follow the clergy and your casket out of the church. I rose from my pew and very stoically walked to the end of my aisle. Your choir closed out the service with 'Cornerstone'. I was paralyzed at that moment. My body would not cooperate. I could not bare to follow your casket out of the church. I wanted to get in that casket with you! Please don't leave me here to carry on without you! I lost it. I was broken emotionally, physically and yes, spiritually. I was unable to remain on my feet, my body gave in or out; they had to roll me out of the church in a wheelchair. I was a broken vessel. (A Song of Praise from the Well of Hope)

By the time the car arrived at the cemetery I guess I was completely anesthetized. I sat through the grave side service feeling completely numb. Perhaps this was God's way of protecting me. When the graveside service was over, we left with the casket above the ground. I kept my eyes on your casket until it was no longer in my sight. I then rested in Louise's arms as we made our way back to the church. God's grace and Louise's presence, comforted me. (from the Well of Comfort, St. Matthew 5:4)

Dinner was waiting for us when we arrived back to the church. Not a whole lot of people returned for dinner, mostly family, close friends and a few co-workers. With the exception of my breakdown, I'm sure you would have approved. You would

234 Gwendolyn D. Persons

have been proud of me. Once I was back at the apartment, I went straight to bed.

11/24-- I did not get out of the bed today. I vaguely remember Martha bringing me dinner. Judy packed up her things today and went over to spend her last night with Carolyn before heading back to Chicago. Sometime today Pat and Frances also left town. I had no clue that they would be leaving so unexpectedly and so soon after the funeral. I did not have much time to spend with either one of them. I would later learn that Frances was concerned about Barnett's health and was anxious to return to her husband, I fully understood.

I expected that Louise would spend the rest of her time here with me. She did not! I so much needed her by my side. Tonight I was alone. I pulled several of your suits from your closet. I placed them on the floor and made a bed out of them. I slept on top of your suits.

11/25-- This morning Joyce, Cliff, and Louise went to church with me. After church service Norma and Heather stopped by. Later that afternoon I took the family to Carl's for dinner. I am sure that is what you would have wanted me to do. We came back home and spent the remainder of the evening celebrating you. We each had our own special remembrances to tell. I pulled out even more photo albums. I thanked God for that brownie camera for I had a wealth of memories to share with them. I walked them back to the hotel around 10:30p.m.

It had been a wonderful day but when it was over I felt like I wanted to crawl into a hole never to come out again.

11/26-- The next day I went over to the hotel around noon. Joyce and Cliff had gotten a cab to take them to the African-American Museum. Louise and I spent the entire afternoon together. I was finally able to spend time alone with my sister-in-law. We had a 'heart -to heart'. Afterwards we took a mini tour downtown. She was anxious to hop aboard the people-mover. I took Louise to B'Anna's to meet Millie. We returned to the hotel about 3:00p.m. Joyce and Cliff had returned and they were sitting in the hotel lobby. Robert would be picking them up to take them to the airport around 5:00, their flight was scheduled to leave at 6:30p.m. It was hard to say goodbye to them. I knew without a doubt that we would stay in touch with one another. But when would I see them again?

11/27-- Today I was alone. Everyone had gone back home. There was much left to be done but I was not up to the task. Thanks to Judy, Carolyn and my Beta Area sorors, most of my condolences have been logged and responded to.

11/30-- The visits have just about stopped. I turned our bedroom into a shrine in your memory. Your picture is everywhere. Cards are everywhere. I reread them daily. I keep your obituary at my bedside. I have just about memorized the names in the visitor's book. I know who was at your home going and who WAS NOT!! Is this normal behavior? I know you would not approve of such behavior. "Let it go, Gwen".

12/02-- I went to church this morning. I tried or rather, the devil tried to get me not to go. Fred, this was the first time since we've been married that I knelt at the altar rail to take communion and you were not by my side. I guess this is just the second of a series of significant 'first' that lie ahead of me. Thanksgiving was the first 'first'. Christmas is just around the corner. Christmas without Fred K?

    I still ask God why He took both you and Mama from me at the same time. I did not have time to mourn her loss before He came for you. I'm sure Mama always thought you'd go before her.

    What will Christmas be like for me? You were Christmas for me!

Fred, I know that God is not to blame for your death, but unfortunately, he is the only target I have. I suppose it is better to question Him that not to be talking to Him at all.

12/04-- Juanita and I went to hear the Harmonaires at Oak Grove's Annual Revival Service. To quote you "They were out of sight." They ended the concert with 'Cornerstone'. Not only did they repeat the resplendent rendition which they rendered at your Home going, but I repeated my performance as well. I was at your funeral all over again. *"Jesus, thou art all compassion. Pure unbounded love thou art. Visit me with thy salvation, enter my trembling heart (Charles Wesley 1707-1788).*

12/05-- Soror Barbara Benford took me to Sinbad's for lunch this afternoon. She gifted me with a bracelet. It reads "Put on the whole armor of God. Ephesians 6:11. I enjoyed spending time with her today. She promised to be there if I need her. That good ol' Delta Spirit keeps showing up!

12/07-- Fred, it's hard for me to be alone, especially at night. Carolyn and Juanita have taken turns spending the night with me this week. The phone rings constantly. I can't stop crying when I am alone. Folks ask me, "Why are you still crying?" Why the heck do they think? I can't believe anyone would have to ask me such a ridiculous question as that! I know Rev. Barbara is right when she says that few woman have been loved or will ever be loved the way I was. How could they be expected to understand? I will cry as much and as long as I feel like crying. I will not let anyone tell me not to cry for you again. (from the Well of Comfort, Psalm 69:20).

12/08-- I tried to go to an academics tournament today. I was only able to stay about an hour. Soror Deborah Sinclair insisted that I come home. She will come by to check on me later. Deborah kept her word, she did come by, but I was not home. As soon as I got here, Terri called. She came and took me out to breakfast. Breakfast turned into three hours of doing Terri 'stuff'. Terri was only trying to be a good friend and I loved her for her efforts, but I just wanted to get back home to you. That good ol' Delta Spirit!

12/09-- Carolyn met me at church today. Afterwards we went for carry-out. Sybil also stopped by this afternoon with dinner. I'm asked all the time, "When are you returning to work? It will do you good." I've decided not to return until after the holidays. If then! Why do people feel that I am suppose to do things according to their time table? This is beginning to get next to me. (from the Well of Love, Hebrews13:1)

12/10-- I displayed this for all to see! It might even become my mantra.

I Need to Be Heard
I need to be heard..
Please don't tell me how you feel!
I need to be heard...
Please don't try to comfort me by telling me, "You'll be better in time.'
I need to be heard...
Please don't pacify me by trying to 'top it" with a hurt of your own.
I need to be heard...
Please don't look away when I mention that precious name!
I need to be heard..
Can't there be anger among sadness and misery?
I need to be heard...
Meet me where I am, and listen to me..
Until I don't need to be heard, anymore.

New Freedom, Pennsylvania (from the Well of Comfort, Psalm 23:4)

12/11-- I feel so low in spirit, I can't hear nobody pray. Fred, it's even hard for me to pray for myself. My faith, my trust in God is being tested. And it looks as though I'm getting failing marks. I am sick and tired of hearing people say that you are in a better place and that the Lord loved you best. NOBODY COULD LOVE YOU MORE THAN I! (from the Well of Comfort, II Corinthians 1:3) Loneliness is overwhelming me. I'm feeling very despondent and all alone. To help me, I try to remind myself where you are. I know it is selfish of me to want you to return to me when I know you are safe with the Lord.

Soror Claudia Hamilton came by and took me to the church this afternoon (that good ol' Delta Spirit keeps showing up). I'm not sure why I went. Or what I was looking for from Pastor Bowman. I took Pastor Bowman a copy of my book draft. I wonder what he will think after reading it! I asked that he hold on to it in case anything should happen to me. I guess that is the reason I went. Fred, I'm not sure if I want to go on without you! I hear you Fred, "Gwen keep the faith." Baby Persons, it ain't easy!!

12/13-- Last Saturday would have been our traditional Saturday (always the second Saturday in December) to decorate the house. I have been telling myself that I do not want to celebrate the holidays this year. I know that's being selfish. You loved the holidays, we loved the holidays. I've always heard that the holidays can be very depressing when you have lost someone special in your life. I felt that sadness the first Christmas without grandma. I am sure that sadness will not compare with what this first Christmas without you and Mama will be like for me.

12/15-- It's done. The place looks like Christmas. But it does not feel like Christmas. I feel nothing but sadness, so empty inside. Life has lost its sweetness. How will I ever get through these holidays, through the rest of my life?"

12/17-- Co-workers stopped by at lunch time today. The last day of school is Friday. Christmas is only a week away. Judy will be coming home for the holidays. I know my sisters and Mama, would want me to spend the day with them. But I'm not sure that is where I want to be. It's not about me or what others need. It's all about you!

I need to be with people who I know loved and cared about you. In all honesty, I'm not sure that's where I will find that love for you!! I think I will spend Christmas Day with the Huggins. (from the Well of Truth, John 8:32)

12/19-- I went out and tried to do a little Christmas shopping today. I came back empty handed. Being in the mall around all those people, I felt even more all alone. I could not get back into this apartment fast enough. I phoned Martha and invited myself to spend Christmas with them.

I am sure Carolyn will be disappointed. Family means so much to her. Mama once said, "I don't think anything can ever come between you and Fred". Mama was right, not in life, and not in death. (from the Well of Love, Romans 8:3)

12/23-- My sisters surprised me and came to church this morning. Carolyn has been to church twice since your home going. You always wanted to see her and Christopher in a church. Maybe you'll get your wish after all Fred. Perhaps Carolyn will come back home.

12/24-- Christmas Eve. This must be the depression people warned me about. I called Mrs. Morris and invited her up to the apartment. She was here just minutes when Mr. Needom came down and invited me up for a Christmas Eve social. In spite of myself I had a good time. Mr. Needom has been a wonderful neighbor.

12/25-- Christmas morning 2001 was here at last! I will spend the day with the Huggins. Today I must be with those who I know for sure loved you! I think this will meet with your approval.

240 Gwendolyn D. Persons

Christmas service was at 9:30.am. Rev. Huggins was there alone. I sat with him but before service was over I went and sat with Georgia Lee. Tomorrow she is scheduled for surgery. I know how much she loved you. I promised her I would check on her in the morning. After service I drove to the Huggins. Martha and I waited for Rev. Huggins to arrive. Once he arrived we took off to Naomi's for Christmas Brunch. It was to be a full day. We spent two or three hours at Naomi's apartment before heading on over to Gloria's for Christmas dinner. We arrived at Gloria's around 3:00 p.m. Dinner was served around 5:30. Although it was not the same without you and Mama here I don't regret I made this decision. It was just where I needed to be today. In the comfort of those who loved you!

12/26-- This morning I went to the hospital to check on Georgia Lee.

12/31-- Another 'first' New Year's Eve. I spent the biggest portion of the evening in your bathroom on the floor crying at the foot of your toilet. I have made your bathroom my sanctuary and your toilet my porcelain altar. Our bedroom is still a shrine in your memory. I miss you Fred. At midnight I knelt my our bedside and continued to pray for strength to keep on keeping on (from the Well of Comfort, St. Matthew 5:4)
  "Even now when your heart is twisted in pain, God is with you. Jesus, too, suffered in anguish and cried out to His Father in heaven. Our loving God and Father gave His only Son the courage and strength to go on. (With Deepest Sympathy)

01/01-- When I woke up this morning I was certain you had been here last night. It was so real. I heard you go into your bathroom and close the door (just the way you always had) When you came out of the bathroom you came into the bedroom and walked over to my side of the bed. I could feel your arms around me. You said that you would not be back. Later in the day I sat down to reread my Christmas cards and my sympathy cards. I ran across one that contained this message, "The greatest gift is to love and to be loved in return." I don't recall having read it before. Perhaps I had, but today the message resonated in my mind. It brought to my mind the December 24, broadcast of the Oprah Winfrey Show.

On this special broadcast her guest said that before we die there are two things we ask ourselves. "Was I loved? and Did I Love well?" I answered on your behalf, yes and yes!

There is no doubt you loved and you were loved in return. The Holy Spirit led me to ask others to mail me their special memories of your love. I will compile these memories into a little book and entitle it, A Gift of Love, the Love Fred K. Persons gave to us all. (from the Well of Love, I Corinthians 13:13) I also stumbled across this card and inside was a small gold angel stickpin with a message that read, "The angel of Reflection will help you to search deep within, for your own personal truth-to reach beyond your own imagination."

I had a visitor over the holidays, Rosa Blake. During the course of our conversation I told Rosa that I had written a book and that it had been published last year, God's Got A Word for Delta Women. I also told her that I was working on another book, Fresh Water from Old Wells.

Rosa prophesied to me that afternoon. She told me that there was yet another book on its way. I guess A Gift of Love will be that book!

Sybil called to invite me over for New Year's brunch, I invented an excuse. I just wanted to be here alone with my thoughts and memories of you. I think she was disappointed but I must do what is best for me right now. However, tomorrow I will return to work. That should make a lot of folks happy.

01/04-- My first week back to work was difficult. I kept waiting for the phone to ring in my office. Waiting for you to call and check on me. I kept wanting to pick up the phone and call you in the middle of the day just to check on you. Nothing will ever be the same again.

Friday I left work at noon. I was driving home and the hurt almost literally blind sided my vision. The tears were pouring from my eyes. The hurt was heavy on my heart today. I came home, crawled into bed, pulled the covers over my head and stayed there all weekend. My groaning has worn me out. At night my bed and pillow are soaked with tears. I never want to leave our bed. I can't live if living is without you. (from the Well of Joy, James 1:2)

01/08-- Soror Erma Henderson called me today. She is just learning about your passing. I suppose it is difficult for me to disguise my feelings. Soror Henderson could feel and hear my pain. She invited me to come over (very soon) so that she could minister to my spirit. She cautioned me that if I continued to stay in this place for too long I will soon be joining you.

I don't quite understand her warnings, it has not even been two months. I am sure she means well (that good ol' Delta Spirit!) but I am still grieving my loss. And I have every right to still be there. Why can't they understand? I read somewhere that when you are working through new struggles, your emotions can help you deal with them in a healthy way. Pretending that you don't feel grief or pain won't help the situation. In fact, it may hurt you in the end. Perhaps I need to share this with all those folks who don't understand.

01/12-- Today is our 14th Anniversary. Happy Anniversary Fred. Another 'first.' It has been one of the hardest first for me. I've been in the bed all day but I will try to go to church tomorrow. All I seem to do is cry and think about you. I found this in one of my catalogs the other day, it seems to say it all "If tears could build a stairway and memories a lane I'd walk right up to heaven and bring you home again." Fred if only I could just see you one more time. My pain is so exhausting. We never had a chance to say goodbye.

PLEASE DON'T TELL ME NOT TO CRY!

01/13--Soror Claudia Hamilton admonished me today for not changing my voice message. She said that it was misleading and that I must change it immediately. I have no doubt Soror Claudia meant well. But I am not ready to accept that I live here alone. Is it natural to feel this way?

I have not joined a support group and I don't have any intentions on doing so either. I did not go to church today as I had planned. This evening however, someone from the Women/ Men's Day committee called to ask permission to sponsor the first annual Fred K. Persons golf classic. I said "Yes" as long as it is done in right order! As you would say "If you can't do it right, don't do it at all."

01/15-- As I was getting dressed for work this morning a commercial captured my attention. I'm not even sure what it was they were advertising, but the words were expressly for me, "Soul mates, buddies, best friends, your better half you're just not you without them." I could not have said it better, those words express exactly how I am feeling since you've been gone.

01/16-- Today I received my first response to my request. It was from my sister Carolyn. I was not quite sure what I was looking for. I did not feel it spoke directly to her love for you or your love for her. Maybe I'm being too sensitive but this is not about her 'gift of love.' It is about you! I still have not forgiven Christopher (and lots of others) for not coming to your home going. I heard you Fred, "Let it go Gwen." "It ain't easy Fred."

1/17-- Today I received my second response to my <u>A Gift of Love</u> request. It was an e-mail from Soror Denise Jackson. Now this is what I'm talking about! A very heartfelt tribute to you and your love. Thanks Soror Denise, it means so much to me! That good ol' Delta Spirit!

01/18-- I stayed home from work today. I was finally able to go back to the funeral home to get the clothes you were wearing on November 17, 2001. I brought the clothes home and put them in the back of your closet. I was not able to look inside that bag. I'm finding it hard to leave this apartment. When I do go out I rush to get back here. Back to a Fred Personless apartment?

01/26-- Today was Delta's Founder's Day, a day you looked forward to as much as I did. How you enjoyed standing at the foot of the escalator with your trusty camera waiting to snap our pictures as we made our way down to greet you! I think the Deltas looked forward to it as much as you did. They will miss you too! Did I mention, I did not attend? I know I am disappointing a lot of people these days. But I honestly don't want to be around a lot of people yet. I want to be left alone. It has become easier and easier to slip into this cocoon like existence. However I did have an unexpected visitor this afternoon, the first one this new year. Soror Barbara Anderson stopped by after she left the luncheon. That good ol' Delta spirit keeps showing up. (from the Well of Kindness, II Peter 7)

01/29-- I ordered your headstone today.

01/31-- The last day of the month. Soror Claudia will be pleased to know I changed the voice mail today. It no longer says, "You have reached the home of Fred and Gwen Persons" it now says "You have reached the home of Gwen Persons." Is this a sign of acceptance? Of healing? Maybe, maybe not. I did it for their sakes. As far as I'm concerned this will always be the home of Fred and Gwen Persons.

02/02-- I put a night light in your bathroom, my sanctuary. Although you said you would not be back, I will keep it on for you anyhow.

Everything seems to be such an effort for me. I don't want to disappoint you and I'm trying to keep the faith Fred, but I often feel so hopeless and lost and I'm made to wonder where is the blessedness I knew when first I saw the Lord. Where is my soul's refreshing view of Jesus and His word? My trips to the wells do not seem to helping me much these days but I know that as long as life endures I will still be growing in God's grace. (from the Well of Joy, Isaiah 12:3)

"There are moments when the suffering is so deep that one can hardly talk to a person. What a joy it is then to know that the Lord understands. No pit is so deep that the Lord is not deeper still. Underneath us are the everlasting arms-and the Lord understands (He Cares, He Comforts).

Fred, I admit, as long as you were here with me you were my earthly King, perhaps God is waiting on me to release you before I can truly feel His presence and His power in my life. As I was going through some of your things today I found this message, it was written in your handwriting, "Does she know how much she means to God?"

Where had I heard those words before? It was one of those overheard conversations that you had with God about me. But now it is so hard to see clearly. Things appear so blurry, but I know that even in my darkest hour, He has not forsaken me.

02/03-- Going to St. Stephen A.M.E. Church without you has been a difficult adjustment. I sat in the balcony today. I just could not bring myself to take that seat down there without you by my side. After church service, I received a wonderful tribute from State Representative Derrick Hale. It was a State Resolution for you. I'm so proud of you! I'm proud to be the widow of Attorney Fred K. Persons!

I still search for the Bethany Hour on Sunday evening even though I know he's no longer on the air. Oh, how I miss him too!

02/14-- "Happy Valentine's Day, Persabol!" You never subscribed to the notion of watching the calendar for those special days of celebration. You celebrated me and life everyday. Like the song says' Everyday is Christmas.' You always said, "Love is a verb. Love is something that you do." You let me know every-day through your words and your actions how much you loved me. Although I may not be able to declare loudly and proudly we were married fifty or sixty years I was loved as few woman will ever know. I was blessed to have been loved by you! And taking care of you has been my greatest reward in life. The verdict is in. I lived my best life, taking care of my husband!! Indeed we were a blessed couple. We shared God's greatest gifts, to love and to be loved in return. People recognized it, they knew it was real. How often did they say to us "Gwen and Fred Persons are the embodiment of God's love!"

I received a surprise at work today. I was summoned to the office for a delivery. It was a beautiful plant. I could not imagine in my wildest dreams, who would be sending me flowers on Valentine's Day? They were from my Soror Joyce Austin. What a thoughtful thing to do, but that's Joyce, a sister in Christ and a sister in Delta too! That good ol' Delta Spirit showed up again!

No one ever could have told me that looking at your picture would bring me so much pain and sorrow. It's so hard to believe I don't have you right beside me. I long to reach for you, to touch you, to hear your laughter. I'd give anything to have you walk through that door once again, to see that smile upon your face. Fred without you I' m just a shadow of someone I used to be.

02/15-- I should not have left you behind that closed door. I should have been here with you. I'm still haunted by the question "Did you have your faithful bottle of Robitussin with you?" Would it have made a difference? Will I ever know the answers?

I am filled with so much guilt and blame, but at the same time I know the passage through this darkness is essential to my grieving process (A song of Praise from the Well of Understanding)

02/16-- Today I received another tribute in the mail. A tribute to the life of Fred K. Persons. It was from the Muic family. Oh how you loved Hattie and Joe. The tribute was a testament to your life. It certainly speaks of their love for you Fred. I was so proud to receive it. I am more excited than ever to complete the book so that I can share your love with the world. (from the Well of Love, Phil 2:2)

I heard that commercial again "Soul mates, best friends, buddies, your better half you're just not you without them. Would you believe it's a commercial for Coffee mate? I still expect to see you sitting in the lobby when I walk through the door each afternoon. I wonder how many of the residents feel the same way?

02/17-- Clara called. Next month Tabernacle will be bringing Yolanda Adams here for their building fund raiser. I told her that I would purchase a ticket. In addition, she convinced me to purchase an ad in the souvenir booklet advertising my book 'God's Got A Word for Delta Women'.

02/19-- And yet another commercial written expressly for me. One of those that ask you to "Ask your doctor." The kind you hated so much. "*You know when you feel the weight of sadness. You may feel exhausted, hopeless and anxious. Whatever you do you feel lonely and don't enjoy the things you once loved. Things just don't feel like they used to.*" I must admit it does describe exactly how I am feeling these days. There just does not seem to be any purpose in my life. I miss fixing your meals. I miss rubbing your 'cabbage patch head', I miss calling you from work to check up on you, I miss our nightly talks, I miss calling your name, I miss hearing you call my name, I miss hearing you say, "You are the best thing that ever happened to me". I miss everything about us!!

Is it still grief or is it now depression? Or are they twin horses?

I still have not sought out a support group. Would you believe, someone actually did suggest medication. Not to worry Perci, I'm not about to 'Ask my doctor." I don't need medication, and you bet your life I am depressed! Who wouldn't be? She has no idea what I'm feeling. She's never had it, she's never lost it! You bet I'm still grieving. I read somewhere "Grief is the price we pay for love." If this is true I have an outstanding bill! It just might bankrupt me!! A good listener would have given me permission to express my thoughts sincerely (from the Well of Patience, James 1:3)

02/23-- Winter break begins Monday. You don't know how many inquiries I have gotten as to whether I'm going to go away? Inquiring minds want to know. Oh, I know what you think. "Don't concern yourself about what other people think Gwen". It's too bad that some widows had to wait until their husbands were gone before they could enjoy his money and enjoy life. I'm so, so thankful, you made it possible for us to enjoy both while you were here. What good is money anyway, if you have no one to share it with! Besides I don't want to leave this apartment.

02/24-- Jennifer spent the night. I know just how fond you were of Jennifer Poole and of course how much she loved you! We went to church this morning. Rev. Huggins and Martha were there. After service the four of us went to Carl's for dinner. I wanted to treat, but he would not let me. I'll fix him.

02/25-- Lest I confess, I have been doing a lot of catalog shopping.. I hear you "Gwen you don't need another thing in this apart-ment." I can't seem to help myself. Fred, I ask myself, "Am I trying to spend my way out of my grief?" I'm reminded of yet another commercial, *"When you know what's wrong, you'll know how to help make it right."* I hear you too, Dr. Jones. "Wrong diagnosis, equals wrong prognosis, wrong prognosis, equals wrong prescriptions." (from the Well of Joy, James 1:2)

I know full well what's wrong with me. What's more I know the correct prescription. It's time that I let Him back into my pot.

02/26-- This afternoon I had yet another 'first'. I had an appointment to file the income taxes. This is was one appointment I was not looking forward to keeping. Some days seem to be better that others. Today is not one of them. I'm suffocating from this feeling of abandonment.

It's greater than when Mama left me at the foot of my dollhouse. It's even greater than the time she left me and moved to L.A. It's greater still than when you left me alone at our dining room table. The abandonment that I'm feeling now is far greater than all of them together.

Perhaps I do need some spiritual counseling. I called Bethany Baptist Church today, I wanted to speak to Dr. Jones. Don't ask me why? I don't even know what I would have said to him had he been there. Fortunately, or unfortunately, he was unavailable. I explained that I was calling from Detroit and that we have not been able to get the Bethany Hour for several months. I then inquired as to Dr. Jones health, knowing that his recent health challenge prevented him from attending Dr. Sampson's funeral last October.

The individual I spoke to informed me that Dr. Jones was doing quite well and that he was in Atlanta for the week. I inquired as to the reason we were no longer able to pick up the Bethany Hour in Detroit? She transferred me to another line. The gentleman on the other end explained to me that our local cable network had dropped the contract. I almost yelled into the phone "You mean we will not be getting the Bethany Hour in Detroit?" "That's correct" he explained to me. "Not unless another cable station picks up the contract." I thanked him for the information and hung up the phone.

I sat down and wrote Dr. Jones a very personal letter. I poured my heart and soul into that letter. Then I had a long talk with God. I confessed my sins to God today. I confessed that I had allowed you, my earthly king to stand between me and God. As long as you were here Fred, by my side, I thought my anchor was secure. (A Song of Praise from the Well of Truth) I need to take a new look at an old word, Proverbs 3:5-6.

02/28-- I had to make another trip to see the tax preparer. She will need even more information before she can complete them. You never involved me with these matters. I am feeling a bit over-whelmed and yes, I'm afraid! (from the Well of Strength, Psalm 27:1)

03/01-- The last day of the winter break. I spent the balance of the week writing. It is difficult to write through the tears, but I am made to realize that I must release my tears and feel my pain.

03/03-- I did not go to church today. I am feeling a certain sense of disconnect from St. Stephen. Could that be one of the reasons I called Dr. Jones and wrote him that letter. Maybe if Rev. Huggins was still there I would not be feeling this way. After all Rev. Bowman did not know you. He can not possibly begin to fathom the depths of my loss.

This evening I spent hours looking through your photo albums. Pictures of a lifetime long before I was a part of your life. As silly as it may sound, I felt a twinge of jealousy that I was not a part of your life then. My, what a rich and full life you had. 'No doot aboot it', Perci, you lived 'the good life'. But I guess it's true, 'All that glitters ain't gold.' Even in the face of this glitch and glamour, you have always said that you never knew real joy, happiness and love until you married me. There are not many people I recognize in these photographs, other than Soror Yvonne

Cathings. I think I will give her a call and offer to share some of these photographs with her. I have no need to hold on to them. They are not my memories. Perhaps we did go from richer to poorer, but our love only grew richer with the years.

03/05-- I know it is deliberate and all by my own design. I make no apologies for it either. I have built a fortress around my life. A wall that no one is allowed to enter without a ticket. The only ticket in, is if they are bringing me some love for the 'you' that lives inside of me. The 'magnetic you' that is in me. Dr. Jones calls it the 'magnetic me connection'. He told me to put that phrase in the hopper of my mind and leave it there. Dr. Jones, I've done just that!

Clinton Hoggard holds that ticket, he has been such a big help to me. His spiritual counsel has helped me through these difficult days on the job. He speaks about you with so much fervor, honor and respect. He holds fond, fond memories of you and I so much delight in hearing him share them with me. It brings so much joy to my heart. (from the Well of Comfort, 1 Thessalonians 4:18)

"We will always need other people and even more so in the darkening hours of personal tragedy." (A Grief Observed)

03/06-- The memories are still coming in. I expected much more of a response, but I am more than pleased with what I have received. They are each so special. I look forward to sharing your love with the world.

03/07-- Clara called today with the best news I've had since you've been gone. Dr. William Augustus Jones is coming to Tabernacle the same weekend of the Yolanda Adams concert. Can you believe it Fred? I had just written him that letter not two weeks ago! And now, I'm learning of his visit to Tab. I had a host of questions for Crowell. Clara responded, "Slow down Mrs. Persons, don't forget who you are. You really are crazy about that man. Fred would have a fit." The only question Clara was able to answer was "He is coming to assist the pulpit committee in their search for a new minister."

My response to her, "No he wouldn't. Fred loved Dr. Jones as much as I do. I hung up the phone and shouted to the rafters! (from the Well of Joy, Psalm 29:13)

03/10-- Tomorrow I have to go with Ms. Sinclair to a two day Academic Games tournament in Southfield. We are expected to stay the night, two nights in fact! I can hardly see myself away from this apartment for two nights! The apartment has now become my refuge. I don't want to be that far away from you. I am not looking forward to this one bit! I know that this might sound strange to some people, but grief is extremely personal. Each person mourns in a different way.

03/14-- I'm not quite sure of the date, but the Barrister's Ball was held recently. I understand that the Wolverine Bar Association honored you at this year's ball. Several weeks ago I was told to expect an invitation in the mail. I was honored and pleased to know that they thought to remember you as the sitting president of the Wolverine Bar Association when it was first inaugurated. I waited anxiously and with lots of anticipation for that invitation to arrive. It never did. I was so disappointed.

After the affair, I was told that I most definitely should have been there to hear all that was mentioned and said on your behalf; I was told to still expect to receive something in the mail. As of today I have not. I find it inexcusable. Well that explains your lack of support and participation. You've always said, "If you can't do it right, don't do it at all." I took the cards and the pictures down today. I opened your closet. I'm not ready to go there just yet.

Adding these final chapters to my book has been a most difficult task, but perhaps my writing will be a form of healing. It certainly has become a true labor of love. When I first began writing it, I thought you would have been here to see it completed. How many times did you walk into the room and ask, "Baby are you working on your book?" I had not planned on these final chapters being a part of my book, 'til Death did we Part' and' Precious Memories.' By the way Fred, did I mention that the Holy Spirit has redirected my steps. A Gift of Love will now be my final chapter and I have renamed it 'Precious Memories'. It appears God had a different plan and a purpose for this book. There was more to this story that He wanted me to tell. We cannot change God's timetable or His plans for us. I am sure I will shed many more tears and feel much more pain before completion. I don't know how long it will be before I complete this book. There are times when my pain is so exhausting. I lose all my strength and I cannot write another word. Times when I just have nothing of me to give to anything or to anybody. Fred, I seem to have no control over my emotions. (from the Well of Strength, Psalm 24:8)

Then I am reminded of what Soror Claudia told me "You must complete your work." With the Lord's help Soror Claudia, I will complete my work. (from the Well of Hope, Psalm 31:24)

03/15-- This is the weekend of our Delta Midwest Regional Founder's Day, which is being held downtown at the Marriott Hotel. I have no interest or desire in participating. I still have not been able to resurrect or reclaim my life. There is only one thing on my mind this weekend and that is seeing Dr. Jones on Sunday. Just as I had settled on the couch for the evening the phone rang. I expected it to be Jennifer Poole or Deborah Sinclair calling from the hotel. Never in a billion years would I have ever expected to hear his voice on the other end of my phone! "Hello, this is Rev. Jones from Brooklyn New York." Was this some kind of joke? I knew it was not a joke, I'd know that voice anywhere! No one could pretend to be him! So was I dreaming? His next words were instantly welded to my mind and my heart, "I received your lovely letter. I was sorry to hear about the passing of your husband." I was paralyzed, I was speechless. Dr. William Augustus Jones, Jr. called me!! He had received my letter, but does he have a clue who I am? Is he just responding to a strangers cry for help? He went on to tell me that he would be in Detroit on tomorrow evening and he would be at Tabernacle for both services on Sunday. At that point I began to introduce myself to him and to tell him all about you. I reminded him that you always greeted him and shook his hand with these words, "Send my regards to Judge Thaddeus Owens in Brooklyn." I told him that we had watched him every Sunday evening until recently as we were no longer able to pick up the Bethany Hour in Detroit. Dr. Jones so graciously responded, "I know who you are?" Fred do you think he really knew? Or was he just being kind?" I told him that I was already made aware of his visit to Tab on Sunday, and how much I was looking forward to his visit. I told Dr. Jones how I shared his tapes with my mother on her death bed. Remember, Perci, I took my tape recorder and a couple of his tapes to the hospital when Mama was in Hospice. When I turned on the tape Mama opened her eyes, smiled and said "That's Dr. Jones." I also shared with Dr. Jones that we had the opportunity to take Mama to hear him when he was in town last year. My how much she enjoyed the service. I'm not sure who borrowed from whom but he simply said 'Bless your heart'.

I hope I didn't sound too forward to the Rev. and most of all I hope I did not embarrass you! But I told him how much you wished you could have had the opportunity to take him out to dinner on one of his visits to our city, especially to Joe Muer. His answer surprised me "Well, I guess I'll have to wait until I get to heaven to have that dinner." Without forethought I blurted out these words," You mean I have to wait that long to have that dinner?" He responded, "No, I mean with your husband, I'll be back that way later in the year." The conversation concluded with Dr. Jones requesting that I shake his hand on Sunday morning. I thanked him for the phone call and told him I was looking forward to both services on Sunday. I hung up the phone, I was in a New York state of mind!! I hollered so loud they probably heard me clear across town. I could hardly believe it! Dr. Jones called me!! I've got to tell somebody!

My first reaction, call Crowell; she'll never believe this!! She was not home, but I left her a frantic message. I can't wait for her to get this message. Who else would appreciate my enthusiasm? Mr. Hoggard. He knows how I feel about Bill Jones. I don't believe it, he's not home either. I left him a message. I've exhausted my list. They are the only two that can really appreciate the gravity of my enthusiasm. If I don't tell it, I will absolutely burst. There has to be somebody I can call. Carolyn, I'll call my sister. She knows how we have followed Dr. Jones over the years. Carolyn answered, I managed to get the words out "Guess who just called me? "Who?" "Rev. Jones." Carolyn replied, "Rev. Jones from New York? Why did he call you?" I told her about the letter I had written to him. Carolyn said "Gwen, he must have read your heart in that letter." She truly seemed to sense my joy. I invited Carolyn to come to Tabernacle on Sunday so that she could see him and hear him for herself. She said she would make every effort to get there on Sunday. (from the Well of Joy, Psalm 30:5)

I didn't expect the next words out of her mouth, "Don't tell me the Lord is sending you another one already. I haven't had my first one yet." "Don't be ridiculous." Although Perci, what have I always said to you? "If there is anybody that could steal me from you, it would be Bill Jones".

I did not have much interest in attending the Yolanda Adams concert from the start. I only agreed to purchase the ticket to support Clara and our affection for Doc. When I woke up Saturday morning, I had one thing and one thing only on my mind. Sunday morning at Tabernacle Missionary Baptist Church. For the first time since you left me, I was excited about something. I was actually looking forward to something. It was almost as though I was expecting you to return to me on tomorrow. I plan to attend both of the services and sit in our usual spot. Up close and personal.

I spent most of the day recalling his last visit to Detroit and preparing a 'goody bag' for him. In it I put a copy of your obituary for him to take to Judge Thaddeus Owens. I included an autographed copy of <u>God's Got A Word for Delta Women</u> and finally excerpts from <u>Fresh Water from Old Wells</u>. It had been nearly one year ago since his last visit to Detroit, March 2001. He was at Tabernacle for the week prior to Easter. I think they call it the 'Week of Challenge'. We had been in attendance all week. We even picked Mama up one night and took her with us. I am certain that I mentioned Mama's passing in the letter I wrote to him. But it was the Thursday night service I called you before leaving work to check in on you. You said that you thought you might sit this one out. I asked if you were okay, I knew that wild horses could not keep you from Bill Jones. You replied in your usual upbeat manner "I'm fine Gwen, just think I'll sit this one out." Upon hearing those words I asked if you needed for me to come home. You assured me that you were fine. I then asked if you would mind if I headed on over to the church right after school and have dinner and sit in on the lecture before the evening service. Of course you did not mind, "Just be careful and pray for me." Like I always said, "Bill Jones and only Bill Jones could take me from you."

I met Clara for dinner. After dinner we attended the lecture. Clara wanted to sit in the rear, but I positioned myself up close and personal. I never imagined just how personal it would get. After the lecture I had an opportunity to speak directly to Rev. Jones. I took a seat next to him and told him all about my book. I confessed that not only had I borrowed the name of one of his sermons to entitle my book, but that throughout the book I had unashamedly borrowed rather freely, many of his words. Without stealing or running the risk of plagiarism I asked Dr. Jones how I should acknowledge that these were his words and not mine? He simply told me to use footnotes. He did not let me off the hook, "And what did you entitle your book my dear?" I replied, "Fresh Water from Old Wells." He repeated those three little words "Bless your heart." I thanked him for the advice and his time. I shook his hand and headed upstairs for what was sure to be another roof raising worship service. What a blessing! I was up close and personal to Dr. William Augustus Jones. Dr. Jones has definitely become my spiritual Father. I arose from that chair feeling as though I had been in the presence of the Lord. I guess this is how Catholics feel in the presence of the Pope! I doubt if I will have that same opportunity tomorrow. But I do want him to leave with something to remember us by. I put the contents in an envelope and sealed it. I got dressed and went to the concert. I left at intermission.

Sunday morning, March 17, 2002, exactly four months from your passing was more than my overactive mind could have ever anticipated. Both messages were powerful, "Stormy Weather" and "A Formula for Living." But never in a million years could I have been prepared for what I heard in 'A Formula for Living'.

Fred, you used to say I was the prettiest when the Holy Ghost got a hold of me. I must have been knock-dead-gorgeous on yesterday. I was full of the Holy Ghost and He showed off! After the first service I did shake his hand and I placed the sealed envelope in his other hand. Before leaving the church I stopped by the office and bought both tapes. Fred, the best way to explain what happened on yesterday lies on the pages of this letter:

Dear Dr. Jones,

I don't know when, I do have an idea how, but I am certain as to why. I am certain that shortly after Fred Persons and Fred Sampson were reunited in heaven, they immediately petitioned God's help to rescue who and what they both loved most on earth. Their mutual plea to God, "Lord heal their broken hearts, their pain, deliver them from evil doers, from their sufferings and darkness. Renew their spirits, O Lord. They both desperately needed to get a message through. Fred Persons, to his beloved wife, and Fred Sampson to his beloved church. Time was of the utmost essence. God granted them their request and the two of them immediately went to work.

Fred Persons queried? Who remained down there that could bring forth this heavenly message? Who could speak to the recesses of their hearts, minds and souls? None other than Bill Jones. Fred Persons had no doubt Bill Jones was the candidate for the job. Fred Sampson quickly agreed. Dr. Jones was no stranger to Tab. He was the only one who could get the job done on the same day, the same time, at the same place. One message, one messenger, two beneficiaries.

They needed a game plan, a strategy, a guarantee. They each retreated to separate quarters. Fred knew his wife was suffering, her heart and her spirit were broken, grief had overtaken her. How best could Fred let his wife know that he was still with her, watching over her. Fred needed to know that his beloved wife had a right relationship with God. He needed to know that her vine connection was all together secure. I'm gone. Gwen must now learn to trust in the Lord with all her heart, and to lean on HIM. Fred was certain that Dr. Jones was the only one left down there (besides Oprah) who could grab hold of Gwen's attention. However, Fred knew he must give Dr. Jones a little assistance.

Now let me see how can I guarantee that Gwen knows the message is from me? Here are a few guarantees. Let's start off with some of her early writings for the sorority. On the cover of her _Random Acts of Kindness_ book, she used Proverbs 31:24, use that in your message. And that little book she put together on depression _Reality Checks and Revelation Clearance,_ she borrowed that title from Doc. She reminds her sisters that "It is better to be on a stormy sea with the master on board, than on dry land without him." That is sure to grab her attention. Now, let's see, why not put a song on the hearts of the choir, put a song on Bill Jones heart. Let me select some of Gwen's favorites from her book (or should I refer to it as their book). 'We are often tossed and driven', 'Blessed Assurance', how many nights did we sing that one together? She had the choir to sing that one at her mother's home going. ' When the storms of life are raging', we must not leave that one out. Oh, and we have to include "His Eye is on the Sparrow', that was her Grandmother's favorite hymn. Now if she still is not convinced that the *message is from me, here is the sure 'nuf clincher, include my prescription for life., my formula for living. Proverbs 3:5-6. Have Dr. Jones lift up Proverbs 3:5-6. She will have to know the message is from me. I think it has become one of her favorite scriptures as well, she used it on one of her sorority campaign literature. But, the question weighed on Fred's spirit. Is it her prescription for daily living?*

This must be my ultimate legacy to Gwen. He and he alone can guarantee delivery. Fred pleaded, "Dr. Jones, give my wife a formula for living the remainder of her days upon earth without me." Well, Doc and Fred came back to the table with their combined requests and gave their petitions to God. The Holy Spirit got busy. The Great I Am went to work. The message was put upon Bill Jones heart and his spirit. Fred attached this post script.

P.S. I owe you one. Time ran out for me on earth, but I will meet you at the gate of glory on your appointed day. We will join Doc and we will feast on manna on high (the one we didn't get to have down there).

Exactly, four months from my husband's departure you came to Detroit and brought to me a message from my beloved husband. I have no doubt, Dr. Jones, that Fred's spirit was hooked up to your spirit yesterday morning. I won't attempt to interpret for Tabernacle, but I pray that their hearts, minds and souls were moved by the profundity of your messages from both services.

Please permit me to tell you how I knew that my husband's spirit was among us. Dr. Jones, Proverbs 3:5-6 was exactly how he lived his entire life (see his obituary) I'm sure if nothing else, this was meant to be his ultimate legacy to me, an assurance policy if you will, a blessed assurance for living the rest of my life. This was my husband's legacy to me and you paid off that policy in full!! I want to thank you from the recesses of my heart.
"God bless your heart."

I mailed this letter on Monday, March 18, 2002.

Fred, thanks for showing up yesterday morning.

03/25-- Each day since I've mailed that letter, I rush to the mailbox with excited anticipation hoping to find a reply. Another phone call would be nice too!! (from the Well of Hope, Hebrews 11:1) The cemetery phoned to say that they have laid your headstone. The family plans on going over to Chicago next weekend to spend Easter with Judy. Stephanie will be flying in from Atlanta and Jimmy and Chrissy will drive over. Carolyn and I will catch a flight Friday afternoon. My heart and mind are not up to it, but I don't want to disappoint the family. After all I did not spend Christmas with them. I know this would make Mommy very happy. Our first Easter without her.

03/28-- Driving home today I saw a couple of little old men walking down the street. I asked God "Why are they still here and not you?" "Why did You see fit to leave them here and take my Fred?" I started to cry all over again. The pain is deeper than my tears. (from the Well of Joy, Psalm 126:5)

03/31-- It's Sunday evening and I'm back from Chicago. Fred, let me try to describe my feelings about the weekend. It was not at all what I had expected. Friday was pretty uneventful. When I got to Chicago I immediately knew that here was not where I wanted or needed to be this weekend. All day Friday my thoughts were with you and Good Friday service in Detroit.

On Saturday we did go downtown, Michigan Ave. I was not in a shopping state of mind. All I wanted to do was to be back in Detroit. Once we were back at Judy's apartment, that dark cloud that still seems to follow me wherever I go ascended over me. I retreated into Judy's bedroom to be alone. It followed me in there too! I tried to force sleep, but sleep would not come. This just did not feel right to me. I had Jimmy to drive me back to the hotel. I wanted to be alone. I guess I thought if I went back to the hotel, Sunday morning would come quicker.

In all honesty, the only reason I agreed to go was out of a sense of guilt and obligation. I felt I needed to do this for Mama.

My body was there, but my spirit and my thoughts were back here. I desperately wanted to be home doing what we have always done, going to Good Friday Service and to church this morning. You have always said "Easter is the Most High day for Christians." For the first time in my saved life I was not in church on Easter Sunday morning. I felt so conflicted and convicted.

This morning they just sat around watching videos. Nobody ever mentioned the significance of the day. They are my family and I do love them but none-the-less it was as though I was among a bunch of non-believers. And to make matters even worse for me, no one mentioned or talked about you the entire weekend!! I did not feel I belonged there.

That old familiar feeling of disconnect returned to me this weekend. I did not feel a part of my own family. I felt like an outsider. I was so anxious to return to this Fred K. Personless apartment. I will not let myself feel so conflicted again. And I don't want to be that far away from you and this apartment anytime soon!

By the way, I did pick up a little something at the airport.

To my Beloved:
When I think of the joy you have brought me
the love and affection you've shown,
I can't help but see just how blessed I have been,
what a wonderful life I have known.
So I'm thanking the Lord,
as always,
for bringing you into my life-
You were a husband who was caring and faithful,
and I was so happy being your wife.
Happy 1st Easter without You
Love Always
Gwen
2002

04/02-- I miss Mama so much. Fred, I'm sure Mama always thought you would go before her. She was so worried that I would not be able to make it without you. Remember when she thanked you during her final days for taking good care of her baby? Mama knew just how much you meant to me Fred. I wonder if Mama was right, will I be able to make it without you?

04/08-- When I got off work today, I stopped at the Harbortown Market to pick up a few items, mostly household items and something from the deli. I don't do much cooking anymore. Going into the kitchen is still hard for me. I don't get any enjoyment out of cooking for one. Sitting down to eat without you is not easy either.

While I was in the market I ran into my Soror Teola Hunter. She asked about you! It's been almost five months and she was not aware of your passing. She expressed her deepest and caring sympathy and had some very kind words for you, as does everyone who speaks of you.

I know you did not share my affection for the Common Council, but I told her that I had written Marianne Mahaffey about getting a resolution on your behalf but she has not responded to my request. I shared with her that Rep. Derrick Hale had given me one from the State of Michigan. Being the gracious lady that she is, Soror Teola said that if I would just get the information to her, she would be more than happy to take care of it for me. I promised her I would have the information in her box the next day. That good ol' Delta Spirit keeps showing up! (from the Well of Kindness Proverbs 31:26)

04/11—I feel so awkward. It is hard to remain in the world and not feel part of it. To watch others rush about like nothing has changed. When every-thing has for me!

04/13-- Well Perci, I am going to give it another shot. The Delta Dears are taking an over night trip to Toronto to see the Lion King on Wednesday. I let Soror Rose Swanson convince me to go along. I know I said I did not ever want to be that far away from you again. I really do want to see it! I will be joining them on Wednesday.

04/17-- As soon as the train departed from Windsor, I knew I had made another impulsive decision. I began counting down the hours for the return trip home. I read it somewhere, "Fake it until you feel it." Well I'm not good at faking it, if I don't feel it, I won't fake it anymore. "To thine own self one must be true," otherwise it is too painful and it will not work (from the Well of Truth John 8:32)

I remained in my room until it was time to go to the theater. Dr. Jones kept me company, I listened to 'The Tree Connection.' I don't leave home without him.

04/22-- Soror Teola called. The resolution is ready for me to pick up. I was somewhat disappointed as I half way expected or looked forward to having the resolution presented to me in person by the council at one of their sessions, the way I've seen it done for so many others. You did more for this city than many of those I've seen come before the Council to receive their resolutions. After all you were Mr. City County Building. Mr. Detroit, an ambassador of 'goodwill' for your city and of course I am one of their biggest fans. In any case I'm thankful to Soror Teola for intervening on your behalf.

04/23-- I picked up the resolution from Teola's apartment and brought it home. I'm sure it would mean precious little to you but like a proud mother I hung it on the wall next to the resolution from the state. Just like a proud mother, I will take them both to work tomorrow.

04/24-- I still have not been to see Soror Erma Henderson. I do want to do that soon but not for the reason she suggested.

"The Lord will wipe away tears from all eyes." (Isaiah 25:8)

05/09-- The cemetery had a memorial service for families with loved ones buried there. I attended alone, and lit a candle for you, Mama and Grandma. After the service concluded I went to visit your grave site for the first time. I suppose I was waiting for them to lay your headstone. Mama's headstone still has not been laid.

My eyes kept shifting to where all three of you laid; Grandma, Mama and now you. All right there together. There lay the three people who I loved and who loved me most in this world. Soon I must reserve the plot between you and Mama for myself. Bill Jones said in one of his sermons, "None of us came here for to stay, we all must get up outta here one day. We all have a reservation and that reservation is without the benefit of cancellation." I don't know how long I languished there but it seemed like hours. I found it to be so peaceful and comforting being there with the three people I loved most in this world. Tonight I was able to be still, be quiet and to know that God is God. Tonight He seemed to vacuum the pain from my soul if only for a little while.

05/10-- The family left today for Christopher's graduation. I knew I would not be going with them. I will acknowledge his graduation once I see him. I know you would have been very proud of him and even prouder of Carolyn. You always spoke of the many sacrifices she made for 'that boy.' Well Perci he has not disappointed her. Her sacrifices have paid off. I am proud of them both! She's been a terrific mother.

05/12-- Mother's Day 2002. Another one of those 'hardest first' for me. I never had a chance to mourn my own mother's death. I feel guilty about this. Only six weeks after her passing, God saw fit to take you. I still ask Him why? Although I am still questioning God, I know He put His arms underneath me to carry me.

I'm sure Mama understands. She always said "Nothing can come between you and your husband." One thing I am most thankful for is for last Mother's Day. I am so thankful that I had a chance to apologize to Mama for that insensitive remark I made years ago.

After church I came home and worked on the final chapter of my book "Precious Memories. The memories stopped coming in a couple of months ago. I expected to receive more than I have gotten. But it is not the quantity of responses I receive but rather the quality. They have each been so, so special.

Perci, I do have a confession. In all honesty I have been very disappointed in the response or lack thereof from the members of St. Stephen. From all places, I expected more from them. I am certain if I had solicited responses from the courts and the City County Building they would have come to me in droves. Just to know you was to love you!

I can still hear you saying "Baby are you working on your book?" "Yes Fred, I am still working on my book."

05/25-- Memorial Day Weekend. Judy is in town. She spent the afternoon downtown with me. After lunch we rode out to the cemetery. Judy was disappointed that Mama's headstone had not been laid.

05/26-- Sunday afternoon I joined the family at Carolyn's. This was our first summer holiday without you and Mama. Unlike last month in Chicago, I did enjoy being with the family. Summer will soon be here. I will be working summer school and of course I still have my position with Marygrove. That ought to at least absorb some of those lonely hours this summer is sure to bring.

05/27-- I heard that commercial again today, about the coffee-mate. You were indeed my better half, you kept me grounded. You saw the best there was in me. But you saw the best there was in everybody. You never engaged in the trivial. Always there to

266 Gwendolyn D. Persons

offer a helping hand or a word of encouragement to others. You saw the bright side to every situation. Fred you never felt discouraged, even during your illness. You remained optimistic and hopeful to the end. We did indeed become one and you were the better half of our oneness. Fred, you were the best thing that ever happened to me too!

I finally, opened the plastic bag that was given to me from the funeral home which contained the clothes you were wearing on November 17. You were wearing that light gray suit and of course your favorite black turtle neck sweater and my favorite shoes of yours, your little black patent ones. The underwear that you were wearing was also inside of that bag. There was also a small paper bag which contained the answer to that nagging question, "Did you have your little brown bottle that morning?" You did have it with you! (from the Well of Patience 11Thessalonians 1:4)

06/07-- The 1st Annual Fred K. Persons golf classic was held today. I took off from work but I did not attend the golf outing. However I did send the committee a donation. I hope it was successful.

Did I mention that in January I made my first payment on your tree of life stone? My goal is to pay $2,000 a year for the next five years. I know you did not embrace the concept when you were here. I am certain you would not approve of me doing it now. I hear you Fred, "Gwen don't spend your money foolishly." Well maybe I won't try to get the stone, maybe just a leaf?

06/13-- Tuesday evening Bishop Vashti McKenzie was in town. She spoke at St. Paul A.M.E. Church. I was quite surprised at the small crowd. You know how much you loved that preachin' woman? I purchased her new book, Journey to the Well how about that title? I Wonder what it is about?

I hope I can finish my book before Celine or Nancy write their May/December memoirs, 'Love letters from Ronnie'.

That's not the only race I'm in; not only is Tabernacle searching for a new minister they will also be erecting a new church. I hope to have my book completed before the new building is completed.

06/15-- Yesterday was the last day of the school year. By the way, I picked up my new car yesterday, a 2002 Cadillac. It's just like the black one, the only difference is the color. This one is pearl white. Fred, without you here to share my life nothing seems to hold much meaning for me. (from the Well of Joy Psalm 16:11)

06/19-- Another hardest 'first' they just keep on coming!!
HAPPY 83rd BIRTHDAY SWEETHEART!!!
What I miss most is the sound of your voice and your laughter, our laughter together. We were buddies, best friends, soul mates. I went to the cemetery today. I thought I was beyond what happened to me today. I had not planned on having another funeral today!
Grief is like a long and winding road that leads you back to the same scene you thought you had left miles behind.
I will not be going to Atlanta for the convention this year. I've missed two national conventions in a row!
My formula for surviving this summer: I will read a little or a lot, I will write a little or a lot, I will exercise a little or a lot, I will cry a little or a lot and above all, I will pray a lot. By the way your golf clubs are still behind your big chair.

06/22-- This morning I was looking for Lila's tape, "God has a plan for your life". Not only did I need to hear the message, I wanted to hear her sing one of your favorite songs, "It's Real." She sang it at your home going. Not only did I find that tape, but I ran across a tape labeled, 'Bro. Persons'. It was the tape from Layman's Sunday in February 1990. You brought the morning message. Your text was taken from Romans 8. Georgia Lee read the scripture. How she misses you, she lets me know each time I see her.

"Look at what you have left in your life; never look at what you have lost." (Robert Schuller)

06/27-- Last night was yet another 'hardest first.' It most definitely was the loneliest one for me. The Freedom Festival Fireworks were last night. How you loved the fireworks and being in the thick of the crowd. People watching, your favorite past time. You were always so young at heart and on the night of the fireworks, you turned into a 'big kid'. However the last two or three years we stood in at the window on the 32nd floor of the Millender Center and watched them from there. The crowds had gotten to be a bit too much for you. Percibol, you were 'just my little boy'.

But last night among those millions of people, I never felt more alone. That old familiar sense of abandonment paid me a visit last night. The invisible essence of your invisible presence was so intense. Suddenly I wanted to be invisible too. I wanted to disappear into the night and so I did. I rushed back inside and watched the remainder of the 2002 Freedom Fireworks from the 32nd floor of the Millender Center. You were here waiting for me when I got back to the apartment.

My buddy, my best friend, my soulmate. (from the Well of Joy Colossians 1:11)

06/29-- When I came in from church this afternoon I sat in the lobby. I sat in your chair for the first time. I did not want to get up. I can't explain it but it felt so comforting. It just felt good. Perci, I am learning that it is not the load that will break you down, but the way you carry it. He is easing my pain.

06/30-- I dismantled your shrine weeks ago. But I still spend hours looking at the volumes and volumes of photographs you took of our life together. That little brownie camera has captured so many precious memories. Thanks for the memories Sweetheart!

07/04-- No cook-out invites today. Frankly I was relieved, I much preferred to be right here! I read most of the day. I started reading Bishop McKenzie's book, Journey to the Well. Wanna hear something ironic? Soror Vashti's book deals with twelve women, one well, my book, twelve wells, one woman.

Fred, I could hardly believe it! Billy's wife, Juanita, called here today, asking for you!! Said she didn't know.

07/07 — Fred, I know I should allow myself to feel the warmth of friendship and to allow others to reach out to me, but unapologetically, I have comfortably retreated into this apartment. I am still only allowing those who are coming to see the magnetic you in me to enter my world.

07/09-- I am doing quite a bit more catalog/telephone shopping. When I pick up the phone and say the words, "I'd like to place an order, I feel convicted, I hear you saying, "Gwen, don't buy another thing for this apartment." I've got a case of the 'can't help it'. I hear you too Dr. Jones, "Wrong diagnosis spells wrong prescription." Am I allowing that intruder to reenter my life? I must proceed with caution!

This summer is finding me wrestling with lots of fears.

I'm afraid to look in the mirror. I'm afraid to get back in the gym. I'm afraid to return to Weight Watchers. I'm afraid to open the closet, (money spent foolishly) I'm afraid to go to the mailbox, bills, bills, bills, more money spent foolishly! I'm afraid to go to the doctor. I'm afraid of looking in the wine rack (too many empty slots). I'm afraid of living without you. I'm afraid of waking up all alone, in the wee hours of the morning. Fred, there is nowhere to run, no where to hide. I'm afraid to face Him face to face! I have much to talk to Him about

07/12-- After summer school ended my days are spent watching "The View" every morning. Then of course I watch 'Oprah' every afternoon, and the Council every evening, (they will soon be going on recess. Fred, you knew how I hated it when they went on recess!)

07/15-- I left my cocoon today. I had to go to 36th District Court. I will have to evict the tenants in Mama's house. On the way home I stopped to see the boys. I discovered the opening of a new downtown five star restaurant, 'Sweet Georgia Brown'. I wish you were here so we could check it out together! It looks like your kind of place. While walking I heard sirens. Whenever I hear those sirens, I still think of you in the back of that E. M. S. vehicle. I still see old men out here and wonder why. Why did my little boy have to leave?

07/20-- I dined at Sweet Georgia Browns this evening. Perci, the restaurant was topnotch!! First class all the way. The ambience was exquisite, the food was out of sight. Definitely, your kind of watering hole. Its owner is an African-American. LaVan Hawkins. Opus One has nothing on this brother. Had it been open during the Joe Muer era, Mr. Hawkins would have given Joe a run for his money, or should I say a run for your money? Simply fabulous. I wish you could have been by my side to enjoy it with me. (from the Well of Peace Thessalonians 5:13)

07/23-- Yet another failed attempt at getting out. I let myself be talked into a girl -to -girl night out. Whatever happened to that promise I made to myself, 'to thy own self be true'. I did not try to fake it and I sure didn't feel it. I almost felt violated. My heart was not in it. I just wanted to get back home to my cocoon. (from the Well of Truth Proverbs 12:19)

07/28-- Why can't I take as good of care of me, as I did you? I need to stop eating out so often. If only I could return to the kitchen and prepare my meals at home. Then perhaps I could begin to lose some of this weight. It is just so hard to return to the kitchen. In many ways it is the loneliest room in the house. The kitchen is where I took care of you. It is where I planned and prepared your meals and dispensed your medicine. It was your favorite room in the house. You took so much pride in keeping it clean, clean like Mr. Wheat called clean. I guess that's why I can't turn on the light when I go in there yet. It needs cleaning!

08/02-- Happy 52nd Birthday to me!! This evening I am going back to Sweet Georgia Brown's. Carolyn will be celebrating my birthday with me this evening. (from the Well of Kindness. 1Peter 3:8)

08/03-- I checked my messages when I got in last night evening, I had several birthday greetings, one was from Joyce and another from Frances.

 08/04-- The Huggins were in church this morning. I invited them to follow me home, I wanted to surprise them and take them to Sweet Georgia Brown's for dinner. They followed me downtown to the Millender Center and we walked down to the restaurant. Unfortunately, the growing popularity of the restaurant now requires reservation for Sunday Brunch. So we were unable to be seated. Rev. Huggins opted for a rain check, we went to Carl's instead. I love them so much as you did too, and they us. You are missed by so many Fred. By the way, it was my treat! I got him back from last February when he treated Jennifer and me. I said I would.

08/07-- Today I had another special reunion. I met Joe and Hattie at Big Fish in Fairlane for dinner. It was so long overdue. It was great to see them. They are both doing fine. They miss you and think about you often! (from the Well of Love Hebrews 13:1)

I thanked them for taking the time to send me that wonderful tribute last February. I told them that I was still writing. I will be so proud when I complete my book. I am so glad they took the time to respond. Of course we spent much time remembering our Friday nights at Joe Muer. Those were some good times. Thanks, sweetheart for the wonderful memories. We missed you! I'm so glad I made the call. The Muic's are certainly among those who see the magnetic you in me! I will make every effort to stay in touch with them throughout the year. It was very sobering and healing.

08/11-- I stayed home from church today, no particular reason why, I just did. I piddled around the apartment for most of the morning. As you know I love to do. Then I spent some quality time at my computer. When I decided to take a break, I sat down in the middle of the living room floor and started reading the September issue of O magazine. The theme of this month's issue was 'Dream Big', something I've been doing since those early years at the foot of my doll house. In essence the article talks about how one can begin to 'live their best life'. In order to realize your full God given potential and to 'live your best life' one must discover what you love, offer it to others in the form of service and then trust God to bring it all to fruition.

Oprah says *"You face the biggest challenge of all when you have the courage to seek your big dream regardless of what anyone else thinks. You are the only one alive who can see your big picture and even you can't see it all..... Dream big, dream very big. And after you've done all you can, you stand, wait, and fully surrender.* (The Oprah Magazine, September 2002)

To that I say "Hallelujah and Amen!

Perci, the article energized, encouraged and inspired me to even greater heights. I must, I shall, I will keep pressing on to complete my work. I do have big dreams for my book and I am trusting God to help to make it happen and to evolve me into the best me He would have for me to be.

After doing a little more piddling and a little more nibbling, I returned to my computer. Somewhere around early evening time, my 'jones' came down. I needed a fix. I put on one of Dr. Jones tapes. Why that particular one I really don't know. Oprah's subject for the month, 'Dream Big', was rescripted when I listened to 'When Your Faith Level is Low''. It was a sermon on 'faith'. Dr. Jones admonishes the listener/believer to check his/ her faith level. He begins by posing these three queries, *"Have you checked your faith gauge of late? When was the last time you weighed yourself on the scale of the gospel? When have you examined your belief system for the purpose of determining the level that your faith in God is presently operating. Dr. Jones says, "We ought be deeply concerned at all times the level of our faith. For 'faith' is primary in the believers dealings with God. 'Faith' is what God is always looking for. 'Faith' is that posture that pleases God. Without Faith it is impossible to please God. Rev. Jones says he has discovered that "God has a special affection for faith folk. Therefore whatever God will do or wills to do, He wants to do, and those who are on the faith frequency have the privilege of seeing it before others see it. They see God doing the 'big thing' before the earthly manifestation occurs. Call it what you will, inside information, big on the inside track, being privy to something unusual, call it whatever you please, it all boils down to seeing it before it gets here.*

Dr. Jones says *"That when you live life at this level, it makes for a certain loneliness of spirit. There are not too many people who operate at such a level. You have to carry great ideas and profound thoughts in the privacy of your own mind and soul. You are reluctant to divulge that which is en route to anybody and everybody for that matter, for the simple reason, most people will not understand. They'll disbelieve, they might even declare you insane." (When Your Faith Level is Low, Dr. William A. Jones)*

Rev. Jones message conjoined in perfect harmony with Oprah's article. One called it 'dreaming big' and the other called it 'faith. In either case the message was the same.

Fred, I can clearly recall the first time we heard Rev. Jones preach this message; it was the weekend I learned you had cancer.

Your faith level was indeed very low that weekend, but that Sunday evening, Dr. Jones preached you back happy with this message. Over the years I have listened to this tape a zillion times. However, today it was as if I was hearing it for the very first time. Today, I got a fresh new meaning from this message. Today I drew 'fresh waters from an old well'.

Even though I did not attend church today, I had two powerful words from above. Similar messages, different messengers. One was from my 'shero' and the other was from my 'hero.'

Well Fred, that's enough for a summer day.

"The faith needed today is a steadfast trust in God come what may- a faith that helps you to be certain, not of things you can see, but of the better realities you cannot see."

08/15-- I've been in workshops for three days this week. The summer has quickly come to a close. This is the first time in many years that we do not return until after Labor Day. Another summer I did not hit the ball, perhaps I'll get back in the 'swing' next summer.

I had an opportunity to hear the African Children's choir this summer. Matter of fact I heard them twice. The first time at Rose's church and again they came to St. Stephen. They are wonderful.

I still cry Fred but the other day I was thinking about my tears.

In the beginning and with regularity anything would find the storm clouds all over me. The storm clouds would ascend over my head and without so much as a warning, they would descend and burst. The tears that filled and flowed from my eyes were likened to a ravaging and tumultuous rain storm.

But now, the crying doesn't come much in the same regularity nor does it last all day. I can even smile in the midst of my crying. The tears that flow from my eyes today are much like a summer shower. Once they are over a rainbow appears in the summer skies. Fred, now when I cry and God wipes away my tears, I look to the skies and there appears a ribbon, 'a ribbon in the sky for our love'. (Stevie Wonder)

08/17 My request for memories stopped coming in weeks ago. Therefore, I went with what I had and completed 'Precious Memories'.

Out of all the memories I received, there were two that got rejected. The very first one that came in was from my sister, Carolyn. When Carolyn's memory arrived, I was still blinded by my grief and still not letting anybody in that was not appealing to the magnetic you in me. At the time I could not see the love for you in what my sister had sent to me. I did not feel that it was centered around you. But rather around her gift from God, her son, my nephew Christopher. Carolyn spoke about how during Christopher's formative years, she did not understand nor did she appreciate then, your firmness, your frankness, and your no nonsense stance in which you dealt with her son, her 'gift from God'. It was many years later that she was made to realize and appreciate your posture at that time in her son's life. Admittedly, my grief blurred the significance of her memory. After all, I was still angry at him for not attending your home going. Consequently, that memory did not make it within the pages of my book!

The other memory that got rejected came from Soror Loretta Dickens and if I'm not mistaken, it was the last memory I received. Her memory was rejected for two reasons. First, she confesses that she can not relate to the Oprah Winfrey Show; to her it is just a T.V. show, a show lacking reality in her life. Now Perci, how many times and how many disagreements have I had with folk over the years (including you, my love) regarding Ms. Winfrey. Loretta's comments clearly qualified as another one of those infractions. Soror Loretta's position is this, Jesus and only Jesus. She did lift up Christ and His teachings in her memory of you and I don't take exception to any of what she writes, but this is about you and your love. Loretta writes, "As you continue your

276 Gwendolyn D. Persons

walk with Christ, I pray that you will see Him more clearly, love Him more dearly, and follow Him more nearly.

Reflectively, I can write most apologetically and admittedly I could not see the love they were each attempting to express for you and about you, Carolyn through her son Christopher, and Loretta through the Lord's Son, Jesus the Christ. I apologize to all four of them. At the time my pain would not allow me to see clearly. My pain ran deeper than my tears.

Fred, you left me nine months ago today, nine months, the time it takes to birth a baby. One might say that over these past nine months I have had a rebirth of sorts. Fred you were my earthly king, but since you have been gone, I have had to stand face to face with God. You are no longer here to stand between me and my God. These past nine months it has been me and God and my hurt, me and God and my tears me and God and my fears, me and God and only me and God.

It is altogether true, no matter how tall I grow in His grace, there will always be room above where I stand. Fred I am still growing his God's grace.

Soror Loretta, I do see Him more clearly, I do love Him more dearly, and I will follow Him more nearly. Today I added my final installment to part six, Precious Memories. This is indeed exactly the way you would want me to celebrate your life and to live the rest of my life.

Sis, because I am able to see more clearly today I thank you for your memory. Carolyn has always been there for me. As a matter of fact Fred, Carolyn was the only one in the family to respond to my request. (A Song of Praise on Understanding)

08/18-- I had to go to church today. So much to thank Him for. These last two weeks of the vacation will probably be spent on Colfax getting the house ready for the next tenant to move in. This is not working out the way I had hoped it would. But I do not want to disappoint Grandma and Mama, they were so proud and they loved that house so much. It was all that either of them ever owned in life.

08/25-- Today is Mama's birthday. I did something that we have not done in years. I walked down to Hart Plaza and stood on the banks of the river. I had so many thoughts about my mother today.

So many regrets I have for my mother, for her life. Maybe I don't even have the right to feel this way. I do regret and perhaps this will be cataloged as one my life's greatest regrets. I regret that we were not closer. I regret all of those missed years, unfortunately time was not on our side. Mama's healing and our marriage each happened around the same time. Once we were united, everyone and everything took a back seat to our marriage. After Mama got well she would often say, "I don't think anything can come between you and your husband." Mama was absolutely correct. I am sure Mama understood and was happy for her 'baby'. Most of all I wish that my mother could have found in her life some of the happiness I found with you. I've been blessed like few woman will ever know. I so wish Mama could have had one half of the happiness you and I have shared. My sisters too! My best friends too! I was blessed in a mighty way! I miss the two of you so much.

Fred, I know the two, no, the three, of you, are looking down on me this day" Joying and beholding my order and my steadfast faith in Christ." (Colossians 1:5)

09/01-- First Sunday in September, the summer is over. I attended church service this morning. When I came home I spent the day enjoying our apartment. I gave a lot of thought about my writing and I did a lot of dreaming about my book (Oprah says dream big). I often wonder where and when did writing become a part of those dreams I had for myself? Even during those early years at the foot of my dollhouse, I never had the slightest notion, thought or inclination that I would ever be a writer of any kind.

Writing was never on my radar screen. Why did I begin to write? Has it been God's plan for my life all along? Had Aunt Cathy prophesied it in 1999? Lila preached about it in her sermon years ago, 'God's got a plan for your life'. Has this been His ultimate plan for my life? It is for certain that all of my writings have been assignments commissioned by God. Dr. Jones said it years ago, "When God tells you to do something, you had better do it." Dr. Jones calls that faith. Fred, you called that trusting in God.

Soror Claudia, however long it takes I will complete my work. I will work hard and get it done! Then Oprah, after I've done all I can do, I will stand and wait and surrender it to God and proclaim unto Him, 'To God Be All the Glory'. (from the Well of Patience Hebrews 10:36)

09/02-- Today is Labor Day, I went to the gym this morning, came back and spent the remainder of the day reading a little, writing a little and dreaming a lot about my book.

I prayed "Lord, don't let me allow those self-righteous, holier than thou, player haters, keep me from my dreams. Amen. (from the Well of Faith Hebrews11:1)

I was pleased to read that Dr. Phil will have his own show this Fall. This was a bit of good news. I can add that to my limited line-up of TV viewing!

Also in this month's issue of O Magazine there was an article entitled, "Does prayer really heal?" You bet it does! I'm a witness!

09/03-- First day back to work. I treated Terri to lunch at Sweet Georgia Browns. When I arrived home and opened the mail box, I almost lost my mind. Finally after all these months a letter from Brooklyn, New York was there. I could not wait until I got into the apartment to open it. I opened it immediately. It was not quite what I had been hoping for all of these months, but it was from Brooklyn nonetheless. Today I received an invitation to the 40th Pastoral Anniversary for Dr. William Augustus Jones. The celebration will be held on Friday, September 13, 2002, in Queens, New York. Was this a personal invitation especially for me? Or did my name just happen to be one among millions across the country on the church's mailing list? Fred, how many times did I say to you, "Fred, I want you to take me to New York, not to shop, or theater hop, I just want to go to Bethany Baptist Church. Your response to my request was always the same, "You got it!" Well we never made it there but you can bet I will not let this opportunity pass me by! This trip is long overdue! I am going to New York!

09/04-- I mailed my check today. You didn't believe me did you, Perci? When I got to work today I shared the invitation and my plans on attending the banquet with Mr. Hoggard. Hoggard was a wealth of information. Hoggard is a native Philadelphian and I learned today that he had practically grown up in the same house with Dr. Jones. He shared with me lots of tidbits about the Jones family. I took copious notes. He told me the name of the first church Dr. Jones pastored in Philadelphia. He took piano lessons under the tutelage of Sylvia, Dr. Jones sister. Sylvia is also married to a preacher, who has one of the largest Baptist Church in Atlanta, Ga., Wheat Street Baptist Church. Their daughter, Crystal Harris, is a renowned vocalist. Lastly, one of Dr. Jones brothers, Rev. Henry Jones, is also a pastor at a large church in Atlanta. Today I had a crash course in the life of Dr. William A. Jones from my Philadelphian connection.

09/05-- Today I had Dontez, a co-worker to help me make my flight reservations on-line. I will be leaving Friday morning at 11:30am and returning Sunday afternoon at 3:00 p.m. I have been on cloud nine all week. I'm actually going out of town and alone no less! I will not know a soul there! I wrote another letter today.

Dear Rev. Jones:

It is my sincere hope that this letter meets you enjoying abundant good health, joy and happiness. May I also take this opportunity to extend congratulations to you on your Fortieth Pastoral Anniversary. My personal testimony to your ministry, "I thank God every day that you came into my life. Although I am no longer able to tune into the Bethany Hour on Sunday evening, you remain a constant in my life. What a mighty, mighty blessing you have been to me." I count it a blessing that last week when I opened my mail, I would receive an invitation to the 40th Pastoral Anniversary. How often did I say to my late husband, "I would like to travel to New York one weekend to visit Dr. Jones at Bethany Baptist Church." Time ran out for us.

In these 52 years I have not done much traveling and precious little alone. I must admit I am just a tad bit nervous but none-the-less I have finalized my reservations for my pilgrimage to 'Mecca''.

I look forward to being in your presence once again and hearing a Word from God, as only Dr. William Augustus Jones can render. I want to shake your hand once more.

Fondly,

(I signed my name)

After I had written the letter, I rewrote the dedication for my book. I then called Bethany Baptist Church. I spoke to a Ms. Audrey Gore. I explained to Ms. Gore that I was from Detroit and that I had received the invitation to Dr. Jones anniversary. Being totally unfamiliar to the city, I was in need of some information to assist me in finalizing my plans. She was very accommodating. Ms. Gore suggested that I may wish to stay at a bed and breakfast near the church, however, she would have to make a couple of calls and get back to me. She asked for my phone number. Gee, she does not know me from Adam. She made me feel like anything but a stranger! The following day I received two calls from Ms. Gore. Both calls were follow-ups to her efforts to book me into the bed and breakfast. Unfortunately, her attempts could not accommodate my needs. Why was she being so accommodating to a total stranger? I thanked her for her kindness and said that I would be in touch (from the Well of Kindness 11 Peter 7). My excitement soared even higher! I can hardly wait to get there.

09/07-- With the help of some more experienced travelers and internet users, I booked my hotel reservations on hotel.com. I will be staying at the Courtyard Marriott in downtown Brooklyn. I called Ms. Gore back to let her know exactly where I would be staying during my stay in Brooklyn. She gave me the itinerary for the entire weekend and asked that I call her once I arrive.

09/13-- Good morning Perci. When you came to see about me New Year's Eve you said you would not be coming again. Thank you for coming to see about me last night. There is no doubt in my mind that somehow we physically connected last night. I'm not sure how it happened and I won't try to give a logical explanation as to how it happened. I just know it happened. Was that your way of telling me it's okay, it's time for me to move on with my life? All I can say is this, "Thanks for coming to see about me." 'God Does Move In Mysterious Ways'.

09/16-- I'm home Perci. Fred, not even my wildest dreams could have compared with what happened to me this weekend in New York. When I arrived in New York I walked out of the airport to hail a taxi to the hotel. I was readily approached by a young man requesting to take me to my destination. I followed him to his car. As it turned out, he was a college student, working underground as a taxi driver. He explained that he was parked a little distance from the airport because he could not afford to be caught by the airport officials. I followed him to his waiting transport. It was a pleasant ride to the hotel. I made every effort to make sure I gave him the impression that this was not my first trip to Brooklyn. I even said to him that "One day I hope to retire to Brooklyn." He gave me his number and asked that I call him on Sunday for my return trip.

My contacts with Audrey Gore before leaving Detroit proved to be invaluable. When I arrived at the hotel I immediately called the church and spoke to Audrey. I announced my arrival to Brooklyn. Audrey welcomed me to Brooklyn and again gave me the weekend's itinerary. Audrey suggested that I get a taxi from the hotel and plan to arrive to the church by 5:30. There will be buses available to take folks out to Queens, where the banquet would be held. I hung up the phone and unpacked my luggage. I had to pinch myself several times. I was actually in Brooklyn, New York on my way to see Dr. William A. Jones. A plethora of questions danced around in my head as I prepared for the evening. Will I get to shake his hand again? Will he even know that I'm here? Will I have an opportunity to discuss our book? Admittedly, I wanted to make a lasting impression. When I was finally satisfied with the results of my efforts I headed down to the lobby. I stepped outside the hotel and hailed a taxi and was asked, "Where to Miss?" I replied "460 Marcus Garvey Boulevard." The words were so utterly familiar to me, but this was not a recording these words came directly from my mouth. I was headed to that Neo-Gothic edifice that we had grown so accustomed to seeing on our TV screen every Sunday evening for all of those years. Riding through the streets of Brooklyn was not unlike riding through certain parts of Detroit, a depressed and forgotten city. Multitudes of flunk-outs, drop-outs and push-outs roamed the streets of Brooklyn, people with nothing to do, no place to be somebody and therefore, no place to go. I'm not sure just how long I had been inside the taxi when I looked out upon a street sign that read Marcus Garvey Blvd. The driver asked me again for the address, and I answered. "460." According to the numbers we still had yet a ways to go. I really sat up and took notice then rode the rest of the way in a state of excited antici- pation. Those desolate, depressed streets now suddenly took on a different meaning for me. I was suddenly made to feel as though I was riding down streets paved with gold. I was traveling down a heavenly highway on my way to the gates of heaven to meet the

King. According to the numbers it won't be long now. We were there at last! There it was in full view, that Neo-Gothic edifice. Fred, at long last I had arrived at Bethany Baptist Church, 460 Marcus Garvey Blvd. in Brooklyn, New York.

When I got out of the taxi I walked around the outside of the church. Oh Fred, how I wished that we could have stood on that corner together. But I know you were with me in spirit. My heart was overflowing with awe, anticipation, wonderment and most of all thanksgiving. I was not in a New York state of mind, I was in a Heavenly state of mind and I was thanking God for helping to make it happen (from the Well of Joy, 1 John 1:4)

When I walked through the doors of the church I found my way to the church office. I asked for Audrey Gore who had already left for the day. I explained to the only gentleman available to me the reason for my presence. He instructed me to go down to the fellowship hall where the people would be gathering to board the buses for the banquet. I followed his instructions. There was not a single person in sight. I took a seat and waited. Although I was alone it felt strangely familiar to me. I felt right at home. I had not been waiting too long when a gentleman appeared, I told him the purpose for my being there that evening. He found that to be remarkable. "You traveled all the way from Detroit?" I was quite surprised by his reaction. Before leaving Detroit, I had just assumed that there would be hundreds of people just like me from all across the country, there to celebrate Dr. Jones 40th Pastoral Anniversary. It was not too long before they started to arrive. I met several very nice people and each time I told them the reason for my visit, their reaction was the same, "You're here all the way from Detroit?" The announcement came as quite a surprise to them. I didn't seem to meet any strangers in that fellowship hall. Everyone treated me kindly. In fact, I do believe I recognized some of the faces that we have grown accustomed to seeing on television during the weekly broadcasts.

It was now time to board the buses. Everyone who had prepaid was allowed to board first. A line began to form for those few who had not prepaid. When it was time for those who had not prepaid to board I took my place in line. I was asked my name. "Gwen Persons" I replied. The lady seated next to the gentleman in charge of collecting the boarding fee looked up at me and repeated my name, "Gwen Persons, from Detroit? I'm Audrey Gore." I felt as though I had just met an old friend. I was a stranger, among strangers, in a strange place. But strangely enough I felt right at home.

The ride from Brooklyn to Queens took about forty five minutes. Once we arrived at the banquet hall we waited in a line over fifty minutes before we could actually enter the dining hall. Seated at the entrance to the banquet room was a single lady whose job was to collect the banquet tickets. The next stop before entering the room was to give your name to yet another single individual who was positioned at the entrance of the door. When I reached the entrance I identified myself, "Gwen Persons." "Mrs. Persons, you are at table #3." I was sure I did not hear her correctly, table #3, so I had her to repeat it. She did not stammer or stutter, her instructions were clear, "You are at table #3 by the dais. I was totally blown away! How did I get seated so close to the dais? I walked through the doors into the largest banquet room I have ever witnessed. The room was practically empty. The majority of the guests were apparently still on the other side of those doors. Following the kind lady's instruction, I spotted the dais and just in front of it I located table # 3. I was the first one to arrive at the table. I claimed my spot at the end of the table. I'll have the best seat at this table, up close and personal!! I could not stop wondering how on earth did this happen for me? How did I get so lucky? What did I do to deserve this? Was this a mere coincidence or was it prearranged? Had Dr. Jones received my letter? Did Dr. Jones arrange this for me? It was most curious to me when my ticket first arrived, there was no assigned table printed or written on the ticket, only a personal note from an

Edith Carson, which read, "Be sure to introduce yourself to me when you get here." I thought to myself then, "How will I ever be able to do that? I was full of questions and no one was there to give me any answers.

Perci, there were food stations strategically positioned all around the room, so once I staked out my spot, I made my way to the food stations. Other than on a cruise ship, I had never witnessed anything like it before. Everything for the most discriminating and diet conscious palate to the most undiscriminating palate was on those tables. The variety of food was limitless.

As I made my selections it was apparent that the plates were not designed to allow one to satisfy an undiscriminating palate such as mine. I made my limited selections and as I headed back to table #3, I thought to myself hmmm, for seventy-five dollars, I would have at least expected a sit down dinner, not a buffet!

The guests were now beginning to fill the room. However, when I reached table #3, no one else had arrived. As my hand approached my napkin, my conscience spoke to me, "This is a church affair, are we to begin eating before saying the grace?" Since there was no one at the table to answer my question, I looked around the room for an answer. When in Rome, do as the Romans do. Well in this case, when in Brooklyn, do as the Brooklyners do. I said a silent grace and just as I picked up my fork to put the first morsel of food into my mouth, a waiter came to the table and inquired as to what I desired for my entree? Well that answered some of my questions. I was humbled in that instant! The choices were, chicken, beef or salmon. You guessed right Perci, I selected the salmon. I then picked up the program that had been placed in my seat. I read half way down the program and there it was, centered, in it's proper place, in capital letters 'DINNER IS SERVED'. Fasten your seat belt Gwen, you're in for what was sure to be an evening you will cherish for the rest your life.

The room was now full of people. My eyes surveyed the entire room. Above my head was an upper tier that circled the circumference of the room. The question still loomed, Perci, "how did I get this lucky?" I am certain that there were folks there who had been members of that church these entire forty years, folk who would have given their eye teeth to be seated where I was. This had to have been God's handiwork! Or was it Bill Jones?

By the time I had finished my first plate of appetizers, the second guest had arrived at table # 3. She introduced herself, as Courtney. Courtney immediately evidenced herself as being well acquainted with the 'Eternal Father'. She had an engaging, endearing and infectious personality. Courtney informed me that she was a close friend to Leslie Jones, Dr. Jones' daughter. I guess I did not give it a lot of thought when she said that she was a close friend to Dr. Jones daughter. I thought it just by chance that we had been seated at the same table together. We each gave a brief history as to how we ended up there that evening. Courtney told me how her relationship with Leslie evolved. They met in a prayer group for young professionals, they are both educators in the Brooklyn school system. As a matter of fact, I recalled a few years back, Clara called me one evening to see if I had been watching Night line that particular week. Ted Koppel was doing a series on 'Master Teachers' throughout the country. Clara informed me that Dr. Jones' daughter had been among one of those selected. When it came my turn to share, I told Courtney how we first became acquainted with Dr. Jones through the 'Bethany Hour', via our local cable network and how over the years Dr. Jones ministry has been such an influence in our marriage and in our lives. I told her about my book and how instrumental Dr. Jones has been in my writing, in fact I even refer to him as my co-author. Dr. Jones has indeed become my spiritual father. When I told her that you had passed away, but that you had always promised to bring me to Brooklyn, to hear Dr. Jones in person, she expressed the same reaction I had received all evening. Courtney was amazed. "What a testimony to your love for one another and to Dr. Jones ministry," she replied. I assured her that I was certain that there were many here this evening that had come from all across the country with their own testimonies of Dr. Jones' influence in their lives.

As we talked on, we discovered that we had another commonality. We were both members of Greek letter organizations. Courtney admitted that she had very little involvement in her sorority (AKA) since her undergraduate years on campus. I could not let the opportunity pass me by. After I finished giving her my testimony about the fulfillment I have experienced in my life through Delta's public service projects, (many of which I initiated) she could not help but sit up and take notice. She found my implementation of the Delta Random Acts of Kindness Days in the city of Detroit, (which I adopted from Oprah) of significant interest. When I told her that this activity garnered my chapter national recognition from the Paul Newman Make -A -Difference-Day in 1995, she appeared even more interested. But above all, she seemed most interested and impressed to hear and applauded my role as the chapter chaplain. When I told her that I had written a book entitled God's Got A Word for Delta Women, she asked if it would be possible for her to get a copy. I do believe that after I got through witnessing to her that evening Courtney would be taking a second look at Alpha Kappa Alpha Sorority. That was just the prelude to what made for a memorable weekend in Brooklyn. (from the Well of Kindness Romans12:10)

Once the remainder of the guests started to arrive at the table, I knew this was no ordinary table. This table had been reserved for Dr. Jones family and close friends. Allow me to call the roll. Of course already seated was Courtney, his daughter's close friend. Next to arrive was a lady and her spouse. She introduced herself as a first cousin to Rev. Jones. A few minutes later two more ladies and a gentleman joined us at the table. They were childhood friends who had grown up in Lexington, Kentucky with Dr. Jones. The ladies, however now resided in Atlanta. The last reserved seats were filled by none other than Leslie Jones and her fiance. Once Leslie arrived, Courtney could not wait to tell her my story. All of the guests assembled within ear shot listened in earnest and seemed to be genuinely impressed and marveled at the fact I had travel all the way from Detroit to celebrate Dr. Jones fortieth Pastoral Anniversary. I found it somewhat odd that throughout the entire evening, no one inquired as to how it was that I, a complete stranger got to be seated at table # 3. Leslie, the epitome of grace and charm and beauty was the perfect hostess. Perci, did I mention that Leslie is a soror? That good ol' Delta spirit!

Upon learning that I hailed from Detroit, the gentleman that had accompanied the ladies from Atlanta rushed to tell me that he had once lived in Detroit and that he too was an attorney. Well that bit of information got the ball rolling between us. I immediately inquired, "You must have known my husband, he practiced law in Detroit for over forty years. "What is your husband's name?" I couldn't wait to say your name "Fred Persons." He offered only a vague recollection upon hearing your name. He became my link or my personal tour guide for the remainder of the evening. Every time a member of Dr. Jones family entered the room or approached our table he pointed them out and cordially introduced them to me. It all seemed so surreal. I just couldn't believe I was with his family. In addition to Leslie, I was introduced to Billy, Dr. Jones son, and Jennifer, another one of his daughters. All of his children were just as warm and gracious and good looking as Leslie. For the rest of the evening I was referenced as "Gwen from Detroit." The evening was now underway, the program opened with the procession of the dais guests. As the guests entered the room and took their respected seat on the dais, my personal tour guide pointed out their relationship to Dr. Jones. Among those who were singled out for my attention were his brother Attorney Clayton Jones from Kentucky, his sister, Sylvia and her daughter, Crystal, also from Atlanta and another brother, Rev. Henry Wise Jones, also from Atlanta. I'm not sure why, but my guide for the evening parenthetically mentioned that the Rev. Henry Jones was single. I quickly referred to the mental notes I had made from my

Philadelphian connection crash course on last week. All of these names sounded so utterly familiar to me. After Dr. Jones entered the room it was clear that there would probably not be a chance for me to shake his hand this evening. Also clear to me was the beautiful drop dead gorgeous individual who preceded him on to the dais. Also clear to me was the conspicuous silence as to her identity by the introducer of the dais guests or by my personal tour guide. Who was that drop dead for gorgeous individual? My ears were on the listen out. Somebody has to reveal her identity. Not a mumbling word was said regarding her identity.

We had made it one third of the way through the programme, "DINNER IS SERVED", and now it was time for the intermission, an opportunity to mingle, to get up and move about before dinner. I took advantage of this opportunity and made my way to the head table. I introduced myself to Sylvia as Gwen from Detroit and gave her Mr. Hoggard's regards. Of course I had to remind her just who Clinton Hoggard was and his connection to the family. She offered a vague recollection of Mr. Hoggard. She then inquired as to the reason I had traveled here from Detroit. I repeated my story again to Sylvia. Sylvia introduced me to her brother seated at her side, Rev. Henry Jones and then turned her attention in the direction of her brother seated in the center of the head table and asked, "Have you had a chance to let my brother know that you are here?" I said, "I had not." Sylvia insisted that I do that before the night was over. Not unlike her niece, such a kind and gracious lady. Once again I was made to feel right at home among strangers in a strange place. (from the Well of Kindness Proverbs 31:26)

As I was making my way back to the table I came face to face with that drop dead gorgeous lady that had been sitting on the dais. She was standing at table #3 talking to Leslie. Also at the table was Dr. Jones's brother, Clayton Jones. My tour guide made the introductions (to Clayton that is.) I hadn't been seated long when I was to learn who the lady was talking to Leslie. She was the mother of Leslie, Billy, Jennifer and Beth. She was the mother of the Jones children.

This was the former Mrs. William Augustus Jones. Admittedly I felt a little foolish, green has never been my best color.

As it was beginning to get late into the evening I began to get concerned about my safety riding from the church back to the hotel all alone. During the intermission I learned that the ladies from Atlanta, my personal tour guide, Clayton Jones and his wife were also staying at the Courtyard Marriott in downtown Brooklyn. Clayton assured me that though his car was full he would see to it that one of the church members would see to me getting back to the hotel safely. We were now two thirds of the way through the programme. Courtney made her apologies, thanked me for my inspiring words and said she looked forward to our meeting again. I also thanked her for her kindness and promised her I would see to it that she got a copy of my book. After a solo by his niece Crystal, the banquet speaker was introduced, Rev. Dr. Wyatt Tee Walker, from New York, New York. After his almost sermonic message, the moment had finally arrived. The man of the hour was standing at the podium. It was time to hear from the honoree himself, Dr. William Augustus Jones. My eyes became transfixed on this tower of a man. I hung on to every word. My enthusiasm was unharnessed with every word from his mouth and that was apparent to everyone around me. At one point someone even turned to see just where all of the unbridled enthusiasm was coming Romans I could not help but wonder, does he recognize me at the table with his family? Would he even remember me from last March when he was in Detroit? Would he recall our telephone conversation? He had my undivided attention. When the banquet ended somewhere around 1:00 a.m. Clayton introduced me to the church member who would be driving me back to the hotel.

Before saying good night, Leslie asked me if I had had a chance to meet or to speak to her father? "Not tonight" I said to

Leslie, but I reminded her that I have had the pleasure of making her father's acquaintance each time he comes to Detroit. I never expected what came next. Never in my wildest dreams would I have imagined being taken by the hand of Dr. Jones daughter and being led to her father on the dais. She stood behind her father, pecking him on his back, and uttering these words to get his attention, "Daddy, daddy, Gwen from Detroit is here."

If that were not enough, I found myself standing right next to Leslie's mother. ' "I extended a feeble smile accompanied by these words, "You have a very lovely family." This was the first time all evening that I felt like a stranger in a strange place. I felt completely out of place. I stood almost helpless and defenseless behind that imposing figure while the chant repeated, "Daddy, daddy, Gwen from Detroit is here." Why did Leslie feel the compulsion to do this? (from the Well of Strength Isaiah 35:3) All evening I sat out there and wondered if Dr. Jones knew or recognized me in the audience. When he did finally turn around he shook my hand. I managed to say some kind words about the evening. Perci, I had no doubt in my mind, Dr. Jones did not have a clue as to who I was! I felt so awkward at that moment. I rushed back to table #3 where I sat for what seemed like an eternity and waited for my driver to come collect me and take me back to the hotel.

The drive back to the hotel unfolded yet another mystery. Seated in the van along with the driver were three ladies. One sat in front with the driver, his wife, the second lady in the van sat in the middle section with me, and in the back seat sat the third lady. Only minutes into the drive, they each made their separate introductions. Now it was my turn, "My name is Gwen, I'm from Detroit." As fate would have it, the lady in the front seat turned all the way around and queried, "Gwen Persons?" You could have purchased me for a penny. "I'm Edith Carson, I mailed you your ticket and enclosed the note." I needed no reminding, I will never forget that name. What a twist of fate, now how did that happen? Out of all of those hundreds and hundreds of people, would you believe I actually met Audrey Gore and Edith Carson? "God does move in mysterious ways, His wonders to perform!! (from the Well of Kindness Psalm 63:3) Saturday was uneventful. If I had been brave enough I should have caught a taxi and gone to Manhattan. After all this was an historic weekend; it was the first anniversary of ground zero. I ate lunch in the hotel and then took a walk in downtown Brooklyn. That was somewhat of a complete disappointment but it still beats what we have to offer in downtown Detroit! When I returned to the hotel I ran into my personal tour guide from Friday night along with Clayton Jones. They invited me to join them in the lounge. They said that the ladies had looked for me to join them for breakfast. They were going to invite me to spend the day with them in Atlantic City. I was sorry I had missed them; although the gambling didn't excite me I'm sure the trip would have made for an eventful afternoon. I again thanked them for all of their hospitality on Friday evening and headed up to my room to prepare for Sunday services.

When I woke up Sunday morning I had resolved that I would not try and attend the second service. I will leave church after the 8:00 a.m. service and come back to the hotel and pack up my things for my return trip back to Detroit.

The weather had taken a turn for the worse. It was a cold and rainy morning. After I finished dressing, I went down to the lobby and called for a taxi to take me to the church. I was among the first of the early morning worshippers to arrive. When I walked into the sanctuary I felt it again. Is this what is meant by deja vu? Although my physical body had never been here, my spirit was anything but a stranger in this place. Everything seemed so utterly familiar to me. There it was Perci, right before my very eyes I beheld that tall imposing lectern that housed that giant of a preacher, who we had grown to love from the Bethany Baptist Church in Brooklyn, New York.

One of the ladies from Friday night before entered the sanctuary and recognized me sitting all alone. She invited me to join her on the other side of the church. The seating could not have been more perfect. I found myself sitting right behind where Dr. Jones' family would sit once they arrived to service. The church was now filled with the parishioners. It seemed so surreal, faces that we have worshipped with every Sunday evening over all those years. I even had the opportunity to meet the face behind those most familiar words *"Welcome to the Bethany Hour. We come to you under the auspices of grace from Brooklyn, New York........".* I know it is beginning to sound redundant, but I was made to ask myself again, "Was it a coincidence or was it divine intervention?

When the announcements were read and the visitors were introduced I stood when my name was called. It was during this time the visitors were invited to go up and shake the preachers hands. I shook the hands of both Dr. Jones and speaker for the hour, his brother, Rev. Henry Jones from Atlanta, GA. Much more composed than I was Friday night, I told Dr. Jones that this was truly a blessing for me to be at Bethany Baptist Church. Dr. Jones responded with these words "No, it is a blessing for us to have you with us." As I took my seat the choir rose to sing one of our favorite hymns, 'Blessed Assurance'. Oh how I wished you could have been there by my side. Throughout the service I wondered if the cameraman had captured me on camera. I could not wait to get back here to order that tape. As much as I enjoyed the morning message, I was disappointed that I did not have the opportunity to hear Dr. Jones preach. When the service was over I made a promise to myself. One day I will return so that I can hear Dr. Jones preach from his own pulpit.

As I was leaving the sanctuary, I ran into Rev. Peyton. I introduced myself to him, I told him I was from Detroit and that we have tuned into 'The Bethany Hour' for many years. I also told Rev. Peyton how much I enjoyed hearing him pray and that over the years I have collected quite an extensive tape library of Dr. Jones sermons. I admitted to him that I have borrowed many of his prayers for private use. He was indeed impressed to hear such a testimony from a total stranger. He invited me to join his Sunday School class. I accepted the invite.

Rev. Peyton introduced me to his class and shared my testimony with them. He told them how much it meant to hear such a testimony from a total stranger. The members of the Sunday school class were very hospitable. They involved me in the morning lesson as one of the members. One again this weekend I was made to feel like anything but a stranger. (from the Well of Love, Hebrews 13:8)

After Sunday school I called for a taxi cab and waited outside for it to arrive. When I walked outside I ran into the two ladies from Atlanta. I had seen them in church but had not been close enough to speak. The ladies were waiting for one of Dr. Jones' nephews to take them back to the hotel so that they could start to prepare for their return trip to Atlanta. They said they had looked for me at breakfast yesterday morning and had wanted to invite me to go with them to Atlantic City. They offered me a ride back to the hotel. I accepted.

Dr. Jones' nephew had one of those infectious and engaging personalities, the kind that does not meet strangers (quite like yours Perci). He had me in stitches the entire drive back to the hotel. Boy, did he have some stories to tell! Whatever he does in life I'm sure he will go far! Back at the hotel, I packed up my things and called the driver who had brought me here on Friday.

As I started off saying to you Perci, "Not even in my wildest dreams could I have dreamed a more perfect trip for myself. Oprah is all together correct, as she said in last months issue of O Magazine, "*Whatever our plans, God can dream a bigger dream for us than we could ever dream for ourselves.*" I'm sure this will sound like such a little thing to most folks, but for me it was huge. I am so proud of myself. Perci, I finally made my pilgrimage to Mecca. Everything was in divine order! The Holy Spirit was a most gracious host this weekend. Perci, I think I may have a new lease on my life! (from the Well of Joy 29:13)

As I wrote this evening, I could hear you asking me, "Baby, are you working on your book?" "Yes Fred, I am still working on my book and with God's help I will get it done!"

09/16-- The first person I looked for when I got to work this morning was Mr. Hoggard. I spent practically the entire morning telling him and anybody else that cared to listen all about my weekend. As the kids would say "I was geeted." Hoggard queried, "Are you going to be the next Mrs. Jones." Why his comment sounded almost as ridiculous as my sister's did last March, remember when she said to me "He's sending you another one already and I haven't had my first." Forgive me Perci but admittedly I did blush at the remark. Someone said that I looked as though a was glowing. She went as far as to call me 'Stella'. I suppose one could say I got my groove back over the weekend!

Percibol, this is what I said to the social worker today. "My dream is to have my hero meet my shero." As you know Fred I have had their pictures hanging side by side here on my bulletin board for years. Oprah Winfrey is 'my soul sister" and I don't mean ethnicity. I feel that we share a kindred spirit. I am sure that once she has the opportunity to hear Dr. Jones preach, she will love him too! "Her response to me, "How do you expect to make that happen?" "I'm leaving that for the Holy Spirit to work out." Well, Dr. Jones warned me, *"When you operate at this level of faith, it can be a lonely walk."* He was right, she just laughed at me and probably wanted to declare me insane. Instead, she very patronizingly said to me, "You're so cute Gwen". (from the Well of Faith Hebrews 11:1)

When I left work today, I stopped by Millie's. I bought a new hat! A 'mean' black one. I think you would like it on me. I know, Perci. I need a new hat like I need a hole in my head. I brought it home and put it in the back of my closet. I've named it my 'first lady hat'.

09/19-- Today I wrote a thank you note to the Bethany Baptist Church Family. In the letter I lifted up the book of the Epistles to the Hebrews 13: 1-8. I also mailed Leslie and Courtney a copy of <u>God's Got A Word for Delta Women.</u>

09/20-- I learned today that Oprah was in town. I can't believe that I did not know she was scheduled to come to Detroit.

10/03-- Today is the first year anniversary of Mama's home going. Sheila phoned first thing this morning to recognize the significance of the day. I had planned to go to the cemetery when I left work. I didn't. I came straight home.

This evening I found myself staring into the mirror and staring right back at me was Jackie. I didn't talk to either one of my sisters today. I wonder if they talked to each other?

As you know there have been many 'first' for me this year and they each have been difficult. Although Fall has always been my favorite time of the year, this Fall is already proving to be yet another difficult 'first'.

When I hear the sounds of football I'm made to remember those lazy Fall Saturday afternoons; you spending the day in your big chair watching football, waiting for me to return from an afternoon of shopping, sorority meeting or some other Delta activity. I'd be anxiously looking forward to rushing back home, knowing you were there waiting for me so that we could spend the remainder of our weekend together. Another one of those little things that brought us each so much joy. How I miss you Fred! My life is forever changed.

10/05-- It is so hard to realize that in less than six weeks you would have been gone one year. Fred, there have been so many times over this past year that I have felt that I've died without dying.

I seem to be crawling back into my cocoon, if indeed I ever came out of it. I felt so rejuvenated when I returned from New York.

I thought my trip to New York would have been my debut back into life. I hear you Fred "Hang in there Gwen and keep the faith."

I missed the first and the second Sunday at church this month. Did I tell you that I have found two TV preachers? I look forward to watching them on Sunday evening. Dr. Charles Stanley and Joel Osteen. I really enjoy their messages. Of course no one can ever replace William Augustus Jones.

10/10-- Someone called here today and asked for you! They still do not know

10/19-- A year ago today you sat with your pretty Juanita in our living room. The two of you shared a moment. She often reminds me of that conversation. "Gwen, Fred was ready to go, he was only concerned about you. He wanted to be sure that you were taking care of yourself?" I promise you I will make an appointment to see a doctor soon!

10/19-- Happy Sweetest Day Perci!

10/27-- I went to Tabernacle today, to hear one of the prospective candidates. While there, Clara gave me some very disappointing news. Dr. Jones was in town all of last week. He preached Monday through Thursday at Corinthian Baptist Church, in Hamtramack. I can hardly believe he was here for nearly an entire week! Soror Charlene Mitchell has always been my Corinthian connection to Dr. Jones. She didn't even call to tell me! I so looked forward to having that dinner with him the next time he came to town, you know the one you never got to have with him? Did I tell you that when I returned from New York, I put his picture in a frame and placed it on the dining room buffet. His picture is sitting there as though it belongs there? What do you make of that? Still dreaming big I suppose? Or should I ask my doctor?

Last month Oprah was in town and this month Dr. Jones. I missed seeing my 'shero' and my hero!

10/30-- I went to the dermatologist today. A first step in taking care of myself.

11/05-- M&M's movie will debut in Detroit this week. I thought, gee, if they can make a movie about his life, someone ought to be able to make a movie about your life. The lawyer famous for his white shirt and white tie and the couple's inspiring May/December marriage. It even has potential for a weekly sitcom, don't you think? Lord knows there is currently nothing of relevance on TV with substance about African-Americans. There is nothing on T.V period but a bunch of mindless reality shows.

I've done most of the work for Hollywood. I've already selected the actors and actresses for the movie. Hally Barry will play me. I heard her say she wants to look for positive African-American roles in the future. She has also admitted that she has never known true love in her life. Well how positive can you get, than a true love story like ours? I also thought about Whitney Houston to play me, I feel so sorry for her. I am sure she has never known real love either. Like so many sisters only that caustic, toxic, 'can't do without him', 'don't know no better' kind of love. I had better get back in the gym pronto if I expect either one of them to be cast in the role of Mrs. Fred K. Persons, Esq. Now to play the role of the preacher is none other than James Earl Jones. Who will we get for the starring role? Who can we cast in the role of the lawyer that everyone loves? Hmmm...now there's a catchy title 'Everyone loves Fred'. On second thought that one has already be taken by Raymond. How would you feel about Glen Turman, Samuel L. Jackson or Kim? Something about them reminds me of you? Could it be their 'cabbage patch' heads? The movie would open with Celine Dion's, 'Because You Loved Me'. It will end with Mariah Carie's, 'Hero.' The theme song embedded throughout the movie will be by none other than Detroit's own Anita Baker 'Giving you the Best that I've Got. Now ain't that dreaming big?

I hear you girlfriend *"Dream big, dream very big, work hard-work very hard. And after you've done all you can, you stand, wait, and fully surrender."* I hear you as well Dr. Jones *"Those who are on the faith frequency see God doing the 'big thing' before the earthly manifestation occurs. Call it what you please, it all boils down to seeing it before it gets here. Faith recognizes hidden reality in route to actuality."*

11/06-- Today I shared my 'big dream' with the social worker. When I told her about my plans for the movie and the sitcom, I added this comment, "I had better go on a diet, I don't want them to cast Queen Latifa to play the role of me." She laughed hysterically and said to me in her signature style "Gwen you are so funny." I'm sure today she was ready in that instant to have me declared insane! We'll see who laughs last!
I think this will be the last dream I share with her!

11/09-- I just got in from the Harmonaires 25th Anniversary Concert. To coin one of your favorite sayings, "It was out of sight." They sang to the glory of God. I'm certain that you were among the angels looking down over the balcony of Heaven with envy. Like fine wine, Sylvia and 'your choir' get better as the years go by. Although the Huggins were unable to be there, Rev. Huggins would have called it 'delicious'. I purchased a full page ad in their 25th Anniversary souvenir booklet (with our picture) I'm certain you would have been proud. The Harmonaires also placed a special dedication to you in the booklet. A beautiful tribute for a beautiful legacy.

Janice Young moved into the Millender last March. She rode with me to the concert tonight so I was not out alone; I'm sure that pleases you. Of course Rev. Martin (Lila) was there and your pretty Juanita. As always, we had a hallelujah good time tonight! You will be forever loved and missed by many!

11/10-- Good morning Perci, last night I had two more 'big dreams' for my book. The first is a play if you will? Here is how it plays out. Next year for their annual concert, Sylvia will write 12 vignettes depicting one woman torn by domestic disaster. After each scene the woman makes her way to the Well. Each time she visits the Well, the choir will sing one of the songs from my book, one that most appropriately speaks to the situation the woman brings to the well. I've given title to the play or vignettes, 'A Woman, A Well, Some Water'. The songs will be recorded that evening, the name of the CD, 'Songs from Fresh Water from Old Wells.' Once the book is published, the CD will then be marketed along with the book, but sold separately. The Harmonaires will hold all rights to the CD, all of the profits from the CD will go to your choir. What do you think Perci? Ain't God good? If folks didn't know how much you loved that choir before, there will be no 'doot aboot it' after this miracle unfolds. (from the Well of Faith 11 Corinthians 5:7) As I get closer to completion, I'll share my vision with Sylvia.

Now for the ultimate dream. To honor your memory and legacy, I would love to be able to set up a Fred K. Persons scholarship fund at Morehouse College for seniors wishing to pursue a career in law. Once I sell the copyrights to the book I will use the profits for the scholarship fund. How does that one grab you Perci?

11/13-- My mind has stayed on you all day. I came home and got on the computer. I lost or misplaced both my keys and my money today. This has been one of those, I think I'm losing it days. Do you recall the last time that I misplaced some money?

Before retiring for the evening I had found both my keys and my money. I thanked the Holy Spirit for showing and rescuing me again! I'm hanging in there Perci!

11/15-- My mind still returns to the events of last November 17. If only I had not left the house that day. Would you still be here with me? Could I have gotten E M S here any faster? Would it have made a difference? I thought I had worked through all of this months ago.

I was up all night talking to God. I stayed home from work today. I walked over to the florist this afternoon and ordered the flowers for the altar on Sunday. I ran into the young lady from the shoe shop. She told me that she thinks about you often. Just the mention of you and I began to cry.

When I came home I went straight to my computer. I began reading over chapter three 'from Health to Sickness'. I was at the part where we were beginning your radiation treatment. You had your first appointment with Dr. Chuba on November 17, 1999 at 2:00pm. to prepare your body for the simulation process. The date never registered before today. Exactly two years later on that date and time you made your transition! He does reveal things to us in His own time!(A Song of Praise from the Well of Understanding)

11/16-- The eve before the anniversary of your death. Sheila sent me flowers. She is so thoughtful, so giving, such a loving and faithful friend. Earlier this week I called Sheila, Jennifer and Juanita and invited them to join me at church tomorrow. I also phoned Rev Huggins, Lila and Barbara and asked if they would plan on going to the cemetery with me after church tomorrow.

I decided to come today alone. This was my first visit since Mama's headstone had been laid. The spot where all three of your bodies had been laid to rest were now clearly marked. The three people who I loved and who loved me most in this world, my husband, my mother and my grandmother. I didn't stay out there too long this afternoon. I knelt, said a prayer and left you with these words "I'll be back tomorrow" (from the Well of Strength Zechariah10:12)

11/17--- Good Morning Perci, Sunday, November 17, one year ago today the lights went out in my life and they are still out. When I got to church the flowers had been placed on the altar. Jennifer telephoned last night to say she will not be able to attend. But Sheila and Juanita were both there. I kept expecting and hoping to see Rev. Huggins and Lila: neither was there this morning. I'm sure they each had commitments that prevented them from coming.

During the service, I did something that I had witnessed you do so often over the years. I interrupted the service and begged Rev. Bowman's permission to allow me to say a few words on your behalf. I rose to my feet and began my remarks with these words "Rev. Bowman, may I have a word," I think that is the way you would have done it? I went to the front of the church and spoke these words to the congregation. I thanked the members who have prayed with me and who have prayed for me over this past year. I also had Sheila and Juanita to stand so that I could publicly thank them for their love and unwavering support. Fred, the two of them have been here for me every step of the way. With them, there has been no shadow of turning. I know how much you loved both of them, and their love for you. I then thanked those who responded to my request for memories of my beloved. I told the congregation that it would take many years before the invisible essence of your spirit ceases to exist not only in this church, but throughout this city. I also warned them that with the help of the Holy Spirit one day you will be celebrated throughout this nation. Of course I was referring to my book and all of the other dreams I have for it.

I have no doubt the Holy Spirit has already ordained it, once my book is completed the gift you gave to so many will one day be spread throughout this land. And the results will all be 'To the Glory of God'. (from the Well of Truth ST. John 16:13)

Did I mention that Barbara preached this morning and the Harmonaires sang? Carl Tucker sang the lead to "I Bowed on my knees and cried Holy', they dedicated it to you. To quote Harold Huggins again "It was a delicious' service." You were a pillar in this church and your physical presence is sorely missed, but your spirit is ever-present!

After service Barbara and I headed off in separate cars to the cemetery. Just the two of us. The same angel who held my hand and prayed with me on that fateful day one year ago, when God called you home, held my hand and prayed with me today. Barbara stood over your grave and lovingly repeated those same words she so sweetly uttered to you one year ago, "My, precious, precious Attorney Persons. We held hands, Barbara prayed. I laid flowers on your grave. As we turned to walk away, Barbara let go of my hand and suddenly ran back and fell on her knees to your grave. She then rejoined me and we got in our separate cars and drove to Southern Fries for dinner. (from the Well of Love 1 Corinthians 13:13)

When I came home, I called Louise. Then I listened to this message for the last time. "Hello Gwen, this is Esther, I'm so sorry, I just heard the news, Jean Reese called and if there is anything I can do please let me know. I will try calling back later this evening. I really loved Fred and he is going to be missed."

I have kept and listened to this message for an entire year. Tonite I erased it. I placed your picture next to my pillow and crawled into bed.

Fred we are soul mates and you will live in me until that day we will be reunited throughout all eternity. I will forever 'love' and 'cherish' your precious memory. I know you will keep your promise and you will be waiting for me when I arrive. In the meantime as I make my journey onward, I will keep a Song of Praise from the Well of Patience and Proverbs 3:5-6 upon the tablet of my heart!

The Journey of A Thousand Miles Begins with the
FIRST STEPS

This Has Been
My
First Year's Journey

"To love and to cherish"
FOREVER YOURS, YOUR LOVING WIFE!

Because The Angels Came

No more grief or sorrow
no more suffering or pain,
now there is everlasting peace
because the angels came.

Only God knows what is best
and He gently holds my hand
guiding me to a better place
because the angels came

When the sun rises tomorrow
and I answer not my name,
please don't cry. rejoice with me
because the angels came.

I now can rest in peace
as I never could before.
I answered the gentle knock
of the angels at my door.

So please don't mourn for me
as new wings I now claim.
 I can take my flight to heaven
because the angels came

by Hannah McCarty

"To love and to cherish"

FOREVER YOURS, YOUR LOVING HUSBAND!

306 Gwendolyn D. Persons

Part Six

Precious Memories

When someone you love becomes a memory
The memory becomes a treasure

EARTH'S LAST PICTURE IS PAINTED
RUDYARD KIPLING

WHEN EARTH'S LAST PICTURE IS PAINTED, AND
THE TUBES ARE TWISTED AND DRIED,
WHEN THE OLDEST COLORS HAVE FADED, AND
THE YOUNGEST CRITIC HAS DIED,
WE SHALL REST, AND FAITH, WE SHALL NEED
IT-LIE DOWN FOR AN EON OR TWO,
TILL THE MASTER OF ALL GOOD WORKMEN
SHALL SET US TO WORK ANEW!
AND THOSE THAT WERE GOOD SHALL BE
HAPPY; THEY SHALL SIT IN A GOLDEN CHAIR;
THEY SHALL SPLASH AT A TEN LEAGUE
CANVAS WITH BRUSHES OF COMET'S HAIR
THEY SHALL FIND REAL SAINTS TO DRAW
FROM---MAGDALENE, PETER AND PAUL;
THEY SHALL WORK FOR AN AGE AT A SITTING
AND NEVER BE TIRED AT ALL!
AND ONLY THE MASTER SHALL PRAISE US,
AND ONLY THE MASTER SHALL BLAME;
AND NO ONE SHALL WORK FOR MONEY, AND
NO ONE SHALL WORK FOR FAME.
BUT EACH FOR THE JOY OF THE WORKING,
AND EACH IN HIS SEPARATE STAR, SHALL
DRAW THE THING AS HE SEES IT FOR THE
GOD OF THINGS AS THEY ARE!

310 Gwendolyn D. Persons

Precious Memories

written January 4, 2002

Dear <u>Friends and Loved Ones of my Dear, Dear Husband Fred K. Persons</u>

On Saturday, November 17, 2001, Attorney Fred K. Persons was summoned by God to his eternal rest. Without time to prepare or to brace myself for this eventual life expectancy (which we each are sure to encounter) the light went out of my life. Fred was ushered from this earthly tabernacle to live with God.

While my heart is still shattered from the brokenness, and his physical absence is ever present. I am able to find solace and comfort in my museum of loving memories for my dear, dear, devoted and loving husband. Just as I relive my special memories daily, I am sure that each of you own, cherish and hold near your special memories of Fred as well.

As a devout follower of the <u>Oprah Winfrey Show</u>, a very poignant and special message was revealed on her December 24, 2001 broadcast. While unable to give proper credit to the guest, the following questions have grabbed hold of my soul and beg to be responded to on behalf of Fred's spirit.

Do we die the way we lived? At the moment of our death, we ask ourselves the following: Was I loved? and Did I love well?

I wish to stress responded to: and not answered. We know the answers, Fred Persons did indeed model his life after the Master's teachings. Fred walked the walk and talked the talk.

Fred loved people, he loved to be around people. People loved being around Fred. Folks, that is exactly the way Fred died.

Fred made his transition from earth to glory in the lobby of the Millender Center. He did not suffer, Fred was surrounded by people who loved him, people who took good care of my sweetheart. Fred died in the bosom and loving comfort and care of others.

Are you a witness? Do you have a personal testimony that speaks to his love? Did he share his love for life, his love for his wife with you? Won't you assist me in compiling "A Celebrated Life," the gift of love that Fred K. Persons gave to us all.

Please let me hear from you.

Forward your special memories to gdpersons@aol.com or return to me at 555 Brush #3206, Detroit, Michigan. 48226.

Thanking you in advance. **To God Be All The Glory!!**

GOD LOVES YOU AND SO DO I!!
 Fred's Loving Wife
Mrs. Fred K. Persons, Esq.

Was I Loved?

"If love could have saved you,
you would have lived forever."

Fred K. Persons Esquire
Our Family Testimonial

Fred was bestowed with a fitting surname for a man who was always interested in the "person". Perhaps we could refer to Fred as: A Man for all Persons

Fred was always genuinely interested in the people he met. He was not only interested in who you were, but what you were doing, how your families were doing, what was new in your world and things of that nature.

From the time we first met Fred until thirty years hence, our family always found Fred to be endearing, caring, and without ill words concerning anything or anybody.

In his business, as perhaps with every business, it is easy for an individual to become dour, jaded, downcast, disillusioned or the like.

Even in our personal lives it is often difficult to masquerade our disappointments, our frustrations, or our true emotions of the day.

Yet, in Fred we always found warmth, a pleasant smile, a gleam of life in his eye, and a little dance in his step before that welcoming hug he always gave.

Whether you know Fred a lot or only knew him a little, he had that ability to always make you feel like a lost friend, suddenly found again.

We will miss him, surely but our loss is the Good Lord's gain. Fred will live in our minds and hearts forever, He achieved his destiny for as Edward Markham once said:

> "There is a destiny that makes us brothers,
> none goes this way alone, All that we send
> into the lives of others comes back into our own."

From our family to yours, with love and peace in the Lord. .
Joe and Hattie Muic
Ray and Geri Achilli & Family
Joe and Delphine Borors and Family
Barbara and Jack Zelazny & Family

Dear Gwennie,
I can't imagine how you must feel without Fred. You certainly had a beautiful marriage full of love and attention. Fred loved you and everyone knew it!
Cherish your sweet memories; they will in time dry the tears you are shedding.
Please know that I share in your sorrow because I loved Fred and I love you.
Sisterly,
Iris (Faye)

Dear Mrs. Persons,
We loved him, but God loved him best!
Doe

Dear Gwen,

I have known Fred for more years than I can recall. In any event, at least since March 12, 1959, around 43 years. That was my beginning at St. Stephen A.M.E. Church Detroit, Michigan. I was hired as an assistant to the Pastor of St. Stephen. The Pastor at that time was the great Dr. Charles S. Spivey. It was there, St. Stephen where I first met Fred. I was young, and a student fresh out of Seminary and did not know anything about the operation of a church, nor a single person in St. Stephen, and I was badly in need of an understanding, reassuring, friendly face, and/or someone to help me adjust to my career as a member of the cloth. Attorney Persons turned out to be among the first persons in that church to make me feel a sense of well being.

I did not know him at that time as I came to know him in later years.

Six years later, I was assigned to pastor my first charge at St. Matthew A.M.E. Church Detroit. I did not know or ever dream that 17 years later I would return to St. Stephen as Pastor of that great congregation. Among those who spoke to Bishop Hubert Nelson Robinson about me as their choice to become the Pastor of St. Stephen was Attorney Fred Persons. I don't know why, but upon learning of my assignment to Pastor St. Stephen the first member of the church I called was Fred. I called Fred and told him how happy and scared I was. In his own way, again, he was that reassuring spirit that made it possible for me to pastor that church for 17 years and ten months, before being assigned to the office of Presiding Elder.

Attorney Fred and Gwen Persons turned out to be very close friends of Martha, my wife, and me. We stood up with Gwen and Fred at their wedding. We have spent times together on many occasions at Fred's special dining spot, Joe Muer. Thanksgving dinner at our home, dinner at their home.

In the last years and months of Fred's life, as it turned out to be. Fred and I had many intimate and personal exchanges of significant importance, filled with mutual healing. Fred loved the church, he loved the Lord, he loved, adored, and appreciated Gwen with all his heart, soul, mind and strength. Fred loved life and life loved Fred. Fred was life and life was Fred.

Fred, God bless your new employ,
The battle is fought, the victory is won
Rest in your Master's Joy

Harold C. Huggins
Brother, Friend, Pastor of
Fred. K., Persons

Dear Mrs. Persons,
Your husband was a special man. He always had a kind word and a big smile for everyone. He will be missed by many. Our thoughts and prayers are with you.

Marc & Shuzuka Regard

Dear Gwen
We were saddened to hear about your dear husband, Fred. We will always remember Fred, not only as a true friend, but as a wonderful member of our extended family and we have many memories that we will cherish.

You have certainly shown a lot of strength with the loving care, concern support during Fred's illness.

Please know you have our deepest sympathy and prayers.

We are as close as a telephone call if you need us.

With love,
Thelma and Magellan

Hi,
There's only one Fred in my life. The one who I used to holler at! "Fred, mama wants you! The one Fred whom I called many times "Come to get me!" Remember? I hurt my knee the year was '31 (smile), I didn't weigh much then, but you carried me from bed to chair to the front porch and back again for four months! 'til school opened again and I could walk on my own again! "I'll

never forget the times I washed a special shirt for you or ironed it for you! And the many times I thought I was earning a nickel and didn't get it (sad face)!

You never came to supper on time! but I kept a plate in the 'warmer 'for you! And you were 'real mean' to me when you wouldn't let me follow you everywhere! ARR- those were the times when I was having the time of my life!

Does all of this raving tell you something! I love you! Talk to me now! I'm still your little sister! Although 150 lbs and much older! ha ha!! You can't pull the wool over my eyes, 'NOW'.
My thoughts and prayers are with you right now as I write- I love you; I hope I don't have to say it to have you know it!

You are special to me. There is never a time when God's mercy and love does not attend you. He is ever present. This is a reminder for I know you know also!

He wills wholeness for each of us and the knowledge that He is able to take care of everything' 'He's all powerful!"

Trust Him... He can and will direct the "medical persons to do and perform His wishes. Believe Him... He has said in His word " I will not forsake you! I will be with you!"

Call me when you have an appropriate moment! I Love You!
Your Sis,
Louise

P.S. Did I mention that God loves you and He's thinking about you too!! And He's 'All Ears' too!!
(sent 10-01-99)

Gwen,
Memories of Fred's Love. His many gifts of love. There are so many precious memories of my beloved Fred that I could spend all day sharing with you, but the most precious ones are his on going encouragement to me to pursue the call of God on my life and the gift of song that God gave to me.

318 Gwendolyn D. Persons

Each time that I preached, Fred would never let me leave his presence when he did not tell me that God has used me on that occasion to speak a Word that came from God. He would always say, "Girl, you keep preaching the Gospel of Jesus and don't let nothing turn you around", and with that way of saying "Hallelujah", that only he could do, he would 'slap the air', and shake his head and say, "God is good."

When I would hear Fred say "Yea," in the response to the Word being preached, I would know that a witness was in the room. His encouragement all of my life that I was beautiful, meant so much to me, especially during the hard times of my life after my divorce. He would share that sometimes life seems unfair, but that if I just HELD ON",

I would be alright and he was right.

I was so blessed to be included in the special group called 'Fred's special ladies', and to share in the celebrations of his life with Gwen, the love of his life. Fred knew how a woman needed to know she was special. He always knew the right words to say and how to say them to women without ever crossing the line that separates gentleman and cads!

Oh, Lord, he set the standard for how a man, a real man, should treat a woman. He treated us all as if he were our 'knight-in-shining -armor', but Gwen was blessed among us all for she would go home with him. We all loved it and the two of them gave us such joy to see love in action.

Finally, Fred's smile and his joy of living is something that I will carry with me the rest of my life. Never will I forget his dapper style and classic dress. Oh did he know how to dress, but unlike so many others, the clothes did not make the man, the man made the clothes look good. The 'white' on 'white' shirt and tie, the suit fitting just so, and the hat tilted just right. Then, enter the man, Fred and the walk that he had full of style ad grace, like a Spanish dancer has that nobody could duplicate. No effort or conscious pretense, just Fred K. Persons, knowing who he was and 'whose 'he was. What a man, what a mighty good man. Oh

thank you Lord for Fred K. in my life. (thank you Gwen for being you and remember you were loved as so few of us have been or ever will be. Let it be your comfort my dear friend and hold on to your precious memories, they will get you through. I love you and thank you for loving Fred)
Love you, my precious
Barbara A. Woodson

Dear Gwen,
We were saddened to hear of Fred's passing; our continued prayers are with you. Knowing Fred for over 50 years we knew he never experienced love and happiness until you became a part of his life. His love for you was so deep and you were the smile on his face and the sparkle in his eyes.
Thank you for making that possible for a great guy.
Cherish your time with him. I know he will always be watching over you. God Bless.
Deepest Sympathy and Love
Samual & Joy Turner

Dear Gwen,
I am deeply sorry to hear of the loss of your husband Fred. He was such a delight to talk to and was very funny. I'll keep you in my prayers and pray that God will continue to give you the strength to get through the coming days.
Love & God Bless
Mary Grace Wilbert
Mrs. Persons,

We really didn't know your husband. My daughter and I spoke to him daily. He was a special person.
Stay Strong, Liz

Dear Gwen
Needless to say, I am so sorry about Fred's passing. I'm sure that you are still in a state of shock and disbelief. It always felt like he was such a larger than life person, who will be missed by many. There was much love between you and I hope that those memories and your strong faith will help to sustain you. Take good care and be well,
 Love,
Your Cousin,
Cheryl

I hope you get this Gwen. As I have shared with you I loved him too. I loved him for always being a smiling face to see. I loved him for the way he ALWAYS continued to encourage me with the things I was trying to do. I loved him wearing his spats during January. I loved his zest and enthusiasm for life, people and the things he believed in. I loved the way he would say "Please pardon me, but I have to say this.".. I loved being considered one for his girls (Fred's Harem of Honeys) But most of all I loved the way he said years ago, ..."Get up Gwen, everyone knows we are dating and that I love you..." without hesitation. To ask was he loved? That is not the question. The question is can I ask that he knew I loved him? The answer is yes. You KEEP ON Keeping on because that is what he expects you to do and I know you won't let him down!
Love
Sylvia Hollifield

Fred was a wonderful person to have known. I'm sure everyone that knew him would agree. It was that winning smile, compliments, and humor I always received from him. I never been in his presence without a smile on his face.

Status and title of a person didn't matter to him. Listening to Gwen, friends and associates, it was like knowing him much more than I really did. I will always remember his saying about his wife, "That's My Baby."

May your memories of Fred always bring a smile upon your face. I believe he would like that.

Your friend,
Shirley Moss

Hi Gwen,
First of all, let me say how wonderful it is of you to remember your beloved husband in this manner. One would have to be blind not to see how devoted you were (and still are) to each other. Though he has gone, your love will continue forever. The following is my tribute to his memory: What can I say about Fred K. Persons? I think all would agree that he was a gentleman's gentleman: suave and debonair, with impeccable taste and a zest for life. You know, the kind of guy people stop and take notice of, the kind of guy who makes everyone feel comfortable and important. The Fred I knew was never negative, he saw the bright side of life and that's the way he lived. Life is filled with trials but Fred met them head on and did not falter. He relied on his strong faith in God and His promises to see him through everything life dealt him. People like Fred do not often cross our paths. I feel honored to have known him and all that he stood for. He will be remembered by many as he lives on in our hearts,

Lorraine Baker

Dearest Gwen,
It was always such a joy to see you and Fred together. You were always beautifully dressed and happily blessed. You were a great team. I thank you for all the love and happiness you gave to him. I knew him for many years. And you made him so happy. He often spoke of it. He would say, "Jan, Gwen is wonderful. And she is not accustomed to all the things I am able to provide for her. I enjoy her and love her so much."

God Bless you Gwen, and in time the sorrow will pass; and only beautiful, happy memories will remain.
Love,
Jan

Dear Mrs. Persons,

The short time I knew Mr. Persons, it was obvious that he was a very special person. I could tell he had a "joy for living". The first time I met him was at Dr. Bright's party. I could see that he was very charming and a special man. I loved the way he greeted me with a smile, kiss on the cheek or hand shake.

I have told you more than once, that I could see why you fell in love with him. If you asked me " was he loved?" I would say "Yes", especially by his wife, Mrs. Persons. I, along with everyone else will always remember Mr. Persons as the 'charming man with the great smile."
Your friend,
Velva Gullatte

Dear 'Auntie Gwen"

My memories of Uncle Fred go way back to my childhood. I can remember in the early years of my life, like age 2 or 3 years old that my mother had tuberculosis and I was sent to live with my Aunt Mae and Uncle Sylvester.

My Aunt Mae's brother was Uncle Fred. Even though I was very young at the time, I remember Uncle Fred constantly coming into the house and playing with me. He always had something funny and kind to say to me. That was when my love for Uncle Fred began. Right there in my high chair on Atkinson Street!

As, the years went by whenever I would see him there was always a kind word, a smile or twinkle in his eye. I never saw his eyes twinkle so much in my life as when he was with my friend, Gwen, who became my 'Aunt Gwen'. His joys in life were at least quadrupled ten thousand fold when she became a part of his life. I could tell he had the highest level of love and respect for her. I was so happy that Gwen and Uncle Fred were going to unite in Holy Matrimony. I had been with them on numerous occasions and was impressed with the love that was shared between them. They both eluded a special magical glow whenever they were together or spoke about the other. I could tell that the way Gwen's eyes twinkled, just like Uncle Fred's, that she was the one for him.

I remember discussing with my cousins, Ronnie and Robert, the special bond that was shared by my friend and our Uncle Fred. I assured them that their's (Fred and Gwen) was a match ordained by God. That it was a relationship that was loving and pure and being around the two of them a special glow or happiness for all those blessed to be around the two of them.

I was pleased at the way Uncle Fred loved Gwen's friends. He was always there with his camera taking pictures of Gwen and her friends. I was so pleased to have been one of 'Fred's girls'. I loved him very much and he will always have a special place in my heart.
Love
Pam

It has been the will of GOD to remove from amongst us Fred K. Persons who has been a valued fighter for a host of social issues.
He richly deserves the esteem and admiration of the community. He stood as a shining example of our American members of society. He was close to the hearts of his associates. He rendered efficient faithful and valuable service.
Myrtle Calliman Moore

Dearest Gwen,
Fred was my special friend. He would always greet me with "Hey boy! I mean Roy," playfully and affectionately.

I remember when our wives went on an ocean cruise. Fred was the last one to leave the airport with a forlorn look of separation from his beloved Gwen. He was also the first to arrive at the airport, impatiently anticipating their return. The reunion was a joyous occasion. Fred would tell me repeatedly about his prowess on the gold course. Unfortunately, I was never able to test his skills because of his illness.

Fred was a devout man. When he became ill his faith never wavered. He was a tower of strength remaining steadfast that he would overcome his illness to the end. A powerful testimony of faith and love for God.

Fred, my special friend
James H. Stephens

Hi Gwen,
I wanted to respond to your note requesting "Am I A Witness to Fred's Love?" Here is one memory forever branded in my heart.
Attorney Fred K. Persons came to my aid back in 1990-1991. My son, Marcel was picked up by the police in the middle of the night in September 1990. He had just celebrated his 17th birthday and was feeling his wild oats and snuck over his girlfriend's house about 1:30 a.m.

In the meantime the police were looking for someone who had held up a man at gunpoint and had taken the man's car. The thief had on a navy blue or black sweatshirt.

Marcel, trying to run back home without me realizing he was gone, was stopped by the state troopers and was taken to jail as a suspect because he was wearing a hooded navy blue sweatshirt.
When I awoke the next morning (Sunday) and found him not home, I prayed to God Marcel was okay, but I wanted to serve (sing) that morning and for 8:00 church service.

In the middle of service, someone came to me and said, "Marcel was in jail and had called the church for me." I rushed home. I prayed again that he would be alright.

After finding out the details, I knew I needed a lawyer. Who did I know? Who could I depend on to keep it on the D.L. (down low)? Attorney Fred Persons!

He did not hesitate to help me and my family get Marcel out of jail, and serve as his lawyer from that moment in September 1990 to when the trial came about in January 1991.

One thing about Marcel, he didn't lie to me. I could get the truth out of him no matter what. I asked him that Sunday at 1300 Beaubien did he do this. He told me emphatically NO!!

He began to cry. I told him don't cry in a place like this. Hold on and be strong...Attorney Persons would have him out very soon. He was out before the day was over. Waiting on the trial to come (the period from (September to January) seemed like a million years, however, knowing Attorney Persons had everything under control was such a relief.

He made me think of Perry Mason or Matlock ...he was so together, so eloquent. He had gathered the evidence (or the lack of evidence) and told me this would be a breeze.

Sho' nuff ..he was a man of his word. Judge Drain was very attentive to Attorney Persons information and the Police Officer's lies. No one picked Marcel out of a Line Up.

He was found not guilty and nothing would be on his record. Your loving hubby shared his love and brilliance with so many. I know you can't help but love him for the rest of your days. I thank God for him and I thank God you had wonderful days and years with such a kind, a blessed man.

I love you Gwen. Continue to find your strength in God.
Marion

Hello Gwen'
"This is Esther, I'm so sorry, I just heard the news, Jean Reese called and if there is anything I can do please let me know. I will try calling back later this evening. I really loved Fred and he is going to be missed."
Esther Bright

Dear Gwen,

What 'A Gift of Love' you were to him, He would let me know daily how much he loved you. As you know he loved me very much also (being his namesake) He shared God's word with me daily, I felt very, very special. I would love to support you any way that I can.

Love, Fred Prime

Dear Gwen

I apologize for taking so long to get this to you. I hope that you will be able to use the thoughts, love and feelings we enjoyed with Fred.

I met Fred in the early 1980's when I joined St. Stephen A.M.E. Church. He welcomed me with a warm smile and made me feel a part of the St. Stephen Church family.

Fred enjoyed life with everything he did. After the Sunday morning service he always stood in the front of the church to welcome and greet the members. He was always impeccably dressed, matching from head to toe. In summer he wore a straw hat, white shirt and white tie which complimented his suit. Fred enjoyed looking good.

As time went by, we, Bettye and Jim, Sam and Henrietta, Ralph and Burnie and Gwen and Fred spent a great deal of time together going to dinner, celebrating birthdays and New Year's Eve. Spending time together was fun for us all. Fred was especially pleased by this because he always wanted the best for Gwen and wanted her to be happy. He often spoke of his love for her and that it made him very happy to see her enjoying her friends.

Fred admired and loved Gwen with all his heart. He always commented about how great she was and how great she looked. He would beam with pride as he showed off the things he bought for her at Christmas or for her birthday. There was nothing too good for Gwen.

Fred was funny, easy to talk to and great to be around. He was a good man who loved the Lord.

I considered Fred to be a very special friend. I'm so glad that I had the opportunity to know him and I do still miss him very much. I smile inside sometimes when I think of him and his humor.

With Much Affection,
Bettye Stephens (5/27/05

Precious Memories from Shirley....
For his love of God, his love of life and the love he shared with others, my memories of Fred Persons are truly special and indeed precious. The foundation of my memories, however, lies not solely in Fred, the individual, but rather most profoundly in the blessed union and loving partnership that was "Gwen and Fred."
I remember Fred best and at his best for the love, the joy and happiness that he gave to his beloved Gwen, and ultimately for the love she gave him in return.

I will confess that at the on-set of their relationship, I was one of those people who had little faith in "May-December" romances. This is a fact and concern that I openly shared with Gwen. She in turn shared with me her happiness and her faith that there was no mistake, no need to be concerned..."We prayed together and God tells me it's right'. I remember saying, "Well, it can't get any better than that." Throughout their thirteen years of marriage no one could ever again doubt that **it was right, and it was beautiful.**

It was right to hear that robust voice on any occasion, at any given moment proclaim, "I love that 'ol piece of chick, Y'all"

It was right that Fred loved not only Gwen but Gwen's friends, especially his "**Delta wives**".

328 Gwendolyn D. Persons

It was right to hear Gwen proclaim, "He has brought joy and purpose to my life"

It was right to hear Gwen say his name with the glee and pride with which only she could say it

It was right to watch them glide as one across the dance floor, Gwen all decked out in one of those fabulously famous Fred 'picked it' outfits. No one could ever doubt his impeccable taste

It was right to share their laughter, the laughter that was heartiest when they were together or when they each spoke of the other.

It was right to share the warmth of their home on the many occasions that they welcomed you through their doors.

It was right to see my friend so happy, enjoying her life, always beaming, always so self-assured, so full of love, caring and giving, her person so enhanced. And it was right that this man called Fred was so much a part of it all. **It was right** and it was my comfort.

And so...as I said in the beginning, my memories of Fred Persons lie not solely in Fred, the individual, but in that blessed union and loving partnership that was "Gwen and Fred".

It was right, and it was beautiful because God said so. It truly doesn't get better than that.

Mr. Fred K. Persons, Esq.
I have such fond memories of Attorney Persons (I never called him Fred because I was so respectful of his stature and his wonderful sense of humility.)

I met Attorney Persons at our church, St. Stephen A.M.E., in 1979, the year my children and I joined the church. I noticed

Attorney Persons because of his high visibility and outstanding leadership. It was obvious that he loved his church and was not embarrassed to express his love through spontaneous testimonies when the Spirit moved him to do so.

Attorney Persons had a way about himself that lifted Spirits and offered hope in difficult situations.

I recall an incident when I chaired a huge event of our church and a question arose about trademark rights when one committee wanted to use some music that had been produced by one of our choirs. In seeking answers to legal questions related to the situation, I reluctantly telephoned Attorney Persons at his home, after business hours, convinced that I was disturbing him from his rest from a hard days work. He addressed me with concern and compassion and assured me that our committee was not violating any legal restrictions in what we were attempting to do.

I remember Attorney Persons for his humor and positive attitude. He will be long remembered for his portrayal in our ' Old Fashioned Pot Luck Supper" where old clothing and covered dishes were the order of the day. Attorney Persons always appeared in an old fashioned gray or black pin stripped suit and white 'spats' to wear over his black alligator shoes, shined to "high heaven'.

Everyone at our church loved Attorney Fred K. Persons and he loved us back! He was always upbeat and happy with a God-centered Spirit!

All rejoiced when he married Sister Gwendolyn Whitaker, another dedicated member of St. Stephen who for years, sat only a few pews behind him, with her Grandmother, my friend, Mrs. Jones.

Attorney Persons' love and dedication for "Gwen" was obvious to the congregation and he 'made no bones' about it!!!

Fondly Submitted,
Brenda L. Rayford

Dear Gwen,

I will attempt to answer your question "was I loved?' I hope I stated it correctly. However, I cannot relate to the Oprah Winfrey Show. To me, the production is just a 'Show', My position is Jesus only and only Jesus.

In memory of Fred, your beloved, he did love people and we will always cherish the photos he made at our get-to-gethers and sorority functions.

Jesus taught men to love their wives and emphasized that the two should become as one. Apostle Paul went on to say that the brethren should love their wives as Christ loved the church. Fred was a follower of the Word, so there should be no doubt in anyone's mind that he loved his wife.

Find comfort in knowing that God so loved us that he sent his only Son that whosoever believes shall have life ever-lasting.
In spite of the void and the present circumstances be encouraged and know that our Savior will make your darkness light and turn your sorrow into joy.

As you continue your walk with Christ, I pray that you will see Him more clearly, love Him more dearly, and follow Him more nearly,

Thank Him for all He has done, for our God is a merciful God. His mercies endureth forever. Exalt His name with the Highest Praises for He is worthy of ALL the praises and the glory.

Blessings in Jesus' name
Soror Loretta

332 Gwendolyn D. Persons

A memory from Gwen

Over the years I coined many nicknames for Fred. 'Baby Cakes', 'Baby Persons', 'Perci', Percibol'! I don't recall just when it happened but somewhere along the way Fred began calling me those same names. But the one he enjoyed calling me the most was "Mrs. Fred Persons", Fred would say, "You're Gwen Persons and don't you ever forget IT!" Fred, I'll never let you out of my heart. You will always be here with me right by my side. I will forever love and cherish my precious, precious memories. We truly did become one.

Did I Love Well?

"If love could have saved you,
you would have lived forever."

Dear Mrs. Persons,

I want to say that I know he loved you dearly. I was in the office most of the time when he would call. He always wanted to know that you made it into work fine and well. He was always worried about your journey to work. I will forever remember Mr. Persons, though I only met him once in person. He greeted kindly at our first and only encounter.

Mr. Persons was truly a man of integrity. I became more acquainted with Mr. Persons through his many calls to Butzel. He would always say "This is her husband."

He would always say he just wanted to make sure you got to work okay since you had left the house.

I hope you hold your memories with you forever. There is a country song called "Should You Go First." It says one thing that I want to forward to you. It says that MEMORIES are the one thing that even death cannot destroy. The Lord gives us these memories to console us. Many times when a loved one dies our first thought is to keep the name out of our mouths and the memories out of our heads. The truth is death is the only thing that we are promised.

P.S. You are right, Mr. Persons was a very nice man. I am glad to have had a chance to meet him before the angels called him home. If there is anything I can do just let me know. I may not have much, but I am abundant in love.

Love,
Dontez

A memory from Gwen

Fred's philosophy on Love,: love is an active verb. Love is something that you do. Fred did it as few men knew how. When describing his love for me, Fred would use these three prepositions, 'For', 'With' and 'To', Fred loved doing things 'for me', 'with me' and to me'.

On our first date, Fred incorporated all three of those prepositions. What he did 'with me' was he took me to the Lansdowne for dinner. After dinner, he took me to his home, I guess I was a bit nervous, I developed indigestion.

Fred gave me a glass of Bromo Seltzer to relieve my discomfort; that is what he did 'for me'.

I was able to relax and enjoy the rest of the evening with him. I learned that evening that Fred Persons loved to dance. We danced all evening. When it was time to take me home. I said to Fred, "This has been one of the best evenings in my life, but I don't think I fit into your world." Fred held out his arms and said to me, "Step into here" I complied, he then said to me, "You fit in here don't you?" That was what Fred did 'to me'.

That was the start of the rest of my life.. and as the saying goes, "The rest is history." What a love, what a love, what a mighty, mighty love!!!

Memories

Memories are your link to me
Memories will always be
Times of me will make you smile
At times you may even cry awhile
But through it all, your memories, you'll see
Your memories will be your link to me
I'm gone but just a moment away
God gave you a memory and you'll be okay
Because as I look down from above at you
I know your memories will see you through
God you He will never forsake
Your memory of me even death can't take
Because your memories are your link to me
Your memories will always be

Written by
Dontez Williams

A memory from Gwen.....

In 1990 I quit smoking and I joined Weight Watchers. As a crutch, I started chewing Carefree sugarless gum (the yellow pack) I chewed it constantly. When Fred caught on to my dependency and could see that it was working for me he kept me supplied with my 'fix'. I recall on more than one occasion walking into the apartment only to find individual packs lined up making a pathway into our bedroom. ending on top of the bed. At the end of the path, would be more gum, boxes and boxes of unopened gum. Fred always did things for me in a BIG WAY!!!

Dear Gwen,

It was wonderful receiving the message from you.

What a beautiful idea to create "A Gift of Love"

My special memories of Fred were all the times I watched him watch you. He would just look at you (his baby) with adoration and respect. That look is a look we don't often see between couples. You could just tell that the two of you were very much in love.

I can truly understand how you must feel at this time. When my husband died, I felt a hole in my very soul. My life has changed drastically. However, believe me when I say the pain will go away.

So, when I say to you my most precious memory of Fred was the demonstration of his love for you-that is a memory that will be with me forever.

May you continue to find comfort in your cherished and blessed memories. Continue to hold on to God's unchanging hand. Continue to believe in Him.

With love, Paulette

MY MEMORIES OF FRED PERSONS

My memories of Fred were brief and pleasant. What I remember most about Fred was the smile he put on his wife's face. The few times we met, he always greeted me with a smile and a comment about my youth. As I extended my hand to shake his, he would gently pull my arm and take a hug instead. I always walked away from each greeting thinking that he was a much younger man in an older man's body who not only truly knew how to enjoy his life, but also bring joy to others.

Arletha A. Brooks

Mrs. Persons,
I hope you will find comfort in knowing how much laughter and joy Fred gave everyday.
Sherril Rodriomc

A Memory from Gwen
Fred did not object to me supporting black businesses and helping to bolster the revenue downtown Detroit. In fact, Fred enthusiastically joined me in my efforts to keep our dollars in Detroit. Whenever I headed out on the weekend to shop, he insisted that I take the People Mover. I do believe Fred thought the People Mover operated expressly for his wife. If he even suspected that I was headed out on foot, it never surprised me to take a backward look and find him trailing behind me.

He always seemed to know where my last stop would be. There he would be, waiting to escort me home, accompanied by his infamous mumblings and grumblings. "Gwen, you can't keep these people in business all by yourself." Then there was always this admonishment, "Gwen, I know what these guys on these streets and what they will do, I'm in court with them everyday."

I remember one year Martha Huggins came down the day after Thanksgiving to shop with me. We headed out on foot. We had not gotten to Woodward Ave. when I turned around and there he was, My-Knight- in –Shining-Armor.

All Fred ever wanted to do was to take good care of Gwen.

Gwen,
 Even though I only met Fred a few times at work, I could tell he was a very special person. He had an engaging personality and was so friendly. You are in my thoughts and prayers.
Marcee Findlay

Dear Gwen,

I'm finally responding to your request of stories about your Fred. I enjoyed reading about him and thought it interesting that although I never met nor laid eyes on him, I know with certainty that he loved you (or as the song says, "Loved him some you." I also thought it interesting that someone like me who never met him would actually have a story to tell. I think that's a testament to his specialness.

I can't say I remember every detail of my one telephone encounter with Fred, but the essence of it, the message I took away from it, remains with me. I don't even remember how long it was that we spoke, but I know it's been years. This is my little story;

I called your home on a professional call one day and Fred answered the phone. When I asked for you, he said, "My Baby (or something like that) isn't home from work yet."
I commented to him how refreshing it was to hear a husband refer to his wife so nicely. He quickly replied, matter-of-factly, "I love her."

That may seem like a small thing, but to me it was huge. It struck me and has stuck with me. I just hadn't had the opportunity to hear a man admit so openly and to a stranger, his love for his wife.

Many men would think the admission would show weakness when of course the opposite is true. It is a poor commentary on the rest of the world, but it spoke very well of your relationship.
I am deeply sorry for your loss.
Love, Cheryl Lang

Mrs. Persons,

On behalf of all of your colleagues in the Department of Communication Disorders, I extend our deepest sympathy to you on Fred's passing. We know that mere words cannot erase your sadness, but we pray that time, and many memories will bring you comfort.

All of us who met Fred in person or talked to him on the phone, remember his total devotion and dedication to you.

We salute his life, We will celebrate his memory with a memorial contribution of your choice.

We love you Gwen. Please don't hesitate to let us know of anything we can do to support you in this most difficult time.

We send you our deepest sympathy.

In love and friendship
Sheila P. Ward, Supervisor
Department of Communication Disorders

A memory from Gwen

Worshiping together. Fred would say to me "You're the prettiest when the 'Holy Ghost' gets a hold of you.

Hi Gwen,

I read your note at school today and started thinking back to when we were at White Orthopedic and I first met Fred up to the last time he came to see you at Butzel. His smile stands out most in my memory. It was sincere and natural and just made me happy to be near him. He will be truly missed by all who knew him.

May God bless you and give you the strength you need to face the changes in your life.

Sincerely,
Barb Baldinger

More Memories from Gwen

Oh how he loved the holidays. They were full of such wonderful surprises, and what special memories they each hold for me now.

However, the one that took the cake in the surprise category has to be Christmas of '89, our second Christmas together as husband and wife.

Two weeks before Christmas we had invited a group of close friends over for a Christmas gathering.

Before the evening ended, Fred left the room, only to return with a large gift wrapped box. I asked Fred why was he giving me this gift tonight? His reason was that he wanted all of my friends to see the bedspread he brought me for Christmas.

I could not have been more embarrassed, (at least that is what I thought at the time) and I think I showed my reluctance to comply. Fred just insisted that I open the box. Never in a billion years could I have prepared myself for what I found inside. I opened the box and laid my eyes upon a full length white mink coat! My embarrassment heightened.

It took my breath away. When I tried it on, I literally fell to the floor (I have the pictures to prove it). I must have fallen on my knees only to thank God for blessing me with this man called "Fred"!

Gwen,

I reflect on the last time Fred and Gwen visited my home; he was vibrant and appreciative of the jazz piece that was playing. At that time, I learned that he was a true lover of music, just as he was of people. He met no strangers. I will always hold that memory of Fred as he appeared that evening with his loving wife, Gwen.

I will dearly miss his presence. He was a joy to be around!

Fondly,
Clara, a dear friend

Gwen,

When I first met Fred it was in the City County Building in downtown Detroit. Fred was wearing a white suit with complimentary accessories. He held a hat in his hand and of course a broad smile on his face. I was turned around, as I usually was in this building and he offered to help me without knowing who I was. Fred greeted me as if i were an African Queen and he made me feel so special and beautiful. Never presumptuous not carnal, but a pure gentleman. Everyone knew him in that place.

We talked briefly together on an IRS issue and he taught me a few things about the system I did not know and needed in order for me to be more effective on my job! It was only a short time after we had made our acquaintance that your name came flowing out of his mouth, which created an instant connection between us. I will always remember his warmth, not just to me but to everyone I know that knew him.

If I called to talk to you we always had our own conversation before he either gave the phone to you or informed me of your supposed short trip somewhere that had turned into hours according to his watch.

Gwen, to have been loved by Fred I can only imagine your joy, but then again I saw it in both of your faces as each of you spoke of one another.

Yes, he walked the walk Jesus wants us to walk and he talked the talk that Jesus wants us to share with each other. In some of our last conversations we had in 2001, he would tell me he was tired but never in a complaining way. He would always flip the conversation to asking about me and how I was, or Robert and 'my Fred'. I say to this "Glory to God." We can rejoice in knowing that Fred earned his place on those golden streets of Heaven and know this Gwen, one day you and I will see him again. He awaits you my sister, so dry up those tears and hold on to the wonderful memories you have around you and inside of you because the physical body is gone but his spirit and love will never leave you. Thank the Lord each day for the blessing of Fred in your life.

Remember God loved him more than you and although it's hard to let go of the earthly shell, it was just that and together we will walk forward until you meet Fred again..

When I think of Fred I will remember the epitome of finesse and pride in oneself and of whom and what he represented.

I saw a real man who knew how to love without show. A man I am so glad I had the opportunity to meet, laugh with, break bread with and share you with.

Always remember the Lord our God will fill whatever void your natural body is missing and will make you whole again.

Wait on Him, yield to Him, call upon Him and He will always be there with you and for you.

I love you.... Denise, your sister!

Gwen,

I can remember the first time I met Fred. He was such a charming and a very well dressed man. I said "Gwen is sure a lucky person to have Fred." I said to myself that Fred must treat Gwen like a 'Princess'. I'm sure I'm right.

Then there was the time Doug and I had dinner at Joe Muer and saw the both of you. We should have had dinner together that night. The four of us would probably have talked the whole evening away. I'm sure he was great company.

Then there was the time Fred brought you to work after you were out for a couple of weeks. Fred gave me a great big hug. Always charming and well dressed. You must have been proud to have someone like Fred to be at your side. I'm sure he was proud to have you at his side.

I will always remember him as the well dressed man with the beautiful smile.

Your Friend, Love,
Jenny

A memory from Gwen....

My first Christmas as Mrs. Fred K. Persons.

We had been invited to two special events over the Christmas season. One, the Alpha's Black and Gold Ball, and the other, the Chums Christmas Brunch. Two weeks before Christmas Fred came home with two beautifully wrapped boxes.

The formal affair was to be the Saturday before Christmas. Fred insisted that I open one of the boxes.

His impeccable taste had evidenced itself once again. Inside was a gorgeous 'drop dead 'for black and gold evening gown.

Christmas morning when I opened the second box, In it I found a supple pink leather suit (of all colors, pink).

The next month, I wore that suit to the Delta's Founder's Day. Now can you imagine what nerve, what arrogance, it took for me to step into a Delta's Founder's Day wearing a pink suit!

To my delight and surprise, I don't think anyone gave a second thought to the color association (AKA). The looks were not of ridicule, but rather of admiration. The suit was a knock-out by anyone's standards, regardless of the color. But as the saying goes, "Delta's look good in any color." Once again, Fred Persons taste and unmatchable style, stood up and took notice!!

Dear Gwen

Thanks for asking me to help you in your tribute to Fred. He was a very nice person. Sorry I didn't know him better. I knew Fred as a Steward of St. Stephen A.M.E. Church. who took the opposite of everything to force people to think about the situation before you took a vote,

Please forgive me for taking so long in responding to your request. Hope this will help you in some way to honor Fred.

I pray that God will guide you as you complete your challenge.

Yours in Christ,

Theresa Johnson

Dear Gwen,

I will remember Fred as a man who greeted me warmly every time we met. He made me feel as if he knew me a long time, not someone he had just met. There were many times that I didn't think he remembered who I was but I was wrong.

He knew me, called me by name, held my hand and gave me a hug. I believe I also shared with you a conversation I overheard when two police officers spoke of Fred and how much he loved his wife. They didn't even know you or me.

It was totally unsolicited. The impact Fred had on people was tremendous and will never be forgotten. I know that I'll not forget the warmth of being in his presence.

Love,
Carolyn Williams

Dear Gwen,

I will always remember the story Fred often told about helping his father saw some wood during a lightening storm at night when he was just a small boy growing up down south. Fred told his father that he was afraid and that he wanted to go inside, his father replied, "Just keep holding the wood, God is lightening up the sky, so I can see how to cut this wood."

Fred said that it was that experience as a small child that affirmed his faith in God. He said he joined church the next Sunday. Fred often told this story. This story truly convinced me of the depth of Fred's spirituality.

Fred was a gentleman and a man in the true sense of the word. His wife, Gwendolyn Persons, was very blessed to have had this special man pass through her life. They had a quality marriage throughout the fourteen years that they were married. One that most people aren't fortunate enough to realize in a lifetime!

Respectfully submitted,
Love
Carolyn Alexander

A memory from Gwen......
In the fall 1991, for some undiagnosed reason, I began to have panic attacks. Many of these attacks occurred on the expressway. From the onset of those attacks, until Fred was no longer able to drive, whenever I had somewhere to go that required freeway driving, Fred insisted on driving me.

Hi Soror Gwen,
Whenever I called your house, your husband was always pleasant and very cheerful. I know he adored you because of the twinkle in his eye whenever I would see the two of you together.

Gwen, I know you miss him so much. Our husbands grow on us....we become one...The longer you are together the stronger the oneness becomes.

I know that this is a time that you will have to draw your strength from God; the Creator...For there is nothing that will ever take the place or fill that void that has been left...

But because God knows your pain, your sorrow. He has promised that He will give you life more abundantly. He will be your strength and your refuge...

With all of the Promises of GOD...You know that you have a great deal of happiness coming to you...Your job now dear soror is just to STAND ON HIS PROMISES. When you are weak, lonely and in pain...JUST STAND.
Love,
Soror Barbara Benford

Dear Gwen,
When I think of Fred I remember his great smile, laughter and pleasant conversations. No one could remain a stranger for very long to Fred it seemed. I was impressed by the close bond I could clearly see the two of you shared,
Renay

A memory from Gwen...
I don't care if it was a stumped toe or a severe backache. The first thing Dr. Persons would do, would be to get his faithful thermometer and take my temp. Fred would say "This is the only gauge I have to tell if there is something wrong."

"Remembering Fred"

The first time I met Fred was at the marriage reception of Fred and his wife Gwendolyn Persons. The reception took place in their downtown apartment in the Millender Center. All in attendance included judges, lawyers, administrators and other Detroit Public School employees; I quickly became aware of Fred's fine taste.

The entire evening Fred could not stop expounding about how happy he was to be married to Gwen, whom he affectionately referred to as 'his baby'.

He displayed impeccable manners and dress and he loved to laugh and have a good time.

You could tell that Fred really enjoyed people and life, but most of all his wife, Gwen. Every time I saw him whether at church or at school, he always had a smile and a kind word. I guess that's how I will always remember Mr. Fred Persons,
Reflectively,
Deborah J. Brown

I often look at the Photo Album of my 40th Wedding Anniversary that you and Fred made of us. Your thoughtfulness has given Earl and me so much pleasure.

It is this thoughtfulness that was Fred's hallmark. He was a warm, fun loving, thoughtful friend who never met a stranger. I feel privileged to have known him.
Dr. Esther Bright

I Remember Fred K. Persons

Attorney Persons was a fellow member of the St. Stephen A.M.E. Church family. I have many pleasant memories of feeling his presence in Sunday morning services. He came to praise God and to join in divine worship. He would 'make a joyful noise' unto the Lord. He would often give testimony of God's goodness to him.

At a recent service, he inspired the congregation with words of thankfulness to God for strengthening him during the time of his illness. He gave particular tribute to his wife for her kindness and devotion throughout this trying time.

In reminiscing about Fred Persons, there comes to mind the scene of a young lady, several years ago, who was legally blind. She had just moved into a downtown apartment and was not thoroughly familiar with her surroundings. She had found a beauty salon nearby. However, as she was returning to her residence, the zig zag pattern of the downtown streets became quite blurry as she used her cane to find the way. Out of the gray mist she heard a voice assuring her that this was Mr. Persons from St. Stephen. In his usual friendly manner he assisted her into his car and took her safely to her new address. She has never forgotten that action on his part.....and neither have I, for she was my daughter! "Let your light so shine before men, that they may see your good works, and glorify our Father which is in heaven." Matthew 5:16.

Attorney Persons was a people person. He enjoyed talking and interacting with those around him. Perhaps this was a factor in his choice of law for a profession.

It is a marvelous blessing to know that he and his wife, Gwen, spent many happy years together in the blessed partnership of holy matrimony. There is no greater fortune in life than 'To love and be loved in return'.

Harriet L. Young

Dear Mrs. Persons,

I sincerely hope and pray that you are feeling well and ready for a fun filled summer vacation!

Today I was thinking about you and your dear husband, who has gone home to communicate with God, his Father recently. All I can say is, your husband's sharing and caring will always live on in your thoughts and in those people who knew and loved him. Remember the beautiful exquisite gown you had a picture of one day at Mercy College which you stated Mr. Persons bought for you along with many other things, etc. This is only one of the many beautiful memories you will always have to cherish and to comfort you over the years.

In addition, Mr. Persons's smile and lovely eyes gave a true picture of his inner soul of love, sharing and caring for you, mankind, and God.

I am very happy God gave you two people such a lovely and happy time together before it was his time to go home to his Father.

Peace to his memory, and blessed be his soul!

God bless you!

 Sincerely,
Ms. Terry Ann Lewis

Gwen,

I celebrate the wonderfulness of your special gift titled 'husband', I admit my heart breaks for you as you journey on but know that Fred is next to you every day. I believe the body leaves us but the love and spirit of those we love (who love us) is as reachable as air. Keep talking to Fred and he will continue to hold you in his arms daily. He is now your angel on the other side.

If I can do anything for you...it.. is a given...then let me know.

Love ya,
Lisa

Dear Soror Gwen

I am extremely sorry that I can not add anything of substance to your precious memoirs of your beloved husband, Fred, The only occasions that I had to be in his presence were brief encounters in lobbies following social events. We had great admiration and respect for each other that was nurtured by his relationship with my brother, a fellow barrister and my relationship with you in the sisterhood.

Whenever I would see Fred, he was standing dressed impeccably waiting for you. I recognized early on that if you were inside, Fred was outside or nearby. His devotion to you was very obvious, and I hope that you will find comfort in that.

I pray most earnestly for your healing and the restoration of your happiness, as life must go on. You must finish your work and you can't be effective depressed or holding on too strongly to your losses.

Sincerely,
Claudia

To Gwen

Mr. Persons, I called him. He would come down to the Health Club, not to work out, but to make all of our day. To see him was a joy. He loved to talk smart and joked around. He talked about his wife, Gwen all the time. How much he loved his sisters and how he loved them since he was the only guy in his family. He was everywhere in the Millender atrium to the Renaissance Center He always welcomed you with a smile. We will miss him dearly.

Courtyard Marriott
Health Club Staff

A memory from Gwen...
I have always gotten the biggest kick out of that Pillsbury 'dough boy' commercial. The one where the little dough boy is poked in the belly and lets out the cutest chuckle. Fred would pretend to be my 'little dough boy 'and allow me to poke him in his belly. He would in turn hold up his arms and give me the biggest chuckle. Fred would do just about anything to put a smile upon my face.

Another precious memory from Shirley...
It was right that permanently etched in my mind is the 75th birthday party Gwen gave for Fred. This was the day he stood so proudly in church, in the presence of God and all of his finite witnesses, and announced to all the world hear..."I love Gwen!, I love doing things for Gwen, and I love doing things with Gwen, and I love doing things to Gwen." In the history of "Fredism," i.e. all things unique to Fred, that was the ultimate. It may well be my most precious memory, and I doubt very seriously that mine was the only inquiring mind that day that dared to wonder what that "to Gwen" was all about.
Wink! Wink! and Hallelujah

Dear Gwen,
We have known Fred for many, many years and cannot recall an occasion when his ebullient spirit and spontaneous smile was not a part of his greeting. He truly exhibited a joie de vivre, and we were warmed by his gregarious manner whenever we encountered him.

What a fitting tribute to Fred that you have chosen to honor his memory by inviting reflections from his many friends and admirers! You may be sure that our memories of Fred (natty dresser, camera in hand) will always be accompanied by a smile.
Sincerely
Rose Marie and Leon D. Stein

A memory from Gwen....

Fred often told me that the Barrister's Ball was inaugurated when he served as President of the Wolverine Bar Association. However, he had not been an active member in several years. I never had the opportunity to attend, but always desired to do so. Our first year dating Fred paid his dues and purchased a table for ten. He told me to invite whomever I wished.

A month before the affair Fred picked me up and drove me out to Chudicks in Birmingham. Apparently no stranger to the salesladies, Fred was given the royal treatment. They assisted him in grand style. I was shown many. many beautiful gowns, before he spotted exactly the one he wanted me to have, a beautiful black and silver silk organza gown.

Needing a few minor alterations, we left the gown in the store. Two weeks later, Fred picked up the gown and delivered it to my home.

When I called my closest friend, Sheila (the same friend who encouraged me to go out with him) to tell her that Fred had picked the gown up from the store and delivered it to my house. She said to me, "He's a keeper"

The night of the ball I felt and I looked like the 'Belle of the Ball'. Fred treated me like a queen. When he arrived to pick me up, he presented me with the most beautiful wrist corsage. Not just any flower however, a corsage of orchids. Every formal affair we attended since and there were many, Fred selected the gowns and on each and every occasion brought me orchids for my wrist. Always the first onto the dance floor, Fred had a special way of making me feel like the envy of all the ladies in the room. As Soror Jo Cleta loved to say "You are Fred's lady and he let's everyone know it!!"

354 Gwendolyn D. Persons

Dear Gwen

As I shared with you, I had a few more memories of my Love for Fred. Often, I would notice how you would look at Fred with eyes so full of love and adoration, I would think of a song I used to sing when I was hoping to sing professionally: the song is called "I'm glad there is you",

The lyric goes, "In this world of ordinary people, extra ordinary people, I'm glad there is you." In this world, where many many play at love, and hardly any stay in love, I'm glad there is you"...I won't go on with the rest of the lyric, but you and Fred truly had what the song talks about. In you and Fred, I saw 'love alive. I saw true devotion and commitment.

Gwen, I think you know me, and I don't say things to just say them. I don't believe in patronizing. If I don't believe a thing, I just stay quiet. Fred rewrote the book on when a man loves a woman! He loved you unashamedly and to find a man like that is almost impossible these days. I long to see men like Fred. I thank God I knew him, and I thank God for you my sister. The God of heaven brought you two together at the right time. He looked down through the annals of time and eternity and He decided on the day and year that was time for Gwen and Fred and the two of you became ONE, praise His name. He was a living example of what a real man is and he left footprints that no one can ever fill!

Thanks for letting me express my hearts thoughts and feelings. I love you precious. I thank God for Fred in my life and your kindness in letting me have a little space in his life.

Thanks
Barbara

Fondest Memories with Fred Persons:
Watching Fred create year after year and event after event, precious KODAK MOMENTS with his camera, that he unselfishly shared with everyone.
Beverly Sneed

A memory from Gwen
Fred loved to take pictures, especially of me. In the early days of our relationship, Fred owned an instamatic camera. He was so proud of his trusty little camera. He took it everywhere we went. Folks looked forward and expected to have Fred take their picture. I'm so thankful for that little brownie camera, for today I have a wealth of cherished memories.

Dear Mrs. Fred K. Persons & family
Just a few lines to express my sympathy and regret in the passing of Attorney Fred Persons. I have known Fred for thirty years or more and I can say with certainty that he was a true friend. Whenever there was a call he would answer and you could be sure that he would be there. As a customer, attorney or friend, Fred was a man who was always willing to help. I will surely miss our checker games, our bantering over any number of topics, including sports and politics, and the wisdom he passed along. It is truly a sad day Fred is no longer with us.
With Sympathy and Love,
Panel L. Spencer & Family
Atlantic Barber Shop

A Memory from Gwen
Whenever I had to attend the funeral of a friend or family member, or visit a sick/bereaved friend/family member, Fred never let me go alone. He was always by side. We never left their presence without Fred lifting them up in prayer. God was at His best when He made Fred K. Persons.

Remembering
Fred Persons

My first meeting with Fred was through the Hospitality Club of St. Stephen A.M.E. Church. I would register the guests to be announced. Fred was the only announcer at the 10:45 a.m. service.

Fred was a great motivational speaker. Sometimes while giving announcements he would become happy and start preaching. The Lord would touch Fred with the Holy Spirit. Before you knew it Fred's spirit would have the church shouting and praising the Lord.

I became a friend of Fred's through his wife Gwen. Gwen, myself and two other women went on our first cruise together and developed a close friendship. After the cruise we included our husbands which strengthened our friendship and enriched our lives.

Fred was always a friendly and humorous person. The most memorable memory I have of Fred is how he dressed. He was a very fashionable and proud man. He loved his white shirts and white ties which made him stand out in a crowd.

He was a loving and devoted husband to his lovely wife, Gwen. He will always be remembered as a wonderful friend.

Always,
Burnack Dowell

Fred Persons

I met Fred in August, 1989. He came into B'Anna's to pick up a package Gwen, his wife, had selected. He gave me the note Gwen had written.

We started talking. As the years passed those trips into my store grew. Fred would drop in my store and ask me, "Does my wife have anything put away? You know, Millie, my wife doesn't need any clothing, but I love her so much. I have to take them, I want to keep Gwen happy".

I would look up and Fred would come rushing through the door with a pink slip in his hand. Fred would then say, "I am taking this suit and hat, but there is no place to put another thing." I would say to him, "Unconditional love never ends."

Fred was a star in my crown, he gave me helpful ideas about the law and my business, how to be successful in business. He was a Christian. He loved his Gwen.

Fred is resting, Peace, He was loved by many.

Power belongs to God.

Mildred Windham

Attorney Fred Persons

In the late 50's Attorney Fred Persons made the announcements each Sunday at St. Stephen A.M.E. Church. His delivery and his dress were always exquisite. Why would anyone need to take his place?

Rev. Spivey, the pastor, decided that young people should be trained to do some of the work in the church. At the time I was a teenager and I was asked to make the announcements on Sunday. WOW! What would Attorney Persons think/do?

On the Sunday that I was to do the announcements I was nervous and unsure of myself. I knew what to do, but I was still very apprehensive. Attorney Persons recognized my fear. He assured me that I would do a great job.

When I completed the announcements that first time, he was the first to stand on his feet in applause of sincere support. I shall never forget that day. Because of Attorney Persons' support and continuous encouragement, I became more self-assured as I became more involved in St. Stephen.

I will always remember Fred (I felt comfortable calling him Fred after he married Gwen) as a dapper, outspoken supportive friend.

Carolyn McKissic

Hello Gwen

I am no longer able to write but I wanted to respond to what you sent me in the mail.

I have so many nice memories of 'my brother'. The year was 1986. My sister had passed and I was trying to sale her house. I needed a lawyer to sign at the closing. I called Fred. He met me at City Hall and signed the papers. When I pulled out my check book to pay him he said to me 'put that up girl'. Tears came and I thanked God. He had even cancelled a dental appointment to come down. He said he could always get another appointment. Tears came to my eyes to know he would cancel his appointment and still not take anything.

Then there was the Christmas after I had loss my husband. My husband always brought me a poinsettia for Christmas. That year you and Fred came to see me and brought me a poinsettia. It meant so much to me Gwen. Keep trusting in the Lord.

Adeans Henley
Class Leader

Dear Gwen

I've been trying to e-mail this to you but it keeps coming back I hope all is well.

It's always difficult to see things in print because somehow it makes things seem so real. In my mind and in my heart Fred Persons will live forever. I have never known a man to love a woman as much as he loved his wife. He always shared that with anyone and everyone he came in contact with on a daily basis. That was just one of the things that made him so endearing. It gave me hope that that type of passion and concern for another person is actually possible. Although I witnessed it the way he showed it for Gwen.

Every time I saw him he made me feel like a great person, capable of anything and the best at what I did. What a motivator. I looked forward to all the times that I saw him in the lobby, the elevator, or in the hallway. It was like running into sunshine. He offered fatherly advice when I didn't express a problem. He could read any expression on my face through a few scenarios of things I shouldn't let bother me. Amazingly he would be offering advice for exactly what was on my mind. He's the only other person besides my mother that could ever read me like that.

I always felt a sense of comfort and strength when he was around, even if I didn't see him, I knew he was there somewhere. When he left I felt an emptiness and deep sense of loss. Without seeing him there in the lobby to start my day, it was like walking into a vacant spot. Nothing was ever the same again.

Love

Eva

Dear Gwen

First I met Gwen, then after our friendships blossomed I remember meeting Fred, initially via telephone conversations then later in person. When Gwen and I first started communicating by telephone Fred on many occasions would answer the phone. When I told him who it was, he always had a kind word to say before he called Gwen to the phone.

Later when I met him face to face on the golf course with Gwen, you could feel the love and concern that radiated from him when he was with her. He always watched over Gwen, never complained about our terrible golf game, but continued to encourage us to stick with it.

Being around Fred one knew he loved God, his wife and truly, he enjoyed life. He was very protective when it came to Gwen. No one in Fred's presence would ever disrespect his "beloved wife." If he was not there and heard of something negative directed toward Gwen, a verbal, but dignified thrashing would await that individual.

Such a gentleman; such a dapper dresser. He was an example of what a true gentleman should be.

This comes from my heart.

Love,

Elaine

Remembering Fred Persons

Remembering Fred Persons evokes a picture of one who truly loved life. First, my girlhood memories were of Fred's active love of God and his church. At St. Stephen A.M.E. Church I remember that he delivered the announcements, morning prayer, gave frequent personal testimonies and was a steward and supported the morning messages with inspired "Amens."

Secondly, I discovered that Fred was meticulous about his appearance. He always had a dapper look and was nattily dressed whenever I saw him. I never saw him in casually dressed. He and his Gwen always made a fashion statement. One memorable occasion was the year the church members were asked to wear the oldest items in their wardrobe. Fred came in spats! I had only seen spats on television and I thought that topped the day. I guess you could say that Fred had a flair.

When I grew into my womanhood, I discovered another love of Fred's; he loved people. Especially woman! Age was not a factor with Fred. Young women, middle aged and seniors all benefited from his positive commentary of appreciation. I would see him in the halls of the City County Building, in the Renaissance Building waiting at the escalator to take pictures and throw out a compliment to women leaving a sorority function and providing words that made each soror beautiful.

My fondest memory was his kind and warm friendship with my mother. His exchanges with her always brought a smile to her lovely face. Even when she could neither speak or walk, he and his beloved Gwen were there asking if there was some way they could provide support.

When the final accounting of Fred's life is reviewed, I am sure that the Great Father will say that Fred did an outstanding job of demonstrating to others that one must always seek the joy of life and be an encouragement for others to do the same.
Barbara Jefferies

It was Saturday afternoon, Labor Day weekend 1979, the eve of the Michigan Annual Conference of the African Methodist Episcopal Church when I first met Attorney, Fred K. Persons. He was one of the Stewards who interviewed me for the position of Director of Christian Education for St. Stephen A.M.E. Church.

Upon accepting the position Fred and I became good friends. He was always there to give me advice. Many times I sought Fred out for legal advice as well. He was my tax preparer in Michigan, offering his services because he said "You are a preacher now and there are certain things you are not aware of." Fred always talked about how he wanted to be a preacher but God never called him. He would talk of growing up in Georgia preaching to the chickens and begging God to call him.

Fred and I had many good laughs together. Whenever I wore something he liked he would say to me,' that's not a preacher's outfit, but you sure are looking good." He would kiss me on the cheek whenever I saw him and say "I kissed a preacher" and smile.

Fred defended me a woman preacher. I will always have great admiration for Fred. My fondest memory is when he stood up for me at Tabernacle Missionary Baptist Church, Detroit, MI at the close of the worship and let everyone know that I was his assistant pastor. I had preached the Second Word at the Westside Ministerial Alliance Good Friday Service. The male clergy had refused to acknowledge me and Fred would not allow them to treat me with such disrespect. He said, "you see that young lady over there. That is the Rev. Lila Martin. She is the assistant pastor of St. Stephen A.M.E. church and she preached the Second Word.
I received a thunderous round of applause from the congregation all because of Attorney Fred K. Persons.

I am proud to say that I had the privilege and pleasure to have been the pastor who united Gwen and Fred in Holy Matrimony. Fred and Gwen Persons embodied God's love. The two did become one!
Rev. Lila Martin

Dearest Gwen

In response to your latest request for memories of Fred. Although mine seem few they are full; full of smiles and love. Love for his wife and love for life. I felt that upon my first encounter with Fred. He seemed just blessed to be alive!

There are a few special sentiments that stand out in my mind about Fred K. Persons:

1) Fred <u>loved </u>his wife! I never saw Fred without him mentioning at some point in the conversation, how much he loved and appreciated his wife, Gwen.

2) He seemed to love people. Through his flirtations, outgoing spirit, he made everyone feel special. It didn't matter whether you knew him or had just met him for the first time; you felt like he had been your friend for awhile!

3) When Fred loved you, he really loved you. Gwen, I told you this many times. Many couples are married a lot longer than you and Fred were, but you do not get the feeling that the love between them would even come <u>close </u>to the love between you and Fred.

God knew what He was doing when He brought the two of you together! How blessed you both were to share a love so strong.

4) Lastly, I am blessed to say that on August 12, 2001 I married a special man I often feel has similar qualities as Fred K. Persons. Gwen, you know I often refer to him as "my little Fred". I pray that Terrance and I can continue to share the kind of love that you and Fred shared and the devotion you two had.

For better for worse, for richer for poorer, in sickness and in health....**<u>God is Good!!!</u>**

Love you Gwen,
    In your loving memory Fred,
        Pam Cantrell

A memory from Gwen

Fred always said to me "KEEP THE FAITH AND TRUST IN THE LORD"

Loving Reflections of ......
Fred K. Persons

A candle provides light and dispels darkness in whatever environment it finds itself. Wherever he was, he let his light shine; always there to cast away the darkness with joy, giving unremitting love to all blessed to know him. He 'shined' in our lives with love and support for twenty-four years. Like a candle burning bright, he let his shine, shine, shine.

A tribute placed in the 25th Anniversary Souvenir Booklet by the Harmonaires of St. Stephen A.M.E. Church

Dear Friends and Loved Ones,

Words are not adequate to begin to express my heartfelt gratitude to you for responding to my call. Thank you for taking a few precious moments to share with me, your special memories of Fred's love.

Your words have helped to ease my pain, strengthen my heart, heal my brokenness, bring laughter to my soul and have renewed my spirit.

It is my prayer that the special memories that lie within these pages will keep Fred's spirit alive in each of your hearts for many years to come. I further pray that his memory will remind each of us to keep God's love commandment, "That we love one another, as God loves us.

My prayer for all the world is that you be blessed to have the two greatest gifts in life; someone to love and someone to love you.

God Loves You and So Do I!
Mrs. Fred K. Persons, Esq.

364 Gwendolyn D. Persons

Here are Forty of
Fred's Famous One-Liners

1. Ain't God Good?
2. You're so late, you're absent.
3. Tougher than a nickel steak.
4. Better now that I've seen you.
   (When asked how he felt)
5. On the first. The first chance I get.
   (If asked <u>when</u> he will do something)
6. I love Gwen worse than a hog loves slop. All he can't eat, he wallows in.
7. You look like damn it to hell I'll bite cha.
   (If he didn't like the way I looked)
8. If you step on my foot it still hurts.
   (If you offended Fred and tried to apologize)
9. Love is a verb, love is something that you do.
10. Out of sight
11. Crying with a loaf of bread under your arm.
12. Your skin is smoother than a spanked baby's butt.
13. If you see me fighting the bear, help the bear.
14. I'm not afraid of a snake, as long as I can see it.
15. You can tell a Morehouse man, but you can't tell him anything.
16. I love doing things <u>to</u> Gwen, <u>for</u> Gwen and <u>with</u> Gwen.
    (Fred's three favorite prepositions)
17. I Dare you to try Him!
18. Throw a rock and hide your hand.
19. No doot aboot it. (no doubt about it)
20. Don't accept any wooden nickels.
21. I Love that 'ol piece of chick.
22. The wicked flee when no one pursueth. (Proverbs28:1)
23. If you can't do it right, don't do it at all.

24. Better to have it and not need it, than to need it and not have it.
25. I'm going to do something that the devil seldom does. Leave you.
26. Won't give a cripple crab a crutch.
27. Kill a flea with a sledge hammer.
28. You can put the board in the barrel. (If he promised to do something)
29. I'd rather wear out than rust out.
30. Gwen, you can't make people do what you want them to do.
31. If I wore loose fitting clothes, he'd say "That covers a multitude of sin"
32. Take me as I am, whether it is standing upside down or sliding down a pole backwards.
33. Three quarters of the earth is water, man can't make it and man can't live without it. (When Fred thought about the goodness of the Lord)
34. You can't be hot and cold at the same time.
35. The only way to say it, is to say it.
36. Gwen, you only get one mother.
37. Meaner than a junk yard dog.
38. Remember who you are and whose you are.
39. You're Gwen Persons and **don't you ever forget it!**
40. Trust in the Lord with all your heart. Lean not onto thy own understanding, but in all your ways acknowledge Him and he will direct your path.   KEEP THE FAITH

" A **HERO** does lie in Me"

Part Seven

A Fresh Start

He has made everything beautiful in its time...."

Eccles. 3:11

A Fresh Start

TO EVERY THING THERE IS A SEASON AND A TIME TO EVERY PURPOSE UNDER THE HEAVEN

Since the first of this New Year, I have made numerous visits to my computer to try and fill the pages of the seventh chapter of my book, the chapter which I have entitled "A Fresh Start". But for whatever the reasons, I've made precious little movement in that direction. Just like the seasons in the natural realm there are seasons in our spiritual life as well. There are spring seasons, fall seasons, summer seasons and there are winter seasons in our life. Ironically, this spring found me in a winter season. What is a winter season? I suppose it is a season where your very foundation is being tested. Everything that can go wrong goes wrong. In the Christian church, the week before Easter is often referred to as the 'Week of Challenge.' My challenges began early this Lenten season.

Thursday morning (the day after Ash Wednesday), I resurrected my 5:30 am fitness program. After my workout I headed straight for the Jacuzzi. The door to the pool area was locked this morning. For no explainable reason, a sudden weight of sadness descended upon me. Within minutes Portia, the attendant, was there to unlock the door. As a rule Portia works the afternoon shift but this week while Graydine was on vacation, Portia was working the morning shift. "Mrs. Persons, I have not had a chance to let you know how your husband talked about you and we all knew how much he loved you. He would often come down here in the afternoon while you were at work and talk about his wife and all kinds of other stuff. There were times we even fell out with each other and I had to put him out. He would say, "I've been put out of better places than this." Portia went on to say that Fred would stay away for a day or two but he always came back, still talking about his wife. I started to cry uncontrollably. "Gwen, don't cry, don't you be sad, you were so blessed. Mr. Persons loved you so much. "When Portia walked away from me, I knew that she had been an angel sent to me from above.

The following week all hell started breaking loose 'round about me. Unanticipated and unexplained negative situations circumstances came like a tidal wave. Least of which another letter from the IRS, I thought all of that was behind me.

Murphy's law was fully operating in my life. I asked God "Why?" I've always heard that He chastens those that He loves. Was God whipping me into shape? "What are You doing to me?" Was He getting me ready to fulfill His purpose in my life? My husband sent me a message that morning, "Gwen, trust in God and keep the faith." That morning I paid a visit to the Well of Faith. The spirit asked "How is your faith relationship helping you to trust God in all the circumstances of your life?"

The week before Easter I found myself tackling my writing with a vengeance. I was a writer possessed; I was on a mission. I was ready to complete my book. I attended a workshop one Friday morning in the Fisher Building but my mind was nowhere near where my body sat. The entire first half of the morning session I sat there writing copious notes concerning my book. During the first break the presenter made her way to where I was sitting and commented, "I observed you taking lots of notes." I wanted to say 'Lady I have not heard a word you have said all morning." But, as Fred would have reminded me, "Remember your rearin'. If you can't say anything good, then don't say anything at all." I remained professional and courteous, thus silent. I simply acknowledged her remarks with a smile, then rose from my seat and headed out into the hall for the morning break.

No sooner than I was in the hall, for the second time that morning I felt a tremendous weight upon me and without warning I found myself on the floor. I don't think I blacked out, but people were all around me assisting me to my feet. They escorted me into a room and sat me in a chair around a large table. I could not control my crying and I could hear myself uttering these words, "My husband, my husband." Someone asked, "What about your husband?" "Is there something wrong with your husband?" "Do you want us to call him?" "Is your husband home?" "No", I said, "My husband is in heaven." The minute those words left my mouth I knew I was suspect. Is this woman having a breakdown of sorts? I could see it all over their faces; I'm sure they thought I was some kind of deranged woman. The next thing I recall was the paramedics taking my vitals. They insisted on a phone number, somebody they could call for me. I asked them to call my supervisor, Sheila Ward. I would not be staying for the afternoon session and I needed to report my absence. I wanted to go home. I tried to assure them that I would be just fine and that I was able to drive myself home. They were not about to let me go that easily. They strongly urged me to allow someone to take me to the workmen's compensation clinic for further evaluation. I absolutely refused. "I'm fine, I just want to go home."

A security guard walked me to the elevator. Just as we got off the elevator, the crying returned. I could feel my body weakening again. This time the security guard was there to prevent my body from descending to the floor. Those all too familiar feelings, the racing heart, the shaking and the uncontrollable crying had returned that fateful morning. I was having a panic attack. "Ms. we cannot let you leave here in this condition." I heard myself repeating those words over and over, "My husband, my husband, he's waiting for me. I have to go." The kind man assured me that I would see my husband again one day, but it is not yet my time. Just as he began to walk me toward Comerica Bank to sit me in a chair, my Soror Gwen Mitchell, walked by. Gwen is an elementary school principal. She had also been in the building attending a workshop that morning. Gwen observed the situation and immediately inquired about my apparent state of distress. The security guard asked, "Do you know her?" Gwen replied, "Of course, she is my soror." He took her to the side. I can just about imagine what he may have said to her. In spite of my actions, I was not going to harm myself.

Gwen took over the situation. She had managed to convince the guard that I was in good hands. "She is going to be okay, she's going with me." Gwen put me in her car so we left my car behind. She told me that I would be hanging out with her for the remainder of the afternoon. Gwen ran some errands before heading backs to her school. En route, she asked, "Would you like me to Soror Rose Marie to see if she is home." When she did not get an answer she then asked, "Would you like to spend the rest of the day at my school?" I told Soror Gwen that I really just wanted to go home. Gwen then telephoned her son on her cell and asked that he meet her back at the location of my car.

When we arrived her son was there waiting for us. The two of us got out of her car and got into mine. Gwen drove me home and her son followed. I assured my soror that I just wanted to get into bed. Once she felt comfortable leaving me, her son drove her back to retrieve her car. I thanked my soror for coming to my aid. Gwen promised she would be checking on me later that evening (that 'good ol' Delta Spirit' keeps showing up!)

Once back home, I went straight to bed I was feeling extremely exhausted. I must have slept a couple of hours. I awoke still feeling a bit uneasy. I called my sister Carolyn who works across the street from my apartment. I was too late. She had already left the office for the weekend. I had hoped that she could stop by the apartment and sit with me a little while before going home. I then called Barbara Woodson. Barbara had been by my side twelve years ago when I had my first panic attacks. She prayed with me and for me through those early episodes. I told Barbara how my day had unraveled. I confessed to Barbara my dreaded fear that the panic attacks were returning. "How would I get through them again without Fred?" "My precious, the devil is a liar. Those panic attacks are not coming back. We won't even think about that! Barbara suggested that I stop my writing for now. Just a month ago, I had e-mailed Barbara asking her to stay yoked up with me during this Lenten Season so that I could complete my work. Barbara admonished me, "My precious friend, stop writing for now, your book is a labor of love, it is a labor from the heart and not from the head. Perhaps now is not the time for you to complete your book." Before hanging up the phone Barbara told me to get lots of rest and to read Psalm 91. I took Barbara's advice and stopped writing for the next little while.

*M*y Lord young Lady, I could hardly hold back the tears of Joy, Pride and Awe as I read this prelude to a new Best Seller.

Dearest Gwen, you are truly gifted. I have always found great solace in reading good books. As a child I literally withdrew into the world of books and the places they opened to me were a mirror to the world far beyond my immediate space. My mom encouraged and took me to the library; often I found such comfort there, even as a child. Later, when I became old enough, I would go with my buddies, and we would spend the day at the Library, DIA and the Historical Museum.

I am yoked up with you during this Lenten Season, my precious friend, and I know that God will continue to guide you as the illumination continues to flow through you as you write. Just from this brief sketch of what's to come in your book, lets me know that wonderful things will come as a result of its publication. How prolific you are. Oh Gwen, truly you are blessed among women. I don't know if I deserve to be mentioned among those listed in your comments, but I do know that I am blessed to call you friend and sister. Press on my friend, I am humbled at what I have already read; your gift of expression is amazing. I keep my card from you and my Fred on my table. You both sent it to me with a gift two weeks before he left us, Jesus how I miss him. The world is a darker place because he's gone. I love you Gwen, and thanks.

Today is Wednesday, June 18, 2003. Nearly three months have gone by since I sat down to write. Yesterday marked the nineteenth month since Fred's home going celebration and tomorrow, June 19, 2003, I will celebrate what would have been his 84th birthday. It's time. It's time for me to stop mourning his death. It's time for me to begin celebrating his life. I can't think of a better way to start that celebration than by completing my journey, a journey which began four years ago with the arrival of these words, "Recall I told you we/you did not know of God's plans for you. It appears that you are to become a talented writer." The note was written June 17, 1999, I received it the following day, June 18, 1999, exactly four years ago today. It's now time. It's time to bring it in. It's time to complete my book.

Can you possibly imagine my reaction when I paused to take a break from my writing this afternoon? I turned on Oprah. Today's show dealt with the problems of overspending, overeating and overworking. You could have knocked me over with a feather! What a coincidence or was it?

After the show I logged on to www.oprah.com. There I found these words. *"When you're stressed, overwhelmed, juggling family and work, do you comfort yourself with eating, shopping or having another glass of wine? Find out how to turn off the desire to overdo it, and find balance in your life.* The website offered up it's own formula and remedies. By now, you could not even knock me over with a wrecking ball. I was paralyzed! Overeating, overspending and having another glass of wine; four years ago those were precisely my self-prescribed remedies my prescriptions for coping. That was indeed my dilemma! I needed an antidote for my trouble. Thus, the genesis for my book, Fresh Water from Old Wells, a twelve-step program for coping evolved.

On the very day I sat down to complete my book, Oprah took me back to where it all began. I could hardly contain myself, sitting at my computer in my bedroom; another 'AHA Moment', no, sorry Oprah, you don't get credit for this one! I stand corrected, this was a 'sho' nuf Holy Ghost moment. All of these months I had been beating myself up feeling as though I had wasted so much precious time. The constant nagging questions, "Why am I unable to complete my book? Why had I run into this writer's block? Why had I not been able to move forward?" I had allowed myself to become discouraged and frustrated because I seemed unable to complete my work.

Today the answers became crystal clear. 'Kirotic Kronos'! Let me make it patently clear for you, that's Greek, which means, in God's time or in other words, **To Everything There Is a Season and a Time for Every Purpose Under Heaven!** Is that plain enough for you?

The spirit reminded me that all these months God had been working a purpose and plan in my life. The Spirit told me that He had a predetermined season or time to give me what He wants to give me, but I must not let present circumstances or situations keep me from my God intended purpose. I must not get discouraged and frustrated because it had not come to pass. When God speaks into eternity, His purposes will eventually come to pass in our lives. When my winter season is over it will bring forth good fruit and God's intended purpose for my life will actualize and manifest itself. The Holy Spirit told me "Wait on the Lord and be of good courage, your season is coming." I had to wait on God's perfect timing.

When I awoke on the morning of June 19th, I was ready to complete my journey. I was ready to complete the final chapter of my book. It was time to bring it in. It was time for a fresh start. The moment I began to write I was reminded of a word I heard some years ago. *"Careful analysis, diagnosis and definition is critical for a 'fresh start. 'Improper analysis spells improper remedies. When the diagnosis is faulty and the analysis is wrong the announced remedies will not work."* (On beginning Anew, Dr. William A. Jones) Having heard that message for the third, fourth, who knows maybe even for the fifth time, caused me to ponder and take a close look at my definition of a fresh start. How does one diagnose, analyze or define a Fresh Start?"

It did not take long before I had the answer to that query. At the risk of sounding like an Oprah Winfrey clone, a fresh start can be nothing less than to begin to live your best life.

Oprah, of this I am positively sure, of all my life experiences taking care of my husband; being there for him when he needed me most; being the best wife that God would have for me to be to Fred was without a doubt living my best life. I promised God and Fred's mother that I would take good care of Fred. I kept that promise. I was the best me that God would have for me to be at that appointed time in my life. I have loved and I have been loved in return and there truly is no greater fortune in life.

Now that Fred is no longer with me I find my life without clear definition. Is it time for me to redefine my life? Or, has God already redefined it for me? The Holy Spirit told me that "God has a divine plan for my life that transcends the human imagination and reflects God's best for me. It is time to begin to live the rest of my life the best that God intended for me.

Dr. Jones, I have no doubt that the analysis is altogether correct. But how do I do it? And what about the announced remedy? Oprah also gave me the answer to both of those queries months ago.'' *In order to realize your full God given potential and to live your best life, one must discover what you love, offer it to others in the form of service and then trust God to bring it all to fruition."* Looking back, all of my early writings were commissioned by Him. Could my writing, particularly, this book, eventuate in redefining 'living my best life'? I don't know.

Of all the things I know for sure, Fred would agree with my announced remedy. Fred gave me that exact formula, prescription or remedy for living my best life practically everyday that we were together, Proverbs 3:5-6. If ever there was a time I needed to be reminded of that formula it was after his home going. Exactly four months after Fred left me, Dr. Jones showed up on Beechwood and Milford at Tabernacle Missionary Baptist Church and brought me a message straight from my beloved husband, 'A Formula Living'. The message was clear. It was the one and only formula, solution, prescription, remedy for how to be the best me God would have for me to be. A formula for living the remainder of my days on earth. It was Fred's ultimate legacy to me. An assurance policy for living the rest of my life without him. Dr. Jones paid that policy off in full on that fateful Sunday morning.

After all these months the spirit of truth has forced me to examine those words from each and every possible angle of my life. Scripture teaches us that there is no point even entertaining a fresh start in the absence of confession. If the bare truth is allowed to keeping marching on, it is with Godly sorrow, I confess that the results are indeed tragic. *"We should never be misled by our own goodness. It matters not how right you are or how well acquainted you are with God. It is easy, almost too easy to stumble and fall. None of us is what God would have us to be"(Dr. William A. Jones)* Since that fateful Sunday morning, I have fallen short. I have missed the mark. I have failed. For in all my ways I have not been able to let go and let God move in my life completely.

This revelation took me back to where my journey began, back to the Wells. It was time for a major tune-up. So Lord here it is.

Thank you Father for all You have been and all You continue to do and all You have yet to do in my life. Forgive me Father for all I have not been that has not been pleasing in Your sight. Help me Father to stop holding on to my past and help me to allow Your will and purpose to manifest itself in my life. I believe O God now help my unbelief. I want a new beginning. I want to know again the joy of Thy salvation. I thank you Father for all I see, now help me O Lord to trust you for all that I don't see. I want to be upheld by Thy clean Spirit. So Lord blot out my transgressions, purge me and I shall be clean, wash me and I shall be whiter than snow. I need a Fresh Start. AMEN

As **I move** ever onward to my God intended future I will trust in the Lord with **all** of my heart. I will lean not unto my own understanding. In **all** of my ways I will acknowledge Him and I will allow HIM to direct my path.

Of this I am absolutely, resolutely, unequivocally sure, that is exactly how Fred would want me to celebrate his life.

"Happy 84th Birthday Fred"

Part Eight

Beyond the Gate

Oh, that one would give me to drink of the water of the well of Bethlehem which is by the gate.

II Samuel 23:15

A Gate That Stands Ajar

380 Gwendolyn D. Persons

Beyond the Gate

I invite all who suffer from an unquenchable thirst of the human spirit to join me each morning at the Wells of salvation.
   At the Wells you'll find:

> **Comfort** that abounds as the days go by
> **Faith** that is fresh every morning
> **Guidance** that directs our every step
> **Hope** that helps you cope with despair
> **Joy** that the world can't take away
> **Kindness** that is free to all
> **Love** that makes you love everybody
> **Patience** that makes you grow in God's grace
> **Peace** that flows like a river
> **Strength** that helps you meet every struggle
> **Truth** that sets you free
> **Understanding** that inspires your thoughts

The
Wells

*But whosoever drinketh of the water that
I shall give him shall never thirst; but the water
that I shall give him shall be in him a well of
water springing up into everlasting life.*

St. John 4:14

384 Gwendolyn D. Persons

........from the Well of COMFORT

Yea, though I walk through the valley of the shadow of death, I will fear no evil; for thou art with me; thy rod and thy staff they comfort me; **Psalm 23:4**

In the day of my trouble I sought the Lord; my sore ran in the night, and ceased not; my soul refused to be comforted. **Psalm 77:2**

But Jesus turned about, and when he saw her, he said, Daughter, be of good comfort; thy faith hath made thee whole, And the woman was made whole from that hour. **ST. Matthew 9:22**

For whatsoever things were written aforetime were written for our learning, that we through patience and comfort of the scriptures might have hope. **Romans 15:4**

If there be therefore any consolation in Christ, if any comfort of love, if any fellowship of the Spirit, if any bowels and mercies. Fulfill ye my joy, that ye be likeminded, having the same love, being of one accord, of one mind. **Philippians 2:1,2**

And Jesus stood still and commanded him to be called. And they call the blind man, saying unto him, be of good comfort, rise; he calleth thee. **ST. Mark 10:49**

Blessed be God, even the Father of our Lord Jesus Christ, the Father of mercies, and the God of all comfort. **II Corinthians 1:3**

Wherefore comfort one another with these words.
I Thessalonians 4:18

Who comforteth us in all our tribulation, that we may be able to comfort them which are in any trouble, by the comfort where-with we ourselves are comforted of God. **II Corinthians 1:4**

Are not my days few? cease then, and let me alone, that I may take comfort a little. **Job 10:20**

In the multitude of my thoughts within me thy comforts delight my soul. **Psalm 94:19**

Blessed are they that mourn; for they shall be comforted.
ST. Matthew 5:4

That their hearts might be comforted, being knit together in love, and unto all riches of the full assurance of understanding, t]o the acknowledgement of the mystery of God, and of the Father, and of Christ. **Colossians 2:2**

Now we exhort you, brethren, warn them that are unruly, comfort the feebleminded, support the weak, be patient toward all men.
I Thessalonians 5:14

Reproach hath broken my heart; and I am full of heaviness; and I looked for some to take pity, but there was none; and for comforters, but I found none. **Psalm 69:20**

To proclaim the acceptable year of the Lord, and the day of vengeance of our God; to comfort all that mourn; **Isaiah 61:2**

Sing O heavens; and be joyful, O earth; and break forth into singing, O mountains; for the Lord hath comforted his people, and will have mercy upon his afflicted. **Isaiah 49:13**

Comfort ye, comfort ye my people, saith your God. **Isaiah 40:1**

Finally, brethren, farewell, Be perfect, be of good comfort, be of one mind, live in peace, and the God of love and peace shall be with you. **II Corinthians 13:11**

A Song of Praise on COMFORT
Blessed Quietness

Joys are flowing like a river, Since the Comforter has come
He abides with us forever, Makes the trusting heart'
His home

Bringing life and health and gladness, All around this' heavenly
Guest, Banished unbelief and sadness, Changed our weariness
to rest

Like the rain that falls from heaven, like the sunlight
from the sky So the Holy Ghost is given, coming on us from on
high

See a fruitful field is growing, Blessed fruit of righteousness;
And the streams of life are flowing In the lonely wilderness

What a wonderful salvation Where we always see His
face! What a perfect habitation, What a quiet resting place!

Refrain
Blessed quietness, holy quietness What assurance in my soul!
On the stormy sea He speaks peace to me, How the billows
cease to roll!

Words: Fannie J. Crosby 1820-1915

.........from the Well of FAITH

If you have faith as a grain of mustard seed, ye shall say unto this mountain, Remove hence to yonder place, and it shall remove; and nothing shall be impossible unto you. **ST. Matthew 17:20**

Then touched he their eyes, saying, According to your
faith be it unto you. **ST. Matthew 9:29**

So that we ourselves glory in you in the churches of God for your patience and faith in all your persecutions and tribulations that ye endure. **II Thessalonians 1:4**

Even so faith, if it hath not works, is dead, being alone. **James 2:17**

And beside this, giving all diligence, add to your faith virtue, and to virtue knowledge. **II Peter 1:5**

Now faith is the substance of things hoped for, the evidence of things not seen. **Hebrews 11:1**

Behold, his soul which is lifted up is not upright in him but the just shall live by his faith. **Habakkuk 2:4**

Knowing this, that the trying of your faith worketh patience. **James 1:3**

And put no difference between us and them, purifying their hearts by faith. **Acts 15:9**

Watch ye, stand fast in the faith, quit you like men, be strong. **I Corinthians 16:13**

(For we walk by faith, not by sight:) **II Corinthians 5:7**

388 Gwendolyn D. Persons

I have fought a good fight, I have finished my course, I have kept the faith. **II Timothy 4:7**

Looking unto Jesus the author and finisher of our faith, who for the joy that was set before him endured the cross, despising the shame, and is set down at the right hand of the throne of God. **Hebrews 12:2**

Wherefore, if God so clothe the grass of the field, which to day is, and tomorrow is cast into the oven, shall he not much more clothe you, O ye of little faith. **St. Matthew 6:30**

Because his compassions fail not. They are new every morning; great is thy faithfulness. **Lamentations 3:22:23**

And he said unto them, Where is your faith? And they being afraid wondered, saying one to another, what manner of man is this? for he commandeth even the winds and water, and they obey him! **ST. Luke 8:25**

And Jesus answering saith unto them, Have faith in God. **ST. Mark 11:22**

For though I be absent in the flesh, yet am I with you in the spirit joying and beholding your order, and the stedfastness of your faith in Christ.   **Colossians 2:5**

But without faith it is impossible to please him; for he that cometh to God must believe that he is, and that he is a rewarder of them that diligently seek him. **Hebrews 11:6**

Not, for that we have dominion over your faith, but are helpers of your joy: for by faith ye stand. **II Corinthians 1:24**

But let him ask in faith, nothing wavering, For he that wavereth is like a wave of the sea driven with the wind and tossed.
James 1:6

A Song of Praise on FAITH
Great Is Thy Faithfulness

Great is Thy Faithfulness, O God my Father, There
is no shadow of turning with Thee: thou changest not, Thy
compassions they fail not: As thou hast been
Thou forever wilt be,

Summer and winter, and springtime and harvest, Sun
moon and stars in their courses above Join with all nature in
manifold witness To thy great faithfulness,
mercy and love,

Pardon for sin and a peace that endureth, Thine own
dear presence to cheer and to guide; Strength for today and bright hope for tomorrow, Blessings all mine
with ten thousand beside !

Refrain
Great is Thy faithfulness! Great is Thy faithfulness!
Morning by morning new mercies I See: All I have
needed Thy hand hath provided; Great is Thy
faithfulness, Lord unto me!   Amen

Words: Thomas O. Chisholm 1866-1960

.........from the Well of GUIDANCE

In all thy ways acknowledge him, and he shall direct thy paths. **Proverbs 3:6**

I will instruct thee and teach thee the way which thou shalt go; I will guide thee with mine eye. **Psalm 32:8**

For this God is our God for ever and ever; he will be our guide even unto death. **Psalm 48:14**

Thou shalt guide me with thy counsel, and afterward receive me to glory. **Psalm 73:24**

Which having no guide, overseer, or ruler. Provideth her meat in the summer and gathereth her food in the harvest. **Proverbs 6:7,8**

And art confident that thou thyself art a guide of the blind, a light of them which are in darkness. **Romans 2:19**

And the Lord direct your heart into the love of God, and into the patient waiting for Christ. **II Thessalonians 3:5**

And the Lord shall guide thee continually, and satisfy thy soul in drought, and make fat thy bones; and thou shalt be like a watered garden, and like a spring of water, whose waters fail not. **Isaiah 58:11**

To give light to them that sit in darkness and in the shadow of death, to guide our feet into the way of peace. **St. Luke 1:79**

Howbeit when he, the Spirit of truth, is come, he will guide you into all truth; for he shall not speak of himself; but whatsoever he shall hear, that shall he speak: and he will shew you things to come. **St. John 16:13**

The integrity of the upright shall guide them; but the perverseness of transgressors shall destroy them. **Proverbs 11:3**

Hear thou, my son, and be wise, and guide thine heart in the way. **Proverbs 23:19**

A man's heart deviseth his way; but the Lord directeth his step. **Proverbs 16:9**

The meek will he guide in judgment: and the meek will he teach his way. **Psalm 25:9**

For I the Lord love judgment, I hate robbery for burnt offerings; and I will direct their work in truth, and I will make an everlasting covenant with them. **Isaiah 61:8**

And he said, How can I, except some man should guide me? And he desired Philip that he would come up and sit with him. **Acts 8:31**

I will bless the Lord, who hath given me counsel; my reins also instruct me in the night seasons. **Psalm 16:7**

I know both how to be abased, and I know how to abound: everywhere and in all things I am instructed both to be full and to be hungry, both to abound and to suffer need. **Philippians 4:12**

Which forsaketh the guide of her youth, and forgetteth the covenant of her God. **Proverbs 2:17**

My voice shalt thou hear in the morning, O Lord, in the morning will I direct my prayer unto thee, and will look up. **Psalm 5:3**

A Song of Praise on GUIDANCE
Guide Me, O Thou Great Jehovah

Guide me, O Thou great Jehovah, Pilgrim through
this barren land; I am weak, but Thou art mighty,
Hold me with Thy powerful hand; Bread of heaven,
Feed me till I want no more, Feed me till I want no more.

Open now the crystal fountain, Whence the healing stream
doth flow; Let the fire and cloudy pillar Lead
me all my journey through; Strong deliverer, Strong
deliverer, Be thou still my strength and shield, Be
Thou still my strength and shield.

When I tread the verge of Jordan, Bid my anxious
fears subside; Death of death and hell's destruction,
Land me safe on Canaan's side; Songs of praises,
Songs of praises I will ever give to Thee, I will ever
give to Thee.   Amen

Words: William Williams 1717-1791

..........from the Well of HOPE

Therefore my heart is glad, and my glory rejoiceth; my flesh also shall rest in hope. **Psalm 16:9**

And now, Lord, what wait I for? my hope is in thee. **Psalm 39:7**

Blessed is the man that trusteth in the Lord, and whose hope the Lord is, **Jeremiah 17:7**

And now abideth faith, hope, charity, these three; but the greatest of these is charity. **I Corinthians 13:13**

For we are saved by hope; but hope that is seen is not hope; for what a man seeth, why doth he yet hope for? **Romans 8:24**

Rejoicing in hope; patient in tribulation, continuing instant in prayer; **Romans 12:12**

To whom God would make known what is the riches of the glory of this mystery among the Gentiles, which is Christ in you, the hope of glory. **Colossians 1:2**

But if we hope for that we see not, then do we with patience wait for it. **Romans 8:25**

Now faith is the substance of things hoped for, the evidence of things not seen. **Hebrews 11:1**

Which hope we have as an anchor of the soul, both sure and stedfast, and which entereth into that within the veil.
Hebrews 6:19

But I will hope continually, and will yet praise thee more and more. **Psalm 71:14**

394 Gwendolyn D. Persons

It is good that a man should both hope and quietly wait for the salvation of the Lord. **Lamentations 3:27**

Now our Lord Jesus Christ himself, and God, even our Father, which hath loved us, and hath given everlasting consolation and good hope through grace. **II Thessalonians 2:16**

Be of good courage, and he shall strengthen your heart, all ye that hope in the Lord. **Psalm 31:24**

Therefore did my heart rejoice, and my tongue was glad, moreover also my flesh shall rest in hope. **Acts 2:26**

And where is now my hope? as for my hope, who shall see it! **Job 17:15**

Beareth all things, believeth all things, hopeth all things, endureth all things. **I Corinthians 13:7**

Behold the eye of the Lord is upon them that fear him, upon them that hope in his mercy; **Psalm 33:18**

For we through the spirit wait for the hope of righteousness by faith. **Galatians 5:5**

And our hope of you is stedfast, knowing, that as ye are partakers of the sufferings, so shall ye be also of the consolation. **II Corinthians 1:7**

The eyes of your understanding being enlightened; that ye may know what is the hope of his calling; and what the riches of the glory of his inheritance in the saints. **Ephesians 1:18**

For our sakes, no doubt, this is written: that he that ploweth should plow in hope; and that he that thresheth in hope should be partaker of his hope. **I Corinthians:10**

A Song of Praise on HOPE
My Hope Is Built

My hope is built on nothing less. Than Jesus' blood and righteousness; I dare not trust the sweetest frame, But wholly lean on Jesus name.

When darkness veils His lovely face, I rest on His unchanging grace; In every high and stormy gale, My anchor holds within the veil,

His oath, His covenant, His blood Support me in the whelming flood; When all around my soul gives way, He then is all my hope and stay,

When He shall come with trumpet sound, O may I then in Him be found! Dressed in His righteousness alone, Fault less to stand before the throne

Refrain!
On Christ, the solid rock, I stand; All other ground is sinking sand, All other ground is sinking sand

Words: Edward Mote 1797-1874

396 Gwendolyn D. Persons

............from the Well of JOY

Therefore with joy shall ye draw water out of the wells of salvation. **Isaiah 12:3**

Thou wilt shew me the path of life; in thy presence is fulness of joy; at thy right hand there are pleasures for evermore. **Psalm 16:11**

They that sow in tears shall reap in joy. **Psalm 126:5**

And my soul shall be joyful in the Lord; it shall rejoice in his salvation. **Psalm 35:9**

These things have I spoken unto you, that my joy might remain in you, and that your joy might be full. **ST. John 15:11**

My brethren, count it all joy when ye fall into divers temptations. **James 1:2**

Thy words were found; and I did eat them; and thy word was unto me the joy and rejoicing of mine heart; for I am called by thy name, O Lord God of hosts. **Jeremiah 15:16**

Restore unto me the joy of thy salvation; and uphold me with thy free spirit. **Psalm 51:12**

In his neck remaineth strength, and sorrow is turned into joy before him. **Job 41:22**

They on the rock are they, which, when they hear, receive the word with joy; and these have no root, which for a while believe, and in time of temptation fall away. **ST. Luke 8:13**

But he that received the seed into stony places, the same is he that heareth the word, and anon with joy receiveth it.
ST. Matthew 13:20

That ye might walk worthy of the Lord unto all pleasing, being fruitful in every good work, and increasing in the knowledge of God. Strengthened with all might, according to his glorious power, unto all patience and longsuffering with joyfulness:
Colossians 1:10;11

Not for that we have dominion over your faith, but are helpers of your joy; for by faith ye stand. **II Corinthians 1:24**

I have no greater joy than to hear that my children walk in truth.
III John:4

Then shall the virgin rejoice in the dance, both young men and old together, for I will turn their mourning into joy, and will comfort them, and make them rejoice for their sorrow. **Jeremiah 31:13**

And these things write unto you, that your joy may be full.
I John 1:4

Oh that I were as in months passed, as in the days when God prepared me; When his candle shined upon my head and when by his light I walked through darkness; **Job 29:3**

Then he said unto them, Go your way, eat the fat, and drink the sweet, and send portions unto them for whom nothing is prepared; for this day is holy unto our Lord; neither be ye sorry; for the joy of the Lord is your strength. **Nehemiah 8:10**

The blessings of him that was ready to perish came upon me: and I caused the widow's heart to sing for joy. **Job 29:13**

For his anger endureth but a moment; in his favour is life, weeping may endure for a night, but joy cometh in the morning.
Psalm 30:5

A Song of Praise on Joy
His Eye Is On the Sparrow

Why should I feel discouraged, Why should the shadows come,
Why should my heart be lonely And long for heaven and home,

When Jesus is my portion? My constant friend is He;
His eye is on the sparrow, And I know he watches me:

Let not your heart be troubled, His tender word I HEAR,
And resting on His goodness I lose my doubts and fears;

Though by the path He leadeth, But one step I may see;
His eye is on the sparrow, And I know he watches me,
His eye is on the sparrow, And I know he watches me,

When ever I am tempted, When ever clouds arise,
When songs give place to sighing, When hope within me dies,

I draw the closer to Him, From care He sets me free;
His eye in on the sparrow, And I know He watches me
His eye is on the sparrow, And I know He watches me,

Refrain
I sing because I'm happy, I sing because I'm free
For His eye is on the sparrow and I know Hewatches me

Words: Civilla D. Martin 1869-1948

.........from the Well of KINDNESS

And to godliness brotherly kindness; and to brotherly kindness charity. **II Peter1: 7**

She openeth her mouth with wisdom; and her tongue is the law of kindness. **Proverbs 31:26**

To shew forth thy lovingkindness in the morning, and thy faithfulness every night. **Psalm 92:2**

How excellent is thy lovingkindness, O God? therefore the children of men put their trust under the shadow of thy wings. **Psalm 36:7**

Put on therefore, as the elect of God, holy and beloved, bowels of mercies, kindness, humbleness of mind, meekness, long-suffering. **Colossians 3:12**

Shew thy marvelous lovingkindness O thou that savest by thy right hand them which put their trust in thee from those that rise up against them. **Psalm 17:7**

Because thy loving kindness is better than life, my lips shall praise thee. **Psalm 63:3**

For his merciful kindness is great toward us; and the truth of the Lord endureth for ever. Praise ye the Lord. **Psalm 117:2**

Let the righteous smite me; it shall be a kindness: and let him reprove me; it shall be an excellent oil, which shall not break my head; for yet my prayer also shall be in their calamities. **Psalm 141:5**

400 Gwendolyn D. Persons

Now therefore, I pray you, swear unto me by the Lord, since I have shewed you kindness that ye will also shew kindness unto my father's house, and give me a true token. **Joshua 2:12**

And rend your heart, and not your garments, and turn unto the Lord your God: for he is gracious and merciful, slow to anger, and of great kindness, and repenteth him of the evil. **Joel 2:13**

And now the Lord shew kindness and truth unto you: and I also will requite you this kindness, because ye have done this thing.
II Samuel 2:6

Charity suffereth long, and is kind; charity envieth not; charity vaunteth not itself, is not puffed up. **I Corinthians13:4**

And be ye kind one to another, tenderhearted, forgiving one another, even as God for Christ's sake hath forgiven you.
Ephesians 4:32

And he said, Blessed be thou of the Lord, my daughter; for thou hast shewed more kindness in the latter end than at the beginning, inasmuch as thou followedst not young men, whether poor or rich. **Ruth 3:10**

In a little wrath I hid my face from thee for a moment; but with everlasting kindness will I have mercy on thee, saith the Lord thy Redeemer. **Isaiah 54:8**

Be kindly affectioned one to another with brotherly love ; in honour preferring one another; **Romans 12:10**

Finally, be ye all of one mind, having compassion one of another, love as brethren, be pitiful, be courteous. I **Peter 3:8**

A Song of Praise on KINDNESS
He Lifted Me

In loving kindness Jesus came
My soul in mercy to reclaim,
And from the depths of sin and shame
Through grace He lifted me

He called me long before I heard,
Before my sinful heart was stirred,
But when I took him at His word,
Forgiven He lifted me.

His brow was pierced with many a thorn,
His hands by cruel nails were torn
When from my guilt and grief, forlorn,
In love He lifted me

Now on a higher plane I dwell,
And with my soul I know 'tis well;
Yet how or why, I cannot tell,
He should have lifted me

Refrain
From sinking sand He lifted me,
With tender hand He lifted me,
From shades of night to plains of light,
O praise His name, He lifted me!

Words: Charles H. Gabriel, 1856-1932

402 Gwendolyn D. Persons

.........from the Well of LOVE

Who shall separate us from the love of Christ? shall tribulation, or distress, or persecution or famine, or nakedness or peril or sword? **Romans 8:3**

Ye that love the Lord, hate evil; he preserveth the souls of his saints; He delivereth them out of the hand of the wicked. **Psalm 97:10**

The Lord hath appeared of old unto me, saying, yea, I have loved thee with an everlasting love: therefore with loving-kindness have I drawn thee. **Jeremiah 31:3**

By this shall all men know that ye are my disciples, if ye have love, one to another. **St. John 13:35**

As the Father hath loved me, so have I loved you, continue ye in my love. **St. John 15:9**

If ye keep my commandments, ye shall abide in my love even as I have kept my Father's commandments and abide in his love. **St. John 15:10**

Owe no man anything, but to love one another: for he that loveth another hath fulfilled the law. **Romans 13:8**

Let brotherly love continue. **Hebrews 13:1**

And to know the love of Christ, which passeth knowledge, that ye might be filled with all the fulness of God. **Ephesians 3:19**

Fulfill ye my joy, that ye be like-minded, having the same love, being of one accord, of one mind. **Philippians 2:2**

I will heal their backsliding, I will love them freely; for mine anger is turned away from him. **Hosea 14:4**

And walk in love, as Christ also hath loved us, and hath given himself for us an offering and a sacrifice to God for a sweet smelling savoir. **Ephesians 5:2**

Husbands, love your wives, even as Christ also loved the church, and gave himself for it. **Ephesians 5:25**

So ought men to love their wives as their own bodies. He that loveth his wife loveth himself. **Ephesians 5:28**

Nevertheless let every one of you in particular so love his wife even as himself; and the wife see that she reverence her husband. **Ephesians 5:33**

But God. who is rich in mercy, for his great love wherewith he loved us. Even when we were dead in sins hath quickened us together in heavenly places in Christ Jesus. **Ephesians 2:4**

For this cause shall, a man leave his father and mother, and shall be joined unto his wife, and they two shall be one flesh. **Ephesians 5:31**

And now abideth faith, hope, charity, these three, but the greatest of these is charity. **I Corinthians 13:13**

Greater love hath no man than this, that a man lay down his life for his friends. **St. John 15:13**

With all lowliness and meekness, with longsuffering, forbear-ing one another in love; **Ephesians 4:2**

And above all these things put on charity, which is the bond of perfectness. **Colossians 3:14**

The grace of the Lord Jesus Christ, and the love of God, and the communion of the Holy Ghost. be with you all.   Amen. **II Corinthians 13:14**

A Song of Praise on LOVE
I Love the Lord; He Heard My Cries

I love the Lord; He heard my cries, And
pitied every groan; Long as I live, when
troubles rise I'll hasten to His throne.

I love the Lord; He bowed His ear, And
chased my grief away; O let my heart no
more despair While I have breath to pray.

The Lord beheld me sore distressed; He
bade my pains remove; Return my soul to
God, thy rest, For thou hast known His love.

Words: Isaac Watts, 1674-1748

..........from the Well of PATIENCE

But let patience have her perfect work, that ye may be perfect and entire, wanting nothing. **James 1:4**

Knowing this, that the trying of your faith worketh patience. **James 1:3**

Remembering without ceasing your work of faith, and labour of love, and patience of hope in our Lord Jesus Christ, in the sight of God, and our Father. **I Thessalonians 1:3**

Now we exhort you, brethren, warn them that are unruly, comfort the feebleminded, support the weak, be patient toward all men. **I Thessalonians 5:14**

So that we ourselves glory in you in the churches of God for your patience and faith in all your persecutions and tribulations that ye endure. **II Thessalonians 1:4**

And the Lord direct your hearts into the love of God, and into the patient waiting for Christ. **II Thessalonians 3:5**

That ye be not slothful, but followers of them who through faith and patience inherit the promises. **Hebrews 6:12**

For ye have need of patience, that, after ye have done the will of God, ye might receive the promise. **Hebrews 10:36**

Add to your knowledge temperance; and to temperance patience; and to patience godliness. **II Peter 1:6**

Take, my brethren, the prophets, who have spoken in the name of the Lord, for an example of suffering affliction, and of patience. **James 5:10**

406 Gwendolyn D. Persons

I know thy works, and thy labour, and thy patience, and how thou canst not bear them which are evil; thou hast tried them which say they are apostles, and are not, and hast found them liars. **Revelations 2:2**

And not only so, but we glory in tribulations also; knowing that tribulations worketh patience.
Romans 5:3

The servant therefore fell down, and worshipped him, saying, Lord, have patience with me, and I will pay thee all.
St. Matthew 18:26

In your patience possess ye your souls. **St. Luke 21:19**

For whatsoever things were written aforetime were written for our learning, that we through patience and comfort of the scriptures might have hope. **Romans 15:4**

Strengthened with all might, according to his glorious power, unto all patience and longsuffering with joyfulness; Giving thanks unto the Father, which hath made us meet to be par-takers if the inheritance of the saints in light: **Colossians 1:11,12**

But thou, O man of God, flee these things; and follow after righteousness, godliness, faith, love patience, meekness.
I Timothy 6:11

But the aged men be sober, grave, temperate, sound in faith, in charity, in patience. **Titus 2:2**

I waited patiently for the Lord; and he inclined unto me, and heard my cry. **Psalm 40:1**

Wherefore seeing we also are compassed about with so great a cloud of witnesses, let us lay aside every weight, and the sin which doth so easily beset us, and let us run with patience the race that is set before us. **Hebrews 12:1**

A Song of Praise on PATIENCE
Time is Filled with Swift Transition
(Hold to God's Unchanging Hand)

Time is filled with swift transition, Naught of earth unmoved
can stand
Build your hopes on things eternal, Hold to God's unchanging
hand

Trust in Him who will not leave you, Whatsoever years may
bring
If by earthly friends forsaken, Still more closely to Him
cling,

Covet not his world's vain riches, That so rapidly decay;
Seek to gain the heavenly treasures: They will never pass away.

When your journey is completed, If to God you have been true,
Fair and bright the home in glory Your enraptured soul will
view

Refrain
Hold to God's unchanging hand; Hold to God's unchanging
hand;
Build you hopes on things eternal; Hold to God's unchanging
hand.
Words: Jennie Wilson

408 Gwendolyn D. Persons

.........from the Well of PEACE

And the peace of God, which passeth all understanding, shall keep your hearts and minds through Christ Jesus. **Philippians 4:7**

And into whatsoever house ye enter, first say, peace be to this house. **St. Luke 10:5**

And if the son of peace be there, your peace shall rest upon it; if not, it shall turn to you again. **St. Luke 10:6**

Peace I leave with you, My peace I give unto you: not as the world giveth, give I unto you, let not your heart be troubled, neither let it be afraid. **St. John 14:27**

For he is our peace, who hath made both one, and hath broken down the middle wall of partition between us; **Ephesians 2:14**

Peace be to the brethren, and love with faith, from God the Father and the Lord Jesus Christ. **Ephesians 6:23**

Those things, which ye have both learned, and received, and heard, and seen in me, do; and the God of peace shall be with you. **Philippians 4 9**

To the saints and faithful brethren in Christ which are at Colosse. Grace be unto you, and peace from God our Father and the Lord Jesus Christ. **Colossians 1:2**

And let the peace of God rule in your hearts, to the which also ye are called in one body; and be ye thankful. **Colossians 3:15**

And to esteem them very highly in love for their work's sake. And be at peace among yourselves. **I Thessalonians 5:13**

Grace unto you, and peace, from God our Father and the Lord Jesus Christ. **II Thessalonians 1:2**

Unto Timothy, my own son in the faith; Grace, mercy, and peace, from God our Father and Jesus Christ our Lord.
II Thessalonians 3:16

There is no peace, saith the Lord, unto the wicked. **Isaiah 26:3**

I will both lay me down in peace, and sleep; for thou Lord, only makest me dwell in safety. **Psalm 4:8**

Grace to you, and peace, from God our Father and the Lord Jesus Christ. **Philippians 1:3**

Now the Lord of peace himself give you peace always by all means. The Lord be with you all. **II Thessalonians 3:16**

Hear my prayer. O Lord, and give ear unto my cry, hold not thy peace at my tears, For I am a stranger with thee, and a sojourner, as all my fathers were. **Psalm 39:12**

Thou wilt keep him in perfect peace, whose mind is stayed on thee; because he trusteth in thee. **Isaiah 26:3**

Depart from evil, and do good, seek peace, and pursue it.
Psalm 34:14

Make the fruit of righteousness is sown in peace of them that make peace. **James 3:18**

Finally, brethren, farewell. Be perfect, be of good comfort, be of one mind, live in peace, and the God of love and peace shall be with you. **II Corinthians 13:11**

A Song of Praise on PEACE
When Peace, Like A River

When peace, like a river, attendeth my way, When
sorrows, like sea billows, roll; Whatever my lot, Thou
hast taught me to say, It is well with my soul,

Though Satan should buffet, though trials should come,
Let this blest assurance control, That Christ has
regarded my helpless estate, And has shed His
own blood for my soul,

My sin-,oh the bliss of this glorious thought; My
sin, not in part but the whole, Is nailed to the cross
and I bear it no more, Praise the Lord, praise the
Lord, O my soul!

And Lord, haste the day when the faith shall be sight, The
clouds be rolled back as a scroll, The trump shall resound and
the Lord shall descend, Even so, "it is well with my soul""

Refrain
It is well with my soul, It is well, it is well with my soul
It is well with my soul

Words: Horatio G. Spatford, 1828-1888

........from the Well of STRENGTH

And he said unto me, My grace is sufficient for thee: for my strength is made perfect in weakness. Most gladly therefore will I rather glory in my infirmities, that the power of Christ may rest upon me. **II Corinthians 12:9**

I can do all things through Christ which strengthened me.
 Philippians 4:13

God is our refuge and strength, a very present help   in trouble.
Psalm 46:1

The Lord is my light and my salvation; whom shall I fear, the Lord is the strength of my life; of whom shall I be afraid?
Psalm 27:1

For thou hast been a strength to the poor, a strength to the needy in his distress, a refuge from the storm, a shadow from the heat, when the blast of the terrible ones is as a storm against the wall.
Isaiah 25:4

He will keep the feet of the saints, and the wicked shall be silent in darkness; for by strength shall no man prevail. **I Samuel 2:9**

With him is wisdom and strength, he hath counsel and under-standing. **Job 12:13**

Strengthen ye the weak hands, and confirm the feeble knees.
Isaiah 35:3

If I speak of strength, lo, he is strong; and if of judgment, who shall set me a time to plead? **Job 9:19**

I am as a wonder unto many; but thou art my strong refuge. **Psalm 71:7**

Who is this King of glory? The Lord strong and mighty, the Lord mighty in battle. **Psalm 24:8**

He staggered not at the promise of God through unbelief; but was strong in faith, giving glory to God. **Romans 4:20**

And I will strengthen them in the Lord; and they shall walk up and down in his name, saith the Lord. **Zechariah 10:12**

For when we were yet without strength, in due time Christ died, for the ungodly. **Romans 5:6**

I will love thee, O Lord my strength. **Psalm 18:1**

Be strong, and quit yourselves like men, O ye Philistines, that ye be not servants unto the Hebrews, as they have been to you; quit yourselves like men, and fight. **I Samuel 4:9**

The Lord is my strength and song, and he is become my salvation; he is my God, and I will prepare him an habitation; my father's God, and I will exalt him. **Exodus 15:2.**

The way of the Lord is strength to the upright; but destruction shall be to the workers of iniquity. **Proverbs 10:29**

My flesh and my heart faileth: but God is the strength of my heart, and my portion for ever. **Psalm 73:26**

They go from strength to strength, every one of them in Zion appeareth before God. **II Corinthians 12:9**

Finally, my brethren, be strong in the Lord, and in the power of his might. **Ephesians 6:10**

A Song of Praise on Strength
When the Storms of Life are Raging
(Stand by Me)

When the storms of life are raging, Stand by me;
When the storms of life are raging, Stand by me;
When the world is tossing me Like a ship upon a sea
Thou who rulest wind and water, Stand by me.

In the midst of tribulations, Stand by me;
In the midst of tribulations, Stand by me'
When the hosts of hell assail, And my strength begins to Fail,
Thou who never lost a battle, Stand by me

In the midst of faults and failures, Stand by me,
In the midst of faults and failures, Stand by me,
When I do the best I can, And my friends misunderstand,
Thou who knowest all about me, Stand by me

When I'm growing old and feeble, Stand by me
When I'm growing old and feeble, Stand by me,
When my life becomes a burden, And I'm nearing chilly Jordan,
O Thou Lily of the Valley, Stand by me.
Amen

Words and tune: Charles A. Tindley, 1856-1933

414 Gwendolyn D. Persons

..........from the Well of TRUTH

And ye shall know the truth, and the truth shall make you free. **John 8:32**

Howbeit when he, the Spirit of truth, is come, he will guide you into all truth: for he shall not speak of himself; but whatsoever he shall hear, that shall he speak: and he will shew you things to come. **John 16:13**

But speaking the truth in love, may grow up into him in all things, which is the head, even Christ. **Ephesians 4:15**

He that saith, I know him, and keepeth not his commandments, is a liar, and the truth is not in him. **I John 2:4**

Jesus saith unto him, I am the way, the truth, and the life. No man cometh unto the Father, but by me. **John 14:6**

And the Word was made flesh, and dwelt among us, (and we beheld his glory, the glory as of the only begotten of the Father) full of grace and truth. **John 1:14**

These are the things that ye shall do: Speak ye every man the truth to his neighbor; execute the judgment of truth and peace in your gates: **Zech. 8:16**

He that walketh uprightly, and worketh righteousness, and speaketh the truth in his heart. **Psalm 15:2**

Behold, thou desirest truth in the inward parts: and in the hidden part thou shalt make me know wisdom. **Psalm 51:6**

He shall cover thee with his feathers, and under his wings shalt thou trust: his truth shall be thy shield and buckler. **Psalm 91:4**

I have chosen the way of truth: thy judgments have I laid before me. **Psalm 119:30**

Therefore let us keep the feast, not with old leaven, neither with the leaven of malice and wickedness; but with the unleavened bread of sincerity and truth. **I Corinthians 5:8**

Mercy and truth are met together; righteousness and peace have kissed each other. Psalms **85:10**

Teach me thy way, O Lord; I will walk in thy truth: unite my heart to fear thy name. **Psalm 86: 11**

Let not mercy and truth forsake thee; bind them upon thy neck: write them upon the table of thine heart. **Proverbs 3:3**

The Lord, The Lord God, merciful and gracious, long-suffering, and abundant in goodness and truth, **Exodus 34:6**

He that speaketh truth sheweth forth righteousness: but a false witness deceit. **Proverbs 12:17**

The lip of truth shall be established for ever: but a lying tongue is but for a moment. **Proverbs 12:19**

For I the Lord love judgment. I hate robbery for burnt offering; and I will direct their work in truth, and I will make an everlasting covenant with them. **Proverbs 61:8**

Run ye to and fro through the streets of Jerusalem and see now, and know, and seek in the broad places thereof, if ye can find a man, if there be any that executeth judgment, that seeketh the truth; and I will pardon it. **Jeremiah 5:1**

416 Gwendolyn D. Persons

A Battle Hymn on TRUTH
Mine Eyes Have Seen the Glory

Mine eyes have seen the glory of the coming of the Lord;
He is trampling out the vintage where the grapes of wrath are
stored;
He hath loosed the fateful lightning of his terrible swift sword;
His truth is marching on.

I have seen Him in the watchfires of a hundred circling camps
They have builded Him an altar in the evening dews and
damps,
I can read His righteous sentence by the dim and flaring lamps:
His day is marching on.

In the beauty of the lilies Christ was born across the sea,
With a glory in his bosom that transfigures you and me;
As He died to make men holy, let us die to make men free!
While God is marching on.

Refrain
Glory, Glory! Hallelujah!
Glory! Glory! Hallelujah!
Glory! Glory! Hallelujah!
His truth is marching on.

Words: Julia Ward Howe, 1819-1910

........from the Well of UNDERSTANDING

Trust in the Lord with all thy heart; and lean not unto thine own understanding. **Proverbs 3:5**

Get wisdom, get understanding: forget it not ; neither decline from the words of my mouth. **Proverbs 4:5**

I have more understanding than all my teachers: for thy testimonies are my meditation. **Psalm 119:99**

Counsel is mine, and sound wisdom, I am understanding; I have strength. **Proverbs 8:14**

Understanding is a wellspring of life unto him that hath it: but the instruction of fools is folly. **Proverbs 16:22**

But there is a spirit in man: and the inspiration of the Almighty giveth them understanding. **Job 32:8**

With him is wisdom and strength, he hath counsel and understanding. **Job 12:13**

And God said unto him, Because thou hast asked this thing, and hast not asked for thyself long life; neither hast asked riches for thyself, nor hast asked the life of thine enemies; but hast asked for thyself understanding to discern judgment; Behold, I have done according to the words: lo, I have given thee a wise and an understanding heart; so that there was none like thee before thee, neither after thee shall any arise like unto thee. **I Kings 3:11,12**

Through thy percepts I get understanding: therefore I hate every false way. **Pslam 119:104**

418 Gwendolyn D. Persons

What is it then? I will pray with the spirit, and I will pray with the understanding also: I will sing with the spirit, and I will sing with the understanding also, **I Corinthians 14:15**

And the peace of God which passeth all understanding, shall keep your hearts and minds through Christ Jesus. **Philippians 4:7**

He that is slow to wrath is of great understanding: but he that is hasty of spirit exalteth folly**. Proverbs 14:29**

Consider what I say ; and the Lord give thee understanding in all things. **II Timothy 2:7**

There is none that understandeth, there is none that seeketh after God. **Romans 3:11**

And to love him with all the heart, and with all the understanding, and with all the soul, and with all the strength, and to love his neighbor as himself, is more than all whole burnt offerings and sacrifices. **St. Mark 12:33**

And though I have the gift of prophecy, and understand all mysteries, and all knowledge; and though I have all faith, so that I could remove mountains, and have not charity, I am nothing.
I Corinthians 13:2

Many shall be purified, and made white, and tried; but the wicked shall do wickedly: and none of the wicked shall understand; but the wise shall understand. **Daniel 12:10**

He that hath knowledge spareth his words; and a man of understanding is of an excellent spirit. **Proverbs 17:27**

And all that heard him were astonished at his under-standing and answers. **St. Luke 2:47**

For this cause we also, since the day we heard it, do not cease to pray for you, and to desire that ye might be filled with the knowledge of his will in all wisdom and spiritual understanding; **Colossians1:9**

A Song of Praise on Understanding
We Are Often Tossed and Driven

We are often tossed and driven on the restless sea of time, Somber skies and howling tempests oft succeed a bright sunshine, In that land of perfect day, when the mists have rolled away, We will understand it better by and by

We are often destitute of the things that life demands, Want of food and want of shelter, thirsty hills and barren lands, We are trusting in the Lord, and according to His word, We will understand it better by and by

Trials dark on every hand, and we cannot understand, All the ways that God would lead us to that blessed Promised Land; But He guides us with His eye and we'll follow till we die, For we'll understand it better by and by

Temptations, hidden snares often take us unawares, And our hearts are made to bleed for a thoughtless word or deed, And we wonder why the test when we try to do our best, But we'll understand it better by and by

Refrain
By and by, when the morning comes All the saints of God are gathered home. We'll tell the story how we've overcome. For we'll understand it better by and by

Words: Charles Albert Tindley, 1851-1933

420 Gwendolyn D. Persons

About the Author

Gwendolyn D. Persons is a published author of <u>God's Got A Word For Delta Women.</u> A native of Detroit, Michigan, she is the widow of the late urbane, distinguished Attorney Fred K. Persons, known and esteemed for many years as Mr. Detroit of this city.

Gwendolyn received a Bachelor's of Science Degree from Western Michigan University and a Master's of Science Degree from Wayne State University. She received the degree of Educational Specialist from the University of Detroit and has devoted her entire professional career to the Detroit Public Schools as a Speech and Language Pathologist.

She is a lifetime member of St. Stephen African Methodist Episcopal Church. She was initiated into Delta Sigma Theta Sorority, Inc. on the campus of Western Michigan University in 1969, is a financial member of the Detroit Alumnae Chapter and has been a Golden Life member since 1993.

Gwendolyn is endowed with a keen sensitivity to the power of words through which she weaves basic principles of faith that deeply impact our innermost emotional cavities. Her straight from the heart soulful writing style reflects the vitality of her extraordinary personal experiences and the healing virtues of faith which she prescribes in the current publication of her latest book, <u>Fresh Water From Old Wells.</u>

422 Gwendolyn D. Persons

From the Author.....

I thank the Holy Spirit for guiding me the 'other side of through'. It has been a long journey. I experienced many bumps, pit stops and detours along the way. I was sometimes happy and sometimes sad. Sometimes I was so close to God I could almost smell the sweet savor of incense burning on the heavenly altar. Then there were times I was so low in spirit I felt way down yonder all by myself and I couldn't hear nobody pray (Dr. William Augustus Jones, A Formula for Living)

My endeavor to write <u>Fresh Waters from Old Wells</u> was an assignment commissioned by God. It was created to touch the hearts and souls of its readers. I have never birthed a child but <u>Fresh Water from Old Wells</u> is my baby, a story conceived by the Holy Spirit from the depths of my heart and soul. I carried (wrote) my baby for five years.

Before I began to write my story I needed to ask the Spirit's permission to transpose or to interchange things if you will. The Spirit granted me that permission and for that I am truly thankful. Ironically, however, the closer I got to completion, it was a certainty that I did not want some literary cleansing or purging process to tamper with or contaminate my story. I did not want the editing or publishing process to alter the content which was conceived from my heart and not from my head.

To that end I will be forever thankful to the Holy Spirit for guiding me to Fran Carter, my editor and to Julia Hunter, my publisher.

To My Editor, Fran Carter:

I went into labor on December 4, 2004. The labor process (editing) was painful indeed. It was without question a 'labor of love'. Each time I had to review my story my heart was made to bleed over again. The editing process took six months resulting in a constantly evolving organism; my baby.

Ms. Carter, I wish to thank you for all of your tender loving care. I could not have been blessed with a more caring, gifted, loving, patient and understanding coach. I could not have gotten it done without you. What a wonderful blessing you have been to me. I will be forever thankful!

To My Publisher, Julia Hunter:

Your unbridled enthusiasm and energy met me in the delivery room (my living room) on Monday, August 15, 2005. The delivery process took exactly four months. Julia your untiring and relentless spirit has been unmatchable. Your meticulous attention to detail was uncompromising. You made certain that every omission, infraction and liability were not overlooked. No promise made was unkept. What a phenomenal midwife you have been. You did not cut the umbilical cord until you felt I was ready to deliver my baby. 'Fresh Water from Old Wells was born (published) on Thursday, December 15, 2005.

Julia, when folk ask me what does the 'G' stand for in G Publishing, I will reply loudly and proudly,

"G stands for God's Gift to Gwen."

Now there's a thought. Triple G Publishing. Thank you from the bottom of my heart.

To my readers:

It is prayer that my story touched your heart and your soul. I hope you felt my joy along with my pain. I hope you were able to laugh when I laughed or cried when I cried or shouted praises unto the Lord when I rejoiced in His name. If you walked with me beyond the gate I pray that you were able to draw fresh water from old wells. If I have been able to help somebody along this journey, then as the songwriter put it "My living has not been in vain." To that I say

"TO GOD BE ALL THE GLORY"

A Post Script from the Author:

How is your faith relationship helping you to trust God in all the circumstances of your life. If you open up and let Him come in, He'll give you eternal life, peace that flows like a river, joy everlasting, a song to sing and a story to tell. Fresh Water from Old Wells is my story. It truly is:

A
Gift of Love
to All

Do you have a song to sing? Do you have a story to tell?

Ask me who I am
I will reply loudly and proudly

"I'm a Child of The King"
Proverbs 3:56

426 Gwendolyn D. Persons

Printed in the United States
42139LVS00002B/73-510

9 780977 326730